AF262772

The publisher and the University of California Press Foundation gratefully acknowledge the generous support of the Fletcher Jones Foundation Imprint in Humanities.

Brand New Beat

The Wild Rise of ROLLING STONE Magazine

Peter Richardson

UNIVERSITY OF CALIFORNIA PRESS

University of California Press
Oakland, California

© 2026 by Peter Richardson

Cataloging-in-Publication data is on file at the Library of Congress.

ISBN 978-0-520-39939-6 (cloth : alk. paper)
ISBN 978-0-520-39941-9 (ebook)

Manufactured in the United States of America

GPSR Authorized Representative: Easy Access System Europe,
Mustamäe tee 50, 10621 Tallinn, Estonia, gpsr.requests@easproject.com

35 34 33 32 31 30 29 28 27 26
10 9 8 7 6 5 4 3 2 1

Contents

Introduction

In the summer of 1976, the 30-year-old cofounder of *Rolling Stone* magazine hosted a party for presidential candidate Jimmy Carter. Held in a townhouse on New York's Upper East Side, Jann Wenner's bash drew prominent figures from politics, publishing, journalism, and entertainment. *CBS Evening News* anchor Walter Cronkite was there. So was Hollywood actor and anti-war activist Jane Fonda. *Washington Post* publisher Katharine Graham was accompanied by actor Warren Beatty. Cyrus Vance, who would soon become secretary of state, was in attendance, as were actor Paul Newman, *Washington Post* Executive Editor Ben Bradlee, columnist Sally Quinn, conductor Leonard Bernstein, *Saturday Night Live* star Chevy Chase, and Gonzo journalist Hunter S. Thompson. Wenner's party was a hot ticket; so hot, in fact, that many invited guests never made it through the front door. Both *The New York Times* and *The Washington Post* devoted full-page stories to the event.

The next night, Jimmy Carter accepted the Democratic Party's nomination for the highest office in the land. When Carter won the election four months later, some observers claimed that *Rolling Stone* had delivered the youth vote for the Georgia Democrat. Whether or not that claim was accurate, one thing was clear: *Rolling Stone* had arrived on the national stage. Only four years earlier, its writers had difficulty obtaining press passes to campaign events. Now the magazine was placed squarely in the center of the action, and decades later, it would be described as "the journalistic voice of its generation."

This book poses a deceptively simple question: How did an undercapitalized San Francisco rock publication, edited by a 21-year-old college dropout, become one of that era's most important magazines? The obvious answer isn't wrong. From the outset, *Rolling Stone* served up generous portions of sex, drugs, and rock and roll to the fattest demographic in American history. Yet the magazine had no monopoly on those topics, and they don't explain its extraordinary success. What else distinguished the San Francisco upstart in a crowded media marketplace? *Brand New Beat* answers that question by situating *Rolling Stone* in its place and time, tracking its turbulent development, and mapping its immense influence on American culture.

The magazine's story is sprawling, but four major themes shaped its early history. The first is *Rolling Stone*'s complex relationship with the counterculture, a term that Bay Area social critic Theodore Roszak popularized the same year *Rolling Stone* was founded. Powered by the Baby Boom and postwar affluence, the youthful counterculture was loosely united by its opposition to the Vietnam War and put off by the nation's rampant materialism, environmental rapacity, and spiritual emptiness. What began as a deep fracture in the white middle class changed the way millions of Americans understood themselves and their society. But as Roszak noted, the counterculture wasn't an organized movement with a coherent message. He compared it to a medieval crusade, a "variegated procession constantly in flux, acquiring and losing members all along the route of march."

That shaggy procession didn't lack for media coverage. During the so-called Summer of Love, reporters from mainstream outlets flooded San Francisco, one of the counterculture's capitals. Their dispatches were usually superficial, dismissive, or even disparaging. In contrast, *Rolling Stone* understood the counterculture's importance and championed its music. At the same time, it wasn't a hippie publication, and it rose to prominence in part by chronicling the counterculture's shortcomings and calamities. By probing *Rolling Stone*'s tangled relationship with the counterculture, this book maintains that one way to understand that movement and its durable legacy is to study the magazine most closely associated with it.

A second major theme is *Rolling Stone*'s conception of rock music and its significance. It wasn't the first magazine, or even the first American one, to cover rock and roll. Long before Jann Wenner and Ralph J. Gleason cofounded it in 1967, major media outlets were reporting breathlessly on Elvis Presley and the Beatles. While much of that coverage treated rock and roll as a fad, curiosity, or social symptom, Wenner and Gleason believed that rock music was animating a social revolution already in progress. That conviction, and the journalism that flowed from it, quickly distinguished *Rolling Stone* from its rivals. By insisting on the significance of its topic, *Rolling Stone* created a brand new beat—the rock music beat—which became the seedbed for a generation of music, cultural, and political journalism.

The third theme goes to *Rolling Stone*'s primary influences. The magazine was largely a creature of the San Francisco counterculture, but it bore the stamp of two other Bay Area phenomena, neither of them musical. The first was the Free Speech Movement (FSM) at the University of California, Berkeley, which made a deep impression on the magazine's founders, editors, and early contributors. Both Wenner and Gleason covered the FSM for other outlets, as did Hunter S. Thompson, who later became *Rolling Stone*'s most popular writer. The other primary influence was *Ramparts* magazine, the legendary San Francisco muckraker that employed Gleason and Wenner immediately before they cofounded *Rolling Stone*. Like *Ramparts*, and unlike its direct competitors, *Rolling Stone* ran major stories on politics and current affairs. In that sense, it was always more than a rock magazine. But *Rolling Stone* also had something that *Ramparts* lacked—a sustainable business model, courtesy of the record labels that advertised in its pages. That revenue stream allowed *Rolling Stone* not only to outlive its precursor, but also to run important political stories and commentary long after *Ramparts* closed its doors.

The fourth theme concerns the nature of *Rolling Stone*'s political coverage, which diverged sharply from the standard fare. In the model scene of that period, major outlets covered the news objectively, but the reality on the ground was always more complex. Strict objectivity is a tall order for profit-maximizing media corporations, whose financial and ideological investments shape their coverage. Yet the notion of objective journalism, then and now, faces an even more basic challenge: namely, that storytelling requires a series of nonobjective decisions about selection, emphasis, tone, and other narrative elements. The so-called New Journalism, which imported techniques from modern fiction, was a contemporary response to that challenge. At a critical point in *Rolling Stone*'s development, Wenner sought out New Journalism's leading lights, including Hunter S. Thompson and Tom Wolfe, to expand his magazine's appeal. Unlike its competitors, however, *Rolling Stone* wasn't content to incorporate first-person narration, dialogue, scene-setting, and other literary elements into its coverage. Even as it strove for accuracy, the magazine challenged the notion of objectivity and its efficacy. Awash in "objective" news, much of it narrow, misleading, or mindlessly neutral, *Rolling Stone*'s readers welcomed that approach. Many were keenly aware of the mainstream media's blind spots and hidden biases, especially on issues that affected them directly. Seeking alternatives to mainstream coverage, they turned to *Rolling Stone* as a source of political news, commentary, and media criticism.

These four factors help us understand *Rolling Stone*'s early success, but they never ensured it. Although the magazine quickly reached large audiences, it struggled to turn a profit. Editorial conflicts led to defections, and one of the magazine's foundational claims died a quiet death well before its tenth anniversary. The social revolution that rock music heralded wasn't ushering in political progress. Rather, the nation was tilting into the Age of Reagan. Meanwhile, San Francisco's intimate rock scene was giving way to stadium shows whose vast scale once again separated musicians from their fans. Along the way, some of these musicians fell victim to drug abuse and other pitfalls. As the 1970s wore on, San Francisco no longer piqued the curiosity of national media outlets, rock icons, or music industry insiders. On his way out of town, Wenner dismissed San Francisco as a provincial backwater.

When Wenner moved the magazine's headquarters to New York in 1977, many readers and contributors were dismayed by the relocation and what it represented. Nevertheless, *Rolling Stone* thrived in its new home and continued to produce award-winning journalism. Meanwhile, the Bay Area was busily reinventing its identity. The same year *Rolling Stone* decamped, a new Bay Area company began marketing the Apple II personal computer. Ardent fans of the Beatles and Bob Dylan, the company's cofounders cast their products as the countercultural alternatives to IBM, which dominated the computer business. The region's technological innovations eventually transformed global communications, commerce, work, politics, and social relations. Although Silicon Valley became a global tech capital, it didn't vanquish the counterculture so much as absorb and refract its hippie ethic.

The story that follows is divided into four parts, each of which reflects a discrete stage in *Rolling Stone*'s early development. The first part surveys the magazine's influences and Bay Area context, with special emphasis on cofounder Ralph J. Gleason and his reporting. It also reviews Wenner's earliest efforts to recruit writers, attract advertisers, and create the first issue in November 1967. The second part highlights the magazine's early growth, the sturdy if sometimes fractious relationships Wenner established with record labels, and the editorial upgrades made during John Burks's brief but eventful stint as managing editor. This part also considers the major stories of that period, most notably the lethal debacle at the Altamont Speedway Free Concert and the Manson Family murders and trial in Los Angeles. The third section recounts *Rolling Stone*'s continued expansion and editorial makeover after Burks's departure in 1970, including the arrival of Hunter S. Thompson and the development of Gonzo journalism. The fourth part features what Wenner considered the magazine's golden age. It charts Gonzo's fortunes during the mid-1970s and considers the magazine's deeper commitment to political coverage and investigative reporting. It also reviews the advances made by women at the magazine as well as the contributions of Cameron Crowe, its youngest writer. The epilogue considers *Rolling Stone*'s fortunes and the counterculture's enduring influence following the magazine's move to New York.

Any fresh review of *Rolling Stone*'s legacy must address Jann Wenner's controversial remarks in a 2023 interview with *The New York Times*. His new book at that time, *The Masters*, consisted of interviews he had conducted with John Lennon, Mick Jagger, Bob Dylan, Jerry Garcia, Pete Townshend, Bono, and Bruce Springsteen. Wenner's introduction acknowledged that the absence of black and female musicians in that list reflected "the prejudices and practices of that time." That he had neglected important black artists was his loss, he wrote, and though rock music in its early years was "irredeemably male," he claimed that discrimination against women was another barrier that rock would tear down in the music business. Yet when journalist David Marchese asked why the book didn't include interviews with black and female artists, Wenner replied that the rock stars he featured articulated "a particular spirit and a particular attitude about rock and roll." Admitting that his selection process was "intuitive," Wenner added that female artists like Joni Mitchell, Grace Slick, and Janis Joplin were less articulate "on this intellectual level," and that black artists like Stevie Wonder, Marvin Gaye, and Curtis Mayfield "just didn't articulate at that level." Wenner's remarks were swiftly and universally denounced. Even before he publicly apologized for them, he was removed from the board of the Rock & Roll Hall of Fame Foundation.

While that story spread across the media universe, I was poring over *Rolling Stone*'s earliest records in a New Jersey warehouse. Perhaps for that reason, I noticed several shortcuts in the media coverage, especially when it came to the magazine's first decade. Not surprisingly, those shortcuts were even more apparent on social media, where hot takes and sweeping dismissals were the order of the day. Taken as a whole, the instant analysis tended to brush Wenner, his remarks, and the magazine into the same trash can. Shortly after the story peaked, however, several former staff members quietly defended *Rolling Stone*'s record while distancing themselves from Wenner's comments. If the interview exposed Wenner's prejudices, which his son Gus described as "upsetting and hurtful," its reception revealed the need for a fresh review of the magazine's early history. In what follows, I've kept that need in sharp focus.

My own interest in *Rolling Stone* informs the following account. Born in 1959 and raised in the San Francisco Bay Area, I read the magazine as a teenager and absorbed its iconoclasm, which the broader culture also reinforced. At the tender age of 14, I watched the televised hearings on the Watergate scandal and learned that the president was a crook. My favorite films, including *The Godfather* and *Chinatown*, also featured corruption in high places. I never missed an episode of *All in the Family*, the nation's most popular television show, which satirized bigotry and outdated thinking. Popular rock anthems were also citing current events. "Watergate does not bother me," Lynyrd Skynyrd sang in 1974. "Does your conscience bother you? Tell the truth." Truthfully, my conscience didn't bother me very much. Even before I possessed a driver's license, President Nixon resigned and Jerry Brown replaced Ronald Reagan as our state's governor. At age 36, Brown was dating singer Linda Ronstadt, living in a two-bedroom apartment in Sacramento, and tooling around town in a Plymouth Satellite. Many of us gave him extra points for his frank and cheerful irreverence. We never suspected that the Age of Reagan was just over the horizon.

Rolling Stone made fewer claims on my attention in the 1980s and 1990s, but when I began teaching American Studies courses at San Francisco State University in 2006, the magazine swam back into my ken. *Rolling Stone*'s early history figured in my teaching and informed my books about *Ramparts* magazine, the Grateful Dead, and Hunter S. Thompson. *Brand New Beat* reflects those personal and professional experiences, but it also draws on scores of new interviews, fresh archival material, and a burgeoning body of memoir, biography, commentary, history, and analysis. As my citations make clear, I've benefited enormously from the work of earlier writers, especially Ralph Gleason, Jann Wenner, Chet Flippo, Robert Sam Anson, Robert Draper, and Joe Hagan. Taken as a whole, their accounts tell a vivid and compelling story about the magazine's origins, development, and major figures. I would argue, however, that they don't always capture the scope of *Rolling Stone*'s achievement, the nature of the culture that spawned it, or the magazine's place in the broader sweep of social, cultural, and media history. I wrote *Brand New Beat* to tell that important story. It presumes some familiarity with the magazine's period and provenance, but as my students often reminded me, this was ancient history for them. As an undergraduate in the late 1970s, I would have said the same about the Roaring Twenties, so I've tried to keep their perspective in mind.

This book also reflects the influence of another one, Theodore Roszak's *The Making of a Counter Culture: Reflections on the Technocratic Society and Its Youthful Opposition* (1969). As I was researching the early days of *Rolling Stone* magazine, I was invited to celebrate the opening of Roszak's archive at Stanford University. That occasion prompted a more searching consideration of Roszak's work, which extended well beyond his analysis of the San Francisco counterculture. Undertaking that research with historian Michael J. Kramer, and with the encouragement of Kathryn Roszak, I've brought the results of that study to bear on *Rolling Stone*'s story.

As I discovered early on in my research, Theodore Roszak was no stranger to *Rolling Stone*. Shortly after Roszak's most famous book appeared, Langdon Winner's review in *Rolling Stone* praised its insights. Soon after that, Winner left the magazine to continue his own academic career and eventually occupied an endowed chair at Rensselaer Polytechnic Institute. Winner was by no means the only

Rolling Stone veteran to make his mark in academia, but his review of Roszak's book is one of many reminders that, even at its outset, *Rolling Stone* ranged far beyond what Joni Mitchell famously called "the star-maker machinery behind the popular song." That the magazine was no slouch in that department made everything else possible.

PART I Roots

1 Hippies

When Ralph Gleason saw the March 1967 issue of *Ramparts* magazine, he felt his shock turn into fury.

Launched only five years earlier, the San Francisco muckraker was hotter than ever. Editor Warren Hinckle had converted the Catholic literary quarterly into a "radical slick" whose circulation and cachet were the envy of more established outlets. Even its chief nemesis, *Time* magazine, conceded that *Ramparts* contained "a bomb in every issue." That concession was also a warning, for *Time* routinely cast the *Ramparts* staff as anarchistic bomb-throwers whose investigative stories on Vietnam and the CIA amounted to reckless attacks on effective governance. Unable to kill those stories, *Time* took direct aim at the messenger. Ironically, those attacks only raised the muckraker's profile.

The 28-year-old Hinckle was a rebel by nature, but he was no flower child, and his cover story that month was an unflattering portrait of the Haight-Ashbury scene. "The Social History of the Hippies" traced the links between Beat writers Allen Ginsberg and

Jack Kerouac, novelist Ken Kesey and the Merry Pranksters, and the so-called Acid Tests that Kesey and the Pranksters hosted. Those public amusements mixed music, multimedia performances, and some of the psychedelic drugs Kesey had ingested as a test subject at a local VA hospital. Hinckle's article also featured the street theater of the San Francisco Mime Troupe, the local activism of the Diggers, the rock concerts promoted by Bill Graham and the Family Dog, and the nerve-rattling presence of the Hells Angels, the motorcycle gang whose members attended many concerts.

Hinckle captured the spectacular nature of hippie culture and its anti-establishment posture, but he faulted his new neighbors for their political disengagement. The hippie community's major organizational effort, the Summer of Love, was expected to draw hordes of young people to San Francisco within months. As city officials braced for disaster, Hinckle predicted a different kind of trouble.

> The danger in the hippie movement is more than overcrowded streets and possible hunger riots this summer. If more and more youngsters begin to share the hippie political posture of unrelenting quietism, the future of activist, serious politics is bound to be affected. The hippies have shown that it can be pleasant to drop out of the arduous task of attempting to steer a difficult, unrewarding society. But when that is done, you leave the driving to the Hell's Angels.

The hippie community's greatest failure, it seemed, was its refusal to endorse the New Left politics that *Ramparts* favored.

The cover story stunned Gleason, who thought the hippie story was his. He was certainly well positioned to write it. He covered popular music for the *San Francisco Chronicle*, but his experience stretched back to the 1930s, when he wrote about jazz for the campus newspaper at Columbia University. That neighborhood was steeped in hot jazz, but it also housed what one historian called "the greatest assemblage of academic progressives and radicals in Depression America." Gleason studied with literary critics Lionel Trilling and Mark Van Doren, read the radical magazine

New Masses, and immersed himself in jazz at the uptown and midtown clubs.

After leaving Columbia, Gleason contributed to *DownBeat* magazine and cofounded *Jazz Information*, one of the first U.S. magazines dedicated to that genre. In 1946, he moved to Berkeley, became *DownBeat*'s West Coast correspondent, and freelanced for the *San Francisco Chronicle* until he became a regular columnist in 1951. In 1958, the *Chronicle* syndicated the column, and though Gleason's strong suit was jazz, he also covered Hank Williams, Elvis Presley, Ray Charles, Odetta, Frank Sinatra, Sam Cooke, and Chuck Berry. In addition to writing his column, Gleason created new ways to feature the music he loved. He cofounded the Monterey Jazz Festival, whose 1958 debut included Louis Armstrong, Billie Holiday, and Dizzy Gillespie. The following year, he began hosting *Jazz Casual*, a public television program that featured his interviews with Duke Ellington, Count Basie, Armstrong, Gillespie, and other luminaries.

A man of the left, Gleason had a personal network that included journalist I. F. Stone, poet Allen Ginsberg, writer James Baldwin, labor leader Harry Bridges, and Marxist historian Eric Hobsbawm, who wrote jazz reviews under a pseudonym. He also befriended Lenny Bruce and testified for the defense in the standup comedian's 1962 obscenity trial in San Francisco. Alert to connections between the arts, popular culture, and social movements, Gleason noted that jazz, poetry, and comedy were "part of a growing body of dissent from the status quo that is gradually effecting a fundamental change in many attitudes." Later he would become the only music journalist on President Richard Nixon's notorious Enemies List, which Gleason proudly displayed on the wall of his Berkeley home.

At the same time, Gleason privately bemoaned "the square, myopic, UNHIP left," which antagonized him "like the banderillas in the bull." Toward the end of his life, he recalled an article written by Dwight Macdonald, one of his heroes. Describing a White House cocktail party held for artists during the Johnson years, Macdonald lamented the absence of American composers before claiming that the highlight of the evening was Duke Ellington's performance. It was a profound shock, Gleason wrote, to realize that Macdonald didn't regard Duke Ellington as a composer, much less the nation's greatest one. In this way, Gleason concluded, the square left blithely ignored the accomplishments of major black artists.

Those artists were Gleason's teachers and idols, but his relationships with them weren't predicated on their celebrity. In addition to interviewing jazz musicians backstage and on television, Gleason hosted long conversations with them at his Berkeley home. In taped chats with John Coltrane, Dizzy Gillespie, Sonny Rollins, and a young Quincy Jones, he asked about influences, apprenticeship, and craft. For all the daunting challenges these musicians faced, especially during the Jim Crow era, they were part of a multigenerational art culture that supported their work and their families. Gleason respected every part of that arrangement, and many musicians respected him for that. "I read him," Miles Davis once said about Gleason. "He understands me." It was high praise, especially from Davis, but Gleason downplayed his personal friendships with the musicians he covered. "I don't care if I make it with musicians," Gleason said. "I wouldn't care if Miles and I didn't get along—it happens that we do, but that could change. The important thing is that I stay straight with myself."

In the mid-1960s, Gleason became a contributing editor at *Ramparts*. In his 1965 article about Bob Dylan, he quoted Malvina Reynolds, the 64-year-old Berkeley folk singer, on Dylan's appeal to younger audiences. "He is saying something and saying it effectively, and the fact that he has no voice and looks like nowhere is incidental," Reynolds said. "These kids have been betrayed by the good voices all their lives, have been told lies by the good voices, I mean social lies—that love is all, you know, and if you're good everything will be wonderful." Because of that betrayal, Gleason added, many young people took nothing on faith from their elders. Noting that the latest topical songs challenged the American intervention in Vietnam as well as Bull Connor, the public official who turned attack dogs and fire hoses on black protestors in Alabama, Gleason concluded that the times were changing, that folk music reflected that change, and that young artists "served notice on their elders to get out of the way." But Gleason, who was already in his late 40s, had no plans to step aside, especially as popular music began an exciting new chapter. That year's releases included "Like a Rolling Stone," "Do You Believe in Magic," "Papa's Got a Brand New Bag," "California Girls," "You've Lost That Lovin' Feelin'," "Stop! In the Name of Love," and "(I Can't Get No) Satisfaction." To that list, the Beatles added several masterpieces from *Help!* and *Rubber Soul.*

Alert to the Beatles' significance, Gleason devoted two *San Francisco Chronicle* columns to them in February 1964. Later that year, he interviewed them backstage at the Cow Palace, the exhibition hall on San Francisco's southern border where the Beatles opened their first North American tour. The audience that night included Ken Kesey and the Merry Pranksters, who absorbed the spectacle while tripping on LSD. To Kesey's kaleidoscope eyes, the Beatles and their surging audience formed a single malignant creature. The concert was wildly successful, but the Beatles had misgivings about it. Mainstream outlets had reported that the Fab Four liked jelly beans, and fans pelted them with candy throughout the show. George Harrison described the concert as thrilling but painful, and the entire experience left John Lennon feeling unsafe.

When Bob Dylan came to San Francisco in December 1965, Gleason hosted a televised press conference at KQED, the local public station. Allen Ginsberg, poet Michael McClure, and City Lights publisher Lawrence Ferlinghetti were in the studio audience. Bill Graham, the business manager for the San Francisco Mime Troupe, was also on hand. Speaking through a cloud of cigarette smoke, Dylan deflected questions about politics and the meaning of his work. He was more forthcoming about his writing process, but unlike the Beatles' cheeky press banter, Dylan's answers were brief, enigmatic, or slyly bemused. His performance enacted a fantasy shared by many young people, some of whom were in the studio. The media's struggle to understand their music, outlook, and heroes highlighted the importance of Baby Boomers, and when Dylan's oracular utterances caught the square reporters flatfooted, it was a minor generational triumph.

Gleason handled his part with aplomb, and Dylan was grateful for his host's support. "I had heard that he interviewed Hank Williams, which was impressive," Dylan said later. "So there was a bit of mystery to him. He wore a trench coat and horn-rimmed glasses and was the type of reporter you'd see around the Broadway area in New York. He wrote about jazz and folk music in the mainstream newspaper, so he was responsible for introducing me to a wider crowd, and his approval meant a lot." The following year, Gleason wrote an appreciative *Ramparts* cover story about Dylan, whom he called "the first poet of that all-American artifact, the juke box, the first American poet to touch everyone, to hit all walks of life in this great sprawling society. The first poet of mass media, if you will."

·   ·   ·   ·   ·

Even before Dylan's visit, Gleason was using his *Chronicle* column to champion local rock groups. He also cast the emergent San Francisco music scene as almost unprecedented. "There has been no point in American history that I know of," he wrote to one colleague, "except the street bands of New Orleans, where music has had such a direct role in the culture of any area as it has in San Francisco at this point in our history." Offered from his perch in Berkeley, such views raised the local scene's profile. Eric Hobsbawm later claimed that Gleason understood young people and was "wonderfully sensitive to the vibes of coming times." Although Gleason was "the least infantile of men, he was himself not a character to grow old." Hobsbawm's description chimed well with the standard joke that the 48-year-old Gleason couldn't decide whether he was composed of two 24-year-olds, three 16-year-olds, or four 12-year-olds.

Gleason's enthusiasm was infectious. After he sang Jefferson Airplane's praises in the *San Francisco Chronicle*, RCA Victor offered the band a recording contract. Its second album, *Surrealistic Pillow*, was released shortly before Hinckle's hippie story appeared. After the album rose to number three on the charts, more Bay Area bands signed deals and produced hit records. Meanwhile, music industry insiders lauded the so-called San Francisco Sound. Ahmet Ertegun of Atlantic Records told Gleason that its commercial appeal was unmatched during this period. "The batting average is sensational," Ertegun said. "No other city has anything like it. Something like fifteen out of the first nineteen albums recorded by San Francisco bands made the bestseller charts. There's something different about the San Francisco bands, some mystique."

As the music scene developed, San Francisco hippies began to attract significant media attention. In January 1967, Gleason attended a key event touted as "A Gathering of the Tribes for a Human Be-In." Announced on the cover of the *San Francisco Oracle*, Haight-Ashbury's underground newspaper, the Human Be-In previewed the size and newsworthiness of the hippie community. On a sunny afternoon, some 20,000 people flocked to Golden Gate Park to hear Jefferson Airplane, the Grateful Dead, Big Brother and the Holding Company, Quicksilver Messenger Service, and Blue Cheer. The bands shared the stage with LSD enthusiast Timothy Leary, Berkeley activist Jerry Rubin, and poets Allen Ginsberg, Gary Snyder, Michael McClure, Lawrence Ferlinghetti, and Lenore Kandel.

Many worked hard to make the Human Be-In a success, but the publicity was minimal. "Everybody felt it," Gleason wrote. "There was something in the air that made it imperative to attend." Thousands of hippies were on hand, but the crowd was unexpectedly diverse. "Everybody came," Gleason reported. "There were state assemblymen, reporters, clergy, university professors, advertising agency executives, a Los Angeles music business lawyer, jazz musicians, little old ladies in tennis shoes, hordes of kids, Berkeley political types, and old-line anarchists." Aside from a pair of mounted patrolmen and traffic cops outside the park, there was no visible police presence, and Gleason was struck by the absence of drunks. The Hells Angels were on hand to guard the power lines to the stage, and when one spectator wandered into their area, they beat him badly. Gleason knew about the incident but left it out of his report to avoid diminishing what was otherwise a peaceful event.

For news organizations, the Human Be-In was irresistible. The combination of rock music, spectacular attire, and ecstatic dancing was a visual feast. "The media delighted in the infinitely photogenic Be-In," former student activist and media scholar Todd Gitlin recounted in his history of the 1960s. "Whatever this strangeness was, it was certainly A Story." Surprisingly large and surpassingly weird, the hippie community was ready for its close-up.

·   ·   ·   ·   ·

Gleason was also a force behind the Monterey International Pop Festival, which took place that summer more than 100 miles south of San Francisco. Conceived in Los Angeles, the festival needed the Bay Area bands and their hip cachet to succeed. Publicist Derek Taylor recruited Gleason, whose endorsement was crucial. Sporting his deerstalker hat and pipe, Gleason joined the music industry executives, publicists, and managers for the three-day concert at Monterey County Fairgrounds. Many had never seen Jimi Hendrix, Janis Joplin, the Who, or Otis Redding perform. Their presence helped make Monterey Pop a showcase as well as the year's signal rock event.

In addition to boosting the careers of its headliners, Monterey Pop was proof of concept for outdoor rock festivals and the films that documented them. D. A. Pennebaker's documentary film was originally supposed to air on television, but ABC executives dropped it from the schedule after watching Jimi Hendrix's hip-grinding performance. *Monterey Pop* (1968) eventually screened at art-house theaters, but even that limited distribution multiplied the festival's impact and paved the way for other concert films, most notably *Woodstock* (1970) and *Gimme Shelter* (1970).

Gleason was convinced that rock music was the key to understanding the American scene. "For the reality of what's happening today," he claimed in *The American Scholar* later that year, "we must go to rock and roll, to popular music." Lifting the article's title, "Like a Rolling Stone," from Dylan's hit song, Gleason cited sources ranging from German philosopher Friedrich Nietzsche to Buffalo Springfield to support his point. He also quoted Plato's claim that musical forms and rhythms were never altered without producing changes in the entire social fabric. According to one observer, that argument was "pure Gleason: gushy, naive, hyperbolic, full of enthusiasm and hope." Perhaps, but Gleason also saw something that eluded his peers. Hippies and their music were far more important than the mainstream media realized. How the social revolution would play out was unclear, but Gleason was convinced that politics was downstream from culture. In a letter to a friend, he asked rhetorically, "You make the social revolution first and politicize it, don't you?" It was inconceivable to him that hippies, or anyone else, could win all the cultural battles and lose all the political ones.

Gleason's argument targeted Warren Hinckle's conception of the hippies, but he was even more upset by the cover story's factual errors and snide tone. At one point, Hinckle mistook the Family Dog, a hippie commune that hosted dance concerts, for a rock group. (Bill Graham once made a similar mistake; assuming that the Family Dog was an animal act, he asked where the dogs were.) Hinckle also claimed that the lyrics to drug songs might constitute the entire literary output of the hippie generation. When combined with Hinckle's decision to preempt him, those errors and snubs infuriated Gleason, who fired off a resignation letter and demanded that it run in *Ramparts*. No one responded, which stoked his rage.

Gleason's break with *Ramparts* was complete. In his *American Scholar* article, he described the magazine as "the white hope of the Square Left." By that time, Gleason was almost ready to unveil a new publication that better reflected his understanding of rock and roll's significance.

.   .   .   .   .

The *Ramparts* story was by no means the only report that disparaged the city's flower children. When national media outlets descended on the Haight to cover the Summer of Love, many were even more scornful than Hinckle. "To their deeply worried parents throughout the country," a *Time* magazine cover story said about the hippies, "they seem more like dangerously deluded dropouts, candidates for a very sound spanking and a cram course in civics—if only they would return home to receive either."

Joan Didion's "Slouching Towards Bethlehem" also took aim at the hippie community. Appearing in *The Saturday Evening Post*, her article nicked the title of W. B. Yeats's poem, claimed that the center was not holding, and cast San Francisco as the place where "the social hemorrhaging was showing up." For Didion, who lived in Los Angeles but had studied at Berkeley, hippies were little more than wayward children and a disturbing example of social disintegration. "At some point between 1945 and 1967," she wrote, "we had somehow neglected to tell these children the rules of the game we happened to be playing." Didion also noted the self-reflexive nature of the media coverage. "There were so many observers on Haight Street from *Life* and *Look* and CBS that they were largely observing one another," she remarked. That point wasn't lost on the hippies, some of whom enjoyed pranking the journalists. The Diggers, for example, introduced reporters from *Time* and *Life* to each other and encouraged both to think they had scored an interview with an elusive Digger leader.

A few profiles were more sympathetic. Writing for *The Atlantic Monthly*, Mark Harris charted a path between Gleason's enthusiasm and Didion's horror. An English professor at nearby San Francisco State College, Harris affirmed Didion's point about the media's reflexivity and extended it to the hippie self-image. The hippies were a hoax, a creature of American journalism, known even to themselves only as they appeared in the media. Yet as the Summer of Love approached, Harris reported, they were beginning to "undertake the labor of community which could be accomplished only behind the scene, out of the eye of the camera, beyond the will of the quick reporter."

Harris held out some hope for that undertaking, but the hippies hadn't impressed him to that point. In their search for community, for example, they never managed to connect with their black neighbors, and they were intellectually unsophisticated at best. When Harris visited a record shop, he discovered an album called *Notes from the Underground*. The cashier informed him that *underground* was a hippie word. "He had not yet heard of Dostoevsky, whose title the record borrowed, or of the antislavery underground in America, or of the World War II underground in France," Harris noted. "A movement which thought itself the world's first underground was bound to make mistakes it could have avoided by consultation with the past." Harris supported the hippies and their project, but his tone was professorial, discerning, alert to hubris and youthful folly.

Freelance journalist Hunter S. Thompson also weighed in on the Haight-Ashbury scene. From his home on Parnassus Avenue, Thompson observed the neighborhood at close range, participated enthusiastically in its drug culture, befriended Ken Kesey, and developed a crush on Jefferson Airplane singer Grace Slick. His brief time in San Francisco also improved his professional fortunes. Only two years earlier, Thompson was begging for assignments, but that changed when *The Nation* asked him to write about the Hells Angels. Thompson parlayed that article into a book contract and spent the following year embedded with the motorcycle gang. When *Hell's Angels: A Strange and Terrible Saga* appeared in January 1967, it was a critical and commercial success.

On the strength of that book, *The New York Times Magazine* invited Thompson to write about Haight-Ashbury. "The 'Hashbury'

Is the Capital of the Hippies" traced the neighborhood's conversion from a quiet bohemian enclave to what Thompson called a "crowded, defiant dope fortress." He also claimed that the statewide election in 1966, which put Ronald Reagan in the governor's office, accelerated that conversion. Many Berkeley activists construed Reagan's victory as a "brutal confirmation of the futility of fighting the establishment on its own terms." Some campus activists shifted their attention to the hippie scene across the bay, which Thompson described as a move "from pragmatism to mysticism, from politics to dope, from the hangups of protest to the peaceful disengagement of love, nature, and spontaneity." Unlike many of his colleagues, Thompson didn't associate hippies with political revolt. They valued artistic, personal, and sexual freedom, but they had little interest in reforming universities, stopping the war in Vietnam, or protecting black neighborhoods from police abuse. When the Vietnam Day Committee invited Ken Kesey to speak on the Berkeley campus, Kesey famously exhorted the audience not to march against the war. Marching is what *they* did, Kesey noted. Instead, young people should turn away from the mainstream culture and create the communities they wished to inhabit.

The split between freaks and activists also surfaced at the so-called Houseboat Summit, which followed the Human Be-In. Organized by the *San Francisco Oracle*, it featured a long conversation between Allen Ginsberg, Timothy Leary, and Gary Snyder. Alan Watts, the popular philosopher who hosted the conversation on his houseboat, announced that the main topic was "the whole problem of whether to drop out or take over." Leary was for dropping out.

> Mass movements make no sense to me, and I want no part of mass movements. I think this is the error that leftist activists are making. I see them as young men with menopausal minds. They are repeating the same dreary quarrels and conflicts for power of the thirties and forties, of the trade union movement, of Trotskyism and so forth. I think they should be sanctified, drop out, find their own center, turn on, and above all avoid mass movements, mass leadership, mass followers.

Leary said he was shocked and alienated by those who wished to build a powerful political movement.

> I see that there is a great difference—I say completely incompatible difference—between the leftist activist movement and the psychedelic religious movement. In the first place, the psychedelic movement, I think, is much more numerous. But it doesn't express itself as noisily. I think there are different goals. I think that activists want power. They talk about student power. That shocks me, and alienates my spiritual sensitivities.

Unlike Leary, Ginsberg called for active political engagement. After he and Snyder pressed Leary on his famous exhortation to turn on, tune in, and drop out, Leary said he meant that young people should drop out in small tribal groups.

If the Houseboat Summit revealed fissures within the counterculture, it also indicated how fluid some positions proved to be. Several years later, for example, Leary called for armed resistance to the establishment.

.   .   .   .   .

Thompson's article about Haight-Ashbury didn't celebrate the hippies, but it was a far cry from Didion's claim that they were wayward children. Moreover, his allusion to the 1966 election raised an important point. If hippies didn't care about politics, politics certainly cared about them. In his stump speeches, Ronald Reagan joked that hippies had haircuts like Tarzan, walked like Jane, and smelled like Cheetah. Because many hippies were too young to vote or ignored electoral politics, such jokes were politically costless. Reagan also knew that Berkeley campus activism was a sore point with voters. "Wherever I went in the state, the first question and literally the first half-dozen questions were about what I would do about the University of California at Berkeley," Reagan recalled later. "You knew that this was the number one thing on people's minds."

In a speech given at the Cow Palace in 1966, Reagan went on the attack. He lambasted "a small minority of beatniks, radicals, and filthy speech advocates" who had "brought shame on a great university." He mentioned a report produced by the California Senate Fact-Finding Subcommittee on Un-American Activities and its conclusion that "the campus has become a rallying point for communists and a center for sexual misconduct." He then brandished a report issued by the Alameda County district attorney that supported the subcommittee's verdict. That report described a dance held in Harmon Gym and sponsored by the Vietnam Day Committee. "The incidents are so bad," Reagan said, "so contrary to our standards of human behavior, that I couldn't possibly recite them to you here from this platform in detail." Nevertheless, Reagan managed to read excerpts about the gym's dark lighting, rock music, marijuana smoke, and lewd dancing. "For this reason," Reagan said, "I today have called on the State Legislature to hold public hearings into the charges of Communism and blatant sexual misbehavior on the campus." In fact, the FBI was already investigating Berkeley campus activism—not to monitor sexual misbehavior or even to prosecute crimes, but rather to disrupt and neutralize lawful political expression.

Reagan's charges were absurd, but his indignation resonated with voters. Many believed that Berkeley students should be thrilled to study at a first-rate university subsidized by California taxpayers. Reagan's attack also shifted the public's attention away from the concerns of campus activists—including systemic racism, police brutality, and the war in Vietnam—to the horrors of rock music, dancing, and weed. Many voters construed the hippie rejection of hard work, marriage, family, and patriotism as an insult. Earlier bohemian communities courted similar reactions, but even compared to the Beats, hippies and their psychedelic worldview rattled parents and voters. The media coverage reinforced their concerns. As Todd Gitlin observed, social deviance was "ordinarily, routinely, and unthinkingly treated as a sort of crime" and covered as such by media outlets. That media framing supported Reagan's charges and boosted his electoral prospects.

Meanwhile, a federal crackdown on LSD targeted hippies directly. Two U.S. Senate committees held hearings in 1966, and the FDA commissioner strongly condemned the drug's widespread use on campus. The media did its part to sound the warning. *Time* and *Newsweek* ran several pieces on the perils of LSD, and *National Review* linked it to the Soviet threat, even though most of the early LSD research was sponsored by the Pentagon and CIA. They hoped that the drug could be used to pacify civilian populations and interrogate Soviet spies. Instead, LSD kick-started the San Francisco hippie scene when Ken Kesey, Allen Ginsberg, Timothy Leary, and others touted its benefits.

Immediately after California banned LSD, the *San Francisco Oracle* organized the Love Pageant Rally, which was held in the Panhandle of Golden Gate Park one month before the gubernatorial election. To protest the LSD ban, many in the surprisingly large crowd swallowed tabs of acid. Kesey and the Merry Pranksters were on hand with their colorful bus, and a free outdoor concert featured the Grateful Dead, Big Brother and the Holding Company, and Wildflower. Governor Pat Brown signed the LSD ban into law, but the hippie protest chimed well with Reagan's claim that Brown was coddling rebellious youths. When Reagan glided to victory in 1966, his first target was public higher education. He and his allies raised fees at the University of California and ousted its president, Clark Kerr.

The conservative backlash did little to curb the hippie community's growth. Several years later, Grateful Dead guitarist Jerry Garcia said he saw more hippies every day, which proved that the revolution he cared about was successful. "Today there is no place without its hippies," Garcia said. "*No* place." The political consequences of the movement were another matter. When asked if rock music was a manifestation of the revolution, Garcia said he didn't think so. In his view, those who were sticking to "an old-line revolutionary tack" were missing the point.

> I think that the revolution that's going to make some sort of dent or some change is already over. It's already happened in principle, and the waves of it are now moving away from ground zero at the rate of about, you know, a mile every four years [*laughs*] or something like that. You know, it's going real slow, but eventually the whole world will be a different place as a result of things that have already happened. It's already gone, it's already past, and the rest of it is like telling everybody who missed it that it's already happened.

Whatever transpired from that point on, Garcia maintained, was a cleanup operation. Ralph Gleason couldn't have said it better.

2 Counter Culture

As national media outlets ramped up their Summer of Love coverage, most reporters focused on drugs, radical politics, and the neighborhood's outlandish street life. In doing so, they overlooked an important cultural story: A relatively small group of San Francisco hippies was reinventing rock music and its live performance.

Ralph Gleason began to report that story the previous year, when members of the Family Dog commune visited his home in Berkeley. One of them, Luria Castell, announced that San Francisco had enough musical talent to become the American version of Liverpool, home of the Beatles. Once an activist at San Francisco State College, Castell had found a new cause. Young people needed a place to dance, she told Gleason, and the Family Dog wanted to furnish it. Their plan was to host dances with light shows, a new art form pioneered in the Bay Area. "Basically we want to meet people and have a good time and not be dishonest and have a profitable thing going on," Castell told Gleason. "Music is the most beautiful way to communicate, it's the way we're going to change things."

The first such dance concert, "A Tribute to Dr. Strange," was held at Longshoremen's Hall in 1965. It featured the Charlatans, Jefferson Airplane, and the Great Society, which included Grace Slick, the sultry-voiced model and debutante. "About 400 or 500 people showed up—it was such a revelation," artist and Family Dog member Alton Kelley recalled. "Everybody was walking around with their mouths open, going, 'Where did all these freaks come from? I thought my friends were the only guys around!'" Describing the event as sensational, Gleason noted the difference between the Family Dog and the impresarios who promoted earlier dances and concerts. "They entered into the occasion as participants, not as organizers," Gleason wrote of the Family Dog. "They danced along with the rest." The crowd was energized by its own forms of self-display, and Gleason compared the event to a giant costume party. "It was orgiastic and spontaneous and completely free-form," he wrote.

As he drove home from the event, Gleason noticed the revelers returning to the East Bay:

> After the dance, on the long bridge over San Francisco Bay, the little Volkswagens with Freedom Now stickers and SNCC and FSM signs in the windows driving back to Berkeley would pass me, packed with long-haired young people, a giant convoy of escapees en route back to real life.

But real life in the East Bay that weekend was no less remarkable than the concert in San Francisco. A large anti-war march, organized by the Vietnam Day Committee, was part of a two-day national protest. Gleason learned about the committee when one of its organizers, Jerry Rubin, visited his home to pitch the concept. Gleason endorsed it and suggested several speakers. But when protestors marched from Berkeley toward the Oakland Army Induction Center, they were confronted by Hells Angels. One of the bikers launched his giant body into the protestors while his friends shouted, "Go back to Russia, you fucking Communists!" Hunter S. Thompson, who was researching his book about the Hells Angels, noted that the anti-war protestors initially hoped the motorcycle gang would support their cause. But when push came to shove, Thompson wrote, the Hells Angels "lined up solidly with the cops, the Pentagon, and the John Birch Society."

The next major event in the hippie community was the Trips Festival in January 1966. The largest of the Acid Tests, the three-day happening at Longshoremen's Hall combined rock music, light shows, dance, film, and plenty of LSD. According to one music scholar, the Trips Festival was "a watershed event in the history of the underground arts scene in San Francisco." Gleason panned the first night's program, which featured no live music, but the festival achieved liftoff when the rock music and light shows kicked in. Like the previous Acid Tests, the Trips Festival blurred the lines between performers and spectators. That participatory energy later fueled rave culture as well as Burning Man, the annual event founded by San Francisco artists. When shifted to the Nevada desert, that spectacle took the "all show, no audience" revelry to new heights.

One of the Trips Festival's organizers was Bill Graham. Born in 1931, the German refugee grew up in the Bronx, served in the Korean War, and spent his summers working at Catskills resorts. An aspiring actor, he moved west and eventually served as the San Francisco Mime Troupe's business manager. When the troupe's founder, Ronnie Davis, was arrested in 1965 for staging a performance in Lafayette Park without a permit, Graham organized benefit concerts to cover the legal fees. For the second benefit, and at Gleason's suggestion, Graham rented the Fillmore Auditorium, an underused dance hall on Geary Boulevard. Some 3,500 people paid $1.50 each to hear Jefferson Airplane, the Grateful Dead, Big Brother and the Holding Company, and Quicksilver Messenger Service.

When Graham proposed more benefits, Ronnie Davis wasn't interested. "We're not in the business of doing benefits," Davis told Graham. "We're in the business of doing plays. You do the benefits. Goodbye." After the Trips Festival, Graham staged three Jefferson

Airplane shows at the Fillmore Auditorium, promising to replicate the Trips Festival's "sights and sounds." He also booked the Grateful Dead, Sopwith Camel, Moby Grape, the Sons of Champlin, Big Brother and the Holding Company, and Quicksilver Messenger Service. Soon he received booking requests from Eric Burdon and the Animals, the Yardbirds, James Brown, and the Byrds. Other musicians visited San Francisco to check out the scene and occasionally sat in with headliners.

Graham was no hippie. He carried a clipboard, wore a wristwatch, spurned psychedelic drugs, and was famous for his moxie and short fuse. He once removed Cream manager Robert Stigwood from a concert for insisting on a seat that Graham had reserved for his visiting sisters. "We thought it was *hilarious*," Cream guitarist Eric Clapton said later. "It was just Bill showing no respect. *Absolutely no respect.*" Graham also berated a local rabbi who sought to close down the Fillmore Auditorium because its customers urinated on the walls of his nearby temple. "What the *fuck* do you know about persecution?" Graham roared. "My family is buried in the camp, I came over here—walked across fucking Europe to get here at the age of eleven—and you're telling me about persecution?"

Graham's rage was frequently performative. "I have heard him scream at the limits of human endurance for fifteen minutes and come out of the room smiling because it was just a maneuver," Grateful Dead publicist Dennis McNally recalled. But Graham preferred his anger, real or manufactured, to hippie pacifism and contemplation. "All that bullshit about vibes, feelings," he told journalist Michael Lydon. "Who needs it? Act! Do something, that's what counts." He was especially contemptuous of slacker rebellion: "You want to rebel, great, but rebel *for* something. Hippies couldn't do that. 'Oh, man, like trip out, man.' Bullshit! They call that changing the world?" For all his outbursts, Graham ran a tight ship, treated the talent well, and put on a good show. Stephen Gaskin, a Marine Corps combat veteran and popular lecturer at San Francisco State College, conceded that Graham fortified the hippie community.

Specifically, he "put a toughness and a grown-upness into our movement that would not have been there without him."

As a promoter, Graham's main competition was Chet Helms, who hitchhiked from Austin to San Francisco in 1962, sold weed, and hosted jam sessions in a boarding house near Golden Gate Park's panhandle. When Big Brother and the Holding Company formed in 1965, the house manager's brother, Peter Albin, became its bass player. Helms helped manage the group and recruited Janis Joplin as its lead singer. A month after the Trips Festival, Helms and the Family Dog joined forces to promote concerts. For a short time, Family Dog Productions shared the Fillmore Auditorium with Graham, but when that arrangement collapsed, the Family Dog leased the Avalon Ballroom on Sutter Street, where it hosted the premier rock bands of that period.

Unlike Graham, Chet Helms was a full-fledged member of the hippie community. He helped organize the Human Be-In and represented the Family Dog on the Council for the Summer of Love. To mitigate problems arising from the influx of young people, the council worked closely with the neighborhood's churches as well as two new organizations, the Haight Ashbury Free Medical Clinic and Huckleberry House, the nation's first shelter for runaways. The council also aided the Diggers in their efforts to serve free food, shelter the homeless, and redistribute usable goods through their Free Store. Compared to Graham, Helms ran a loose operation, but he had his own ambitions. In 1967, the Family Dog expanded to Denver, only to withdraw several months later due to financial mismanagement and pressure from the city. That pressure included the arrest of Canned Heat, one of the venue's headliners, for drug possession. At the same time, Helms was seeking an editor for the music magazine he planned to publish. Its title, he told job candidates, was *Straight Arrow*. The same title had been used for comic books and a radio series that began airing in the late 1940s.

The concerts hosted by Helms and Graham contrasted sharply with their precursors. Only a year earlier, the Beatles played their final public concert at Candlestick Park. Dressed in matching suits, the Fab Four ran out to the stage and played 11 songs over a chorus of 25,000 shrieking teenyboppers. Barely a half hour after they started, the quartet clambered into an armored truck and sped away from the stadium. The Beatles were by no means a typical band, but their brief recital was rooted in the rock-and-roll conventions of that time. Across town, San Francisco bands and audiences were creating something more improvisational, participatory, and psychoactive. At some venues, the low stages barely separated the audience from the musicians, who wore their street clothes. There were no spotlights; instead, light shows bathed musicians and spectators alike and blurred the distinction between them. Some of the jams ran longer than the Beatles' entire performance, and the audience was more likely to dance than to scream.

LSD supercharged those concerts and shaped their conventions. "These were tribal rites," author Joel Selvin noted, "often conducted under the influence of exotic and wonderful potions." Partly because those potions made additional theatrics unnecessary, the Grateful Dead politely ignored Graham's exhortations to ramp up the showmanship. "He always had this rap about showbiz," Jerry Garcia said, "how you've got to give them the sword swallower first, and we'd say, 'Right. Yeah, Bill. Sure.' You know, '*Right.*'" Psychedelic drugs influenced live performances in other ways as well. "In the first days," one musician said, "the length of the sets was due to the LSD because that gave you that unlimited amount of energy. You didn't even know when you were tired, and you couldn't go to sleep." The long sets allowed spectators to trip freely and reassemble themselves before the show's conclusion.

LSD also influenced the posters Helms and Graham commissioned to promote those events. The top artists experimented with intense colors, revolving patterns, and wild typography that evoked psychedelic experiences. Often required to produce posters on a few days' notice, the artists nevertheless appreciated the immediate and broad dissemination of their work. Their psychedelic style, which quickly spread to album art and eventually into advertising, became the San Francisco scene's visual signature.

City officials made several attempts to rein in that scene, mostly on the grounds that the concerts corrupted minors. Enacted in 1909, the city's dance hall ordinance forbade minors from attending events unless accompanied by an adult. But when the chairman of the Juvenile Justice Commission objected to the concerts, Gleason eviscerated him in his *Chronicle* column. Gleason added that he would prefer to see his children attend those concerts rather than a fraternity party.

When out-of-town journalists filed their reports on hippie culture, they usually focused on Haight-Ashbury's street life. If they were looking for the community's heart and soul, however, they were more likely to find it at the Fillmore Auditorium, Avalon Ballroom, or Winterland Arena. Paul Williams, the founder of *Crawdaddy* magazine, understood the significance of those venues. After visiting San Francisco in the spring of 1967, he described them as "induction centers."

·   ·   ·   ·   ·

As the Summer of Love wore on, its scale and intensity overwhelmed the Haight. The influx of young people was accompanied by public health risks, drug trafficking, and runaway minors. In his history of Haight-Ashbury, Charles Perry linked that influx to the Summer of Love media coverage, which served as "an advertisement for the neighborhood, but not the kind that had been hoped for."

> The press advertised free love, free lunch in the Panhandle, tolerance for the crazy and outcast, and a New Age governed by the power of love and innocence. So it brought in not only visionaries but insecure young people unable to find a place for themselves, dropouts content with the basics of life, outcasts, and crazies.

In Perry's account, the mainstream media reports altered, and did not merely describe, the facts on the ground. As more Americans learned about the Summer of Love, more young people flocked to the city, creating what Jerry Garcia described as an ecological disaster. After moving to Colorado, Hunter S. Thompson also lamented the neighborhood's transformation. The Haight, he wrote, had become "a cop-magnet and a bad sideshow."

The drug crackdown that followed was a predictable consequence of that media attention. In October, members of the Grateful Dead were arrested for marijuana possession at their home on 710 Ashbury Street. In a press statement released the next day, one of the band's managers criticized the media as well as the state's drug laws. His statement claimed that the Haight-Ashbury coverage depended on "the long-haired dropout who performs his exotic rites for the convenience of visiting cameramen." That ritual encouraged police officers to arrest young people who fit the profile. Meanwhile, respectable citizens in other neighborhoods were allowed to smoke their weed in peace. The statement concluded that the drug law was a lie, and that "the hippie, as created by the media, is a lie as well." Three days later, on the first anniversary of the Love Pageant Rally, the Diggers made a similar point by performing "Death of Hippie," a mock funeral that identified the deceased as "Hippie, devoted son of Mass Media." That trope turned Mark Harris's claim on its head. Whereas Harris argued that hippies derived their identity from media accounts, the Diggers claimed that the media had created the very stereotype it purported to describe.

Despite the mock funeral, Hippie was alive and well. If national news outlets scolded, nagged, and mocked their devoted son, they also made him a celebrity. Other parts of the media figured in this family romance as well. In a bid for younger viewers, television networks introduced programs with hippie characters and themes. After *Easy Rider* became a top-grossing film in 1969, mystified Hollywood executives turned to a new generation of directors to attract younger audiences. Many of their films questioned, subverted, or rejected the American Dream that Hollywood studios had fashioned and popularized. Advertisers also used hippie attitudes, styles, and music to sell everything from vodka to Volkswagens. But that relationship wasn't merely instrumental. A cohort of advertising mavericks joined—and in some cases anticipated—the youthful rebellion that was underway. In addition to casting brands as symbols of defiance and revolt, some ad executives mocked their own industry's hidebound norms and customs. One of their prophets was Howard Gossage, Hinckle's mentor, who was said to have produced "as harsh an attack on American commercial culture as any generated by the Frankfurt School." Gossage would never be mistaken for a hippie, but he and his followers shared the counterculture's impatience with cant and hypocrisy.

.   .   .   .   .

The media landscape was changing in other ways as well. In the 1950s, Top 40 radio emerged as the primary way to market music to young people. Beginning as a survey of popular jukebox recordings, the format shifted to ranking singles by their radio play. With its slick patter, jingles, and youth-oriented advertising, Top 40 radio became a popular format, especially when half the U.S. population was under the age of 25. But the format was also prone to abuse. Music labels routinely paid radio hosts to play specific releases, and Congress began investigating the so-called payola scandal in 1959.

Shortly after that, Top 40 host Bobby Mitchell relocated from Philadelphia, a focal point of the payola scandal, to San Francisco. Mitchell also lured his colleague, Tom Donahue, to the Bay Area. In his mid-30s, Donahue quickly established himself at KYA, a popular Top 40 station in San Francisco. His mission, he told his young listeners, was to "clear up your face and mess up your mind." With his deep voice and massive body, Donahue was an impressive figure. "I loved listening to him," one of his protégés said. "He always had wonderful opinions. . . . And what a voice. You shut up and you listened." Donahue and Mitchell also promoted dances and concerts, including the Beatles at Candlestick Park and the Rolling Stones at the Cow Palace. When they started a record label, they hired 19-year-old Sylvester Stewart as a producer. Raised in Vallejo, some 25 miles north of Oakland, Stewart wrote and produced a top-ten single, Bobby Freeman's "C'mon and Swim," the following year. He also notched two hits by the Beau Brummels, a San Francisco band that rode the wave of Beatlemania; collaborated with Billy Preston on *The Wildest Organ in Town* (1966); and produced an early version of "Somebody to Love," which became a hit after Grace Slick joined Jefferson Airplane.

In the evenings, Stewart hosted a popular radio program, first at KSOL in San Francisco and later at KDIA in Oakland. Both stations targeted black audiences, but Stewart also spun records by the Beatles, Rolling Stones, Bob Dylan, and other white artists along with R&B favorites. "In radio, I found out about a lot of things I don't like," Stewart said later. "Like, I think there shouldn't be 'black radio.' Just radio. Everybody be a part of everything. I didn't look at my job in terms of black." Some white musicians raised in the Bay Area, including John Fogerty of Creedence Clearwater Revival and Ron "Pigpen" McKernan of the Grateful Dead, probably saw it Stewart's way. As youngsters, they listened faithfully to the Bay Area's R&B stations, whose music shaped their later work.

In 1966, Stewart formed his own band, Sly and the Stoners, whose gigs he often joined after completing his radio shifts. He soon merged that band with his brother's group, Freddie and the Stone Souls. The new group's members were black and white, male and female, and the band blended rock, soul, funk, and gospel. Their first album flopped, but their subsequent work vaulted Sly and the Family Stone to the top ranks of popular music and broadened the appeal of the Bay Area counterculture.

Meanwhile, Donahue left KYA but was considering a return to radio. "Do you realize that we sit here every night and smoke dope and play records for each other?" he asked his friends. "I wonder why nobody's done this on the radio." He voiced the same question in March 1967 at a Mills College rock symposium that included Gleason, Bill Graham, and record producer Phil Spector. After the panel, Gleason told Donahue about Larry Miller's midnight show at KMPX, an FM station that specialized in foreign-language programming. A former musician from Detroit, Miller was playing long cuts from blues, folk, and folk-rock albums. Donahue also learned that FM stations could broadcast in stereo, a huge improvement over the tinny AM sound.

In April, Donahue offered his services to KMPX, took the evening slot, and helped develop free-form radio. After his program attracted listeners and advertisers, Donahue filled the daytime slots with rock music, this time without the frantic patter and predictable playlists of Top 40 radio. Instead of playing hit singles by the Monkees and Herman's Hermits, KMPX programs sampled Jefferson Airplane's *Surrealistic Pillow*, Jimi Hendrix's *Are You Experienced*, and the Grateful Dead's eponymous debut album. One show played the Beatles' *Sgt. Pepper's Lonely Hearts Club Band* in its entirety and without commercial interruption. KMPX also played tapes and test pressings, which irked the musicians union but made the station a destination for rock groups seeking airtime. It wasn't unusual, Gleason said, to see touring bands in the KMPX lobby or wandering through the studios, tapes in hand. By previewing the music of Country Joe and the Fish and Creedence Clearwater Revival, KMPX stoked demand for their successful releases. It also became the first FM station to break hits, including the Youngbloods' "Let's Get Together" and the Chambers Brothers' "Time."

KMPX sounded like underground radio, but it sold advertising, played releases from major labels, and remained a commercial enterprise in every way. In effect, historian Michael J. Kramer argued in *The Republic of Rock* (2013), Donahue created a new market segment by packaging and selling a revolt against mass consumerism. The format's success also pointed to a broader, hipper, and more freewheeling imagined community. By giving voice to local hippies, their music, and their outlook, KMPX amplified the effects of the Acid Tests, ballroom shows, psychedelic posters, and other changes on the ground in San Francisco.

In his 1967 *Crawdaddy* article, Paul Williams registered the cumulative effect of those innovations.

> If you examine San Francisco closely, you'll find major changes taking place in almost every aspect of city life. New attitudes towards jobs, towards education, towards entertainment and the arts. Basic shifts in the relationships between man and his environment, shifts that have affected every facet of that environment.

It was a variation on Plato's claim, frequently endorsed by Gleason, that changes in musical form and rhythm altered the entire social fabric. In the Bay Area, new musical forms and rhythms were accompanied by shifts in the presentation, dissemination, and consumption of that music.

While San Francisco was birthing a new form of hip capitalism, many locals claimed that the music belonged to the people and should be free. That notion emerged from a 1966 symposium at San Francisco State College, where poet Kenneth Rexroth appealed to young artists to take art out of the museums and into the neighborhoods. Shortly after that, the San Francisco Mime Troupe hosted a meeting—attended by Gleason, Ferlinghetti, Graham, and Rexroth—whose participants founded the Artists Liberation Front (ALF). Taking up Rexroth's proposal, the ALF called for Free Fairs, which led to free rock concerts in the park. During this time, the Diggers evolved out of the Mime Troupe and focused on using the world as a stage to challenge the dominion of money. That effort included serving free food in Golden Gate Park, establishing Free Stores to redistribute used goods, and staging a "Death of Money" parade in December 1966. Claiming that money was an addictive and unnecessary evil that led to violence, the Diggers invited responsible citizens to turn in their cash for redistribution. "No questions will be asked," the Diggers assured potential donors.

The Grateful Dead played many times without receiving payment, but Jerry Garcia challenged the idea of free music as such. "There was never a free concert," he told one interviewer. "Money is only a symbol for energy exchange. . . . But if it's going strictly an energy rip-off trip, where the musician gets up there and sweats like hell for three hours, and everybody in the front row gets off, and it's all for the purpose of illustrating some philosophical point, fuck it." In another interview, Garcia dismissed "that bullshit about the people's music." The people weren't around while he learned to play the guitar, he noted, nor did they pay their dues as artists. "I mean, if the people think that way, they can fucking make their own music," he said. Garcia also wondered who, exactly, the people were in that formulation. "When somebody says *people*, to me it means everybody," he said. "It means the cops, the guys who drive the limousines, the fucker who runs the elevator, everybody. All that."

.   .   .   .   .

In 1967, Bay Area professor and peace activist Theodore Roszak surveyed these changes and named the community that gave rise to them. In a series of articles for *The Nation*, Roszak argued that the hippies represented a *counter culture*. When that term stuck, it lengthened the list of Bay Area coinages, including *beatnik* and *hippie*, both of which were popularized by *San Francisco Chronicle* columnist Herb Caen. Roszak lived and taught in the East Bay, but he was editing *Peace News* in London when he wrote his articles for *The Nation*. Youthful protests abroad, he noticed, drew from a leftist tradition that was largely absent from American politics. At first, Roszak agreed with his European colleagues that hippie culture was politically immature, but he eventually concluded that the counterculture's indifference to leftist orthodoxy made room for other important questions about consciousness, quality of life, and environmental sustainability.

Drawing from social theory, media accounts, and direct observation, Roszak's description of the counterculture was by no means uncritical. He called out hippies for their rhetorical excesses, unforced political errors, and histrionic resistance to traditional values. He took a dim view of the drug culture, including its quest for "counterfeit infinity," and he never overestimated the counterculture's sophistication. "The young, miserably educated as they are, bring with them almost nothing but healthy instincts," he wrote. Roszak acknowledged that the Summer of Love was essentially a media event that highlighted the hippies' weirdest aberrations, but he faulted hippies for reacting narcissistically or defensively to what he called the fun-house mirror of the media. The mass media was culpable for its distortions, Roszak concluded, but so was the counterculture for playing the media's game.

Nevertheless, Roszak was sympathetic to the youthful revolt against technocracy, materialism, environmental rapacity, militarism, and spiritual emptiness. Indeed, he believed that hippies were the best hope for an alienated and denatured society. The media presented hippies as kooks, weirdos, and oddballs, but Roszak's analysis raised a simple question: Compared to whom? Despite its faith in rationality and efficiency, the establishment had brought the planet to the brink of military, environmental, and humanitarian disaster. For many young people, that was proof enough that mainstream American culture was off its rocker. Moreover, the corporate media had damaged its credibility by misleading the public about the conflict in Vietnam, the nature of the counterculture, and the dangers of marijuana, possession of which was still a serious felony.

When Roszak's book, *The Making of a Counter Culture*, appeared in 1969, it was nominated for a National Book Award. Much later, however, Roszak identified a key omission. "If there is one aspect of the period that I now wish had enjoyed more attention in these pages, it is the music," he wrote. "Music inspired and carried the best insights of the counter culture—from folk protest ballads and songs of social significance at the outset to the acid rock that became the only way to reflect the surrealistic turn that America was to take at the climax of the Vietnam War." That remark qualified Roszak's earlier assertion that hippies brought nothing but healthy instincts to their youthful rebellion, but it fell well short of Gleason's hunch about the new music's transformative power. Roszak didn't expect the establishment to yield any political ground to the counterculture in the absence of effective organizing and determined advocacy.

The hippie community didn't require adult approval, but Roszak's analysis was a welcome break from the media stereotypes. Meanwhile, Gleason, Graham, Donahue, and others were fashioning a symbiotic relationship between rock music, independent labels, print media, live shows, poster art, and radio programming. Neither the mainstream media nor hostile politicians hindered the hippie community's growth and development; indeed, they probably helped popularize it. But there was nothing inevitable about the confluence of social, political, artistic, and commercial forces in the San Francisco Bay Area of that period. Nor was there a road map for the way forward. From the outset, the counterculture was an improvisation, a series of experiments, one step after another into the unknown.

3   Plan B

Throughout the Summer of Love, Gleason remained optimistic about the San Francisco hippies and their music. After resigning from *Ramparts*, he began working with his 21-year-old protégé, Jann Wenner, on a new magazine. In effect, Gleason and Wenner meant to solve the problem of media saturation with more and better media.

Although Wenner was smitten with rock and roll, it wasn't his first love. Raised in affluent Marin County, he was steeped in electoral politics at an early age. His parents, who owned a successful baby food business, brought their liberal politics from New York to California. In his memoir, Wenner noted that his father coordinated Adlai Stevenson's presidential campaign in Northern California, and that his mother was among the founders of the California Democratic Council. As a child, Wenner said, he stuffed envelopes and walked precincts on behalf of Democratic candidates.

An ardent reader of the *San Francisco Chronicle*, Wenner published his own newsletter while still in elementary school. At age 12, he shipped out to a private boarding school in Southern California, where he wrote for the school newspaper and edited the yearbook. He also published an underground newspaper whose title spoofed the school's nautical theme. *The Sardine* reported on Wenner's successful bid for student office and ran his gossip column, "Random Notes."

After graduating from high school, Wenner enrolled at the University of California, Berkeley, where he planned to major in English and minor in political science. By that time, his parents were divorced and his family splintered. Wenner's father moved to Los Angeles, his mother maintained homes in San Francisco and Hawaii, and his sisters attended boarding schools in Colorado and Vermont. In Berkeley, Wenner rented an apartment near campus. With the help of a family friend, he also landed a part-time job at KNBR, the NBC radio affiliate, where he monitored traffic and wrote copy for the broadcasters. He was crushed when his idol, John F. Kennedy, was assassinated that November, but his interest in politics and journalism was undiminished. That summer, NBC hired him to work at the 1964 Republican National Convention, which was held at the Cow Palace only a month before the Beatles launched their North American tour there. As a gofer in the broadcast booth, Wenner fetched cigarettes and ripped wire copy for NBC anchormen Chet Huntley and David Brinkley.

One observer described the GOP convention that year as "a bar fight that lasted four days." Senator Barry Goldwater, the party's nominee, touted liberty and free markets to counter the spread of communism, but his candidacy also reflected a major political realignment. As the civil rights movement gained traction in the South, Dixiecrats were already abandoning the Democratic Party, swelling the Republican ranks, and subverting the GOP's historical support for civil rights. At the convention, white Republicans openly taunted black delegates. One NBC reporter found an elderly black delegate leaning against the wall, weeping. The Goldwater delegates had put out their cigarettes on his suit. That sort of mistreatment led Jackie Robinson, the GOP delegate who had courageously broken the color barrier in Major League Baseball, to describe the convention as "one of the most unforgettable and frightening experiences of my life." The GOP also targeted the media. When Dwight Eisenhower's speech scorned "sensation-seeking columnists and commentators," many delegates rose from their seats and waved their fists at the broadcast booths. Black reporters were especially vulnerable to their wrath. Belva Davis, who later became a prominent Bay Area news anchor, recalled the racial epithets hurled at her and her boss after Eisenhower's speech.

Hunter S. Thompson obtained a floor pass to the convention and witnessed Senator Goldwater's acceptance speech. It climaxed when Goldwater praised extremism in defense of liberty, and Thompson described the audience's response.

> The Goldwater delegates went completely amok for fifteen or twenty minutes. He hadn't even finished the sentence before they were on their feet, cheering wildly. Then, as the human thunder kept building, they mounted their metal chairs and began howling, shaking their fists at Huntley and Brinkley up in the NBC booth—and finally they began picking up those chairs with both hands and bashing them against chairs other delegates were still standing on.

The delegation's ferocity rattled Thompson, but Wenner was struck by his own place in the spectacle. "I was in the heart of the machine, watching it toss and spin, thousands of people screaming and cheering, and millions watching it on television," he recalled in his memoir. "I was a part of making it all happen."

That same summer, Wenner belatedly discovered the Beatles. They were featured on *The Ed Sullivan Show* earlier that year, but Wenner wasn't among the 73 million viewers who watched the group's first U.S. television appearance on the popular variety show. When his friends took him to see *A Hard Day's Night*, however, Wenner found the Beatles irresistible. "We didn't realize it then," he recalled, "but they alleviated the heaviness and cynicism of a society that had killed its beautiful young president and had peeled back the mask on its racism."

For the American public, the British Invasion was as unpredictable as it was welcome. Having absorbed rock and roll and its precursors, English groups sold their music back to receptive U.S. audiences. As Beatles scholar Tim Riley noted, it was as if a Danish baseball team had appeared out of nowhere and won the World Series. On the journalistic front, English rock magazines were also far ahead of their American counterparts. *Melody Maker*, which began as a jazz magazine, shifted its sights to rock and roll in the 1950s. Founded in 1952, *New Musical Express* was another early rock champion. It would take years for the United States to produce a comparable publication.

.   .   .   .   .

During Wenner's sophomore year, the Free Speech Movement began to attract significant media attention, but the underlying issues weren't new. For decades, Cal had effectively barred communists from teaching and speaking on campus. During the 1930s, its president wrote that he and his peers had a duty "to silence those engaged in spreading the mustard gas of class warfare." No such policy targeted fascists, even when they launched the bloodiest war in the history of the planet. During the Second World War, the Board of Regents began requiring all university employees to sign an oath of allegiance to the constitutions of California and the United States. After the war, the regents called for an explicitly anti-communist loyalty oath. When the administration fired professors for refusing to sign it on principle, the university tipped into crisis. Many who lost their jobs sued the university and eventually regained their positions, but other careers were spoiled.

After steering Cal through the loyalty oath crisis, Berkeley chancellor Clark Kerr loosened some of the university's restrictions on speech, but students still weren't permitted to engage in political activities on university property. Activists argued that their rights should be at least as robust on campus as off, but as civil rights protests heated up in the Bay Area, Kerr faced pressure from local businesses, which charged that students were using the campus to organize attacks on them. Those businesses included hotels, auto dealerships, supermarkets, and restaurants that refused to hire or promote black workers.

In the end, an unlikely discovery launched the Free Speech Movement. For years, students had distributed leaflets on the university's southern border near Telegraph Avenue. In the summer of 1964, *The Oakland Tribune* learned that a strip of land near that intersection belonged to the university, not to the city of Berkeley. The university immediately forbade political activity in that space, but many activists continued to use it for that purpose. On October 1, 1964, some of those activists were arrested. "It was a torch thrown into a gas station," Wenner recalled. When one activist was dragged to a nearby police car in Sproul Plaza, students gathered around it. One speaker after another mounted the car to address the crowd, and they were still there the next day, when Joan Baez sang "We Shall Overcome" on the steps of Sproul Hall. For the next several months, FSM rallies and sit-ins drew substantial media coverage.

Meanwhile, Wenner joined SLATE, the student group whose members helped launch the Free Speech Movement. He also edited the *SLATE Supplement to the General Catalog*, a guide to course offerings based on student questionnaires. Although Wenner welcomed the opportunity to rate professors and shape student opinion, he quickly realized he was less radical than his colleagues, whom he later claimed were notable for "their beards, thrift-shop wardrobes, work boots, and bad breath." Many SLATE members had misgivings about President Kennedy's wealthy background, but Wenner was openly intrigued by San Francisco high society. "The wealth was on display, the booze, the big settings, young kids in black ties," he recalled. "I was just dazzled by it." When he returned from a ski trip with his ankle in a cast, his SLATE colleagues teased him about his bourgeois tastes.

If Wenner was more interested in socialites than in socialism, he understood the importance of Berkeley campus activism. The Free

Speech Movement, he recalled, "was the moment it began, the student protests of the sixties, in front of my eyes." He began to report on those protests and was at the Greek Theatre when police hauled off FSM leader Mario Savio for trying to address a campus audience without permission. An Associated Press photograph showed Wenner in a trench coat, microphone in hand, only yards behind the apprehended FSM leader. Gleason devoted a *Chronicle* column, "The Tragedy at the Greek Theatre," to the same event. By that time, Gleason was hosting FSM leaders at his home. "In Ralph, we found someone who spoke our language more fully than any other observer," Michael Rossman said later.

.   .   .   .   .

The following semester, Wenner met Denise Kaufman, a San Francisco native whose affluent parents were active in progressive causes. Kaufman attended public high school in the city, but after she sneaked out of the house to catch concerts, her parents enrolled her in a Palo Alto boarding school for girls. On the peninsula, she took in the local folk music scene and played with the Stanford Music Club. For her high school graduation party, she hired a band that included Ron "Pigpen" McKernan, who would help form the Grateful Dead the following year. Having chosen to attend Cal for its political climate, Kaufman joined the Free Speech Movement. She also guided Wenner through his first acid trip and introduced him to the region's burgeoning music scene. "Denise and LSD changed my life," Wenner wrote later. "I became an evangelist for music and psychedelics." He was especially drawn to her background and disposition. "She combined those two worlds so perfectly for me," Wenner said. "She was from a straight background, wealthy background, the proper background. The good Jewish girl, and the wild child thing. And that was perfect for me."

Kaufman was also developing her musical chops. While attending the Berkeley Folk Music Festival, an annual event held on campus, Gleason heard Kaufman play harmonica at an impromptu blues jam. He complimented her performance in his *Chronicle* column and later introduced himself to her on Telegraph Avenue. They quickly formed a close friendship. Toward the end of her freshman year, Kaufman met Ken Kesey and later appeared in Tom Wolfe's *The Electric Kool-Aid Acid Test* as Mary Microgram. As Kaufman's involvement with the Pranksters deepened, Wenner saw her less frequently but continued to value their relationship.

That fall, Wenner attended his first Rolling Stones concert at the San Jose Civic Auditorium. As he left, he was handed a flyer for a party several blocks away. It turned out to be the second Acid Test. Looking for ways to increase the turnout, Ken Kesey and the Pranksters had posted flyers on the Cal campus and invited the Grateful Dead to perform. Wenner also attended an Acid Test at the Fillmore Auditorium as well as the Trips Festival, where Kaufman introduced him to Gleason. Wenner revered Gleason's *Chronicle* column and later described it as "the only place I knew to find a certain social, cultural, and political mix that was coming to define my world."

Months later, Wenner began writing a weekly column for the Berkeley campus newspaper, *The Daily Californian*. Both his pseudonym, Mr. Jones, and the column's title, "Something's Happening," riffed on Bob Dylan's "Ballad of a Thin Man." For his photograph, Wenner wore a wig and fake mustache, hippie sunglasses, and a harmonica rack. Wenner wrote about his psychedelic adventures and championed Dylan, the Beatles, and the Rolling Stones. He also touted local bands, the best of which was Jefferson Airplane. "Their sound is very tight and very beautiful," Wenner wrote. He also praised another band for its haunting sound. "The group which, if it ever makes it, will make it the biggest, is the Grateful Dead," he wrote. "The lead guitar of Jerry Garcia (Captain Trips) will make your head its own reverb unit."

That same semester, Wenner again crossed paths with Gleason, this time at a Grateful Dead concert in Harmon Gym. Flattered to learn that Gleason was aware of his *Daily Cal* column, Wenner became a regular visitor at Gleason's home on Ashby Avenue. "Ralph liked that I was an enthusiastic student and acolyte, eagerly soaking up everything he had to offer," Wenner recalled. By that time, Gleason had met John Lennon, Bob Dylan, and many other rock stars. Perhaps Wenner, too, would meet his idols.

.   .   .   .   .

One of Wenner's *Daily Cal* readers was Jonathan Cott, a New York transplant and graduate student at Cal. Cott studied with an English professor who wrote about the Beats and helped organize KPFA, the nation's first listener-sponsored radio station. Established by pacifists in 1949, the FM station featured Kenneth Rexroth on literature, Pauline Kael on film, and Alan Watts on Eastern religion and philosophy. Cott, who interviewed guests on a program called *Coconut Grove*, invited Wenner to join him in the studio. The two became friends, and both were embraced by Gleason and his family.

Another reader of Wenner's column was Greil Marcus, a political science major from the peninsula whose dormitory roommate introduced him to Wenner in 1964. Marcus's adoptive father served in the Franklin D. Roosevelt administration, was founding president of Congregation Beth Am in Los Altos Hills, and cochaired Pat Brown's gubernatorial campaign in 1962. An avid music fan, Marcus read in the *San Francisco Chronicle* that an English group called the Beatles would appear on *The Ed Sullivan Show*, a popular television program that aired on Sunday nights. "I thought that sounded funny," he said later. "I didn't know they had rock and roll in England." When he went to the dormitory's commons room to watch the program, he was surprised to see that 200 other people were there for the same reason.

Marcus's classes also intrigued him. Taught by charismatic professors, an American Studies seminar created what Marcus called "an atmosphere of great intellectual intensity." As the Free Speech Movement gained traction, the seminar's key ideas became tangible. "Everything we were doing in that seminar was playing out in public," Marcus recalled. After one class, Marcus and his classmates ventured down to Sproul Plaza, where they saw a police car surrounded by students. They watched for hours as speakers mounted the car with care, sometimes removing their shoes. According to Marcus, the speeches were proffered and received with civility and mutual respect. Such events left a deep impression on Marcus and his cohort. "The Free Speech Movement had an enormous effect on everyone and in many ways," Marcus recalled. "We measured ourselves against it and its values."

Like Wenner, Marcus read Gleason's column in the *San Francisco Chronicle*, but with mounting irritation. In his view, Gleason "wrote the same three columns, over and over again." Marcus was "absolutely sick of reading these columns," he said. "First of all, it was all promotion. Promotion of the scene." When Marcus began writing about music, his articles included digs against Gleason. "My view was, let the young guys take the floor now," Marcus said later. "Let the old guys shuffle off the stage." But when Marcus needed a photograph of the Coasters, who produced a string of hits for Atlantic Records, he called Gleason and was invited to his home. Gleason was familiar with Marcus's work, including the digs, but he thrilled Marcus with the free-ranging conversation that followed. "I left walking on air," Marcus recalled.

Marcus later claimed that the Free Speech Movement made *Rolling Stone* possible, and that much of his formative experiences on campus found expression at the magazine. "Everything that I had learned at Berkeley, that I had learned to care about, there was room for that at *Rolling Stone*," he said.

·   ·   ·   ·   ·

After Wenner and Kaufman attended a concert in 1966, she expressed doubts about their future as a couple. Meanwhile, Wenner discovered that some Berkeley friends were planning to visit London, and he decided to make the same trip. London was a major node in the global rock network, and *Time* magazine's 1966 cover story, "London: The Swinging City," roughly coincided with Wenner's departure. Upon his arrival, he visited the offices of *Melody Maker* and presented a letter of introduction from Gleason. It didn't lead to a job offer, but the magazine ran Wenner's article about a new Beach Boys record. During that time, Wenner also attended shows by the Yardbirds, John Mayall & the Bluesbreakers with Eric Clapton, and the Spencer Davis Group with Stevie Winwood. After watching a Simon & Garfunkel show, Wenner met the duo backstage and introduced himself to their manager, another friend of Gleason's.

With no job offers in sight, Wenner wasn't planning to stay in London. After receiving a conciliatory letter from Kaufman, he returned to New York that August, but she wasn't ready to see him. A disappointed Wenner stayed with a friend in Westchester County, where he drafted an autobiographical novel, smoked weed, and listened to the Beatles' *Revolver*. Meanwhile, Gleason was trying to track down Wenner. Through Kaufman, Gleason obtained his address and wrote that the editors at *Ramparts* magazine were launching a weekly newspaper "roughly in the *Village Voice, New Republic* bag."

> We will cover the local stories the metros don't cover, full coverage to the movement, literary, social, etc. etc. etc. I am going to be on the board of editors of this project. I would like to propose that you might be available for a part or full-time job as a reporter when we get going in October. You would fit into this whole thing very well. We are going to need coverage of flicks, art, books, plays, etc., etc., etc. Wide Open.

Wenner returned to San Francisco and waited for Gleason's call.

.   .   .   .   .

In October 1966, Wenner reported to work at the *Sunday Ramparts* at 301 Broadway, a short walk from City Lights Bookstore as well as the cafés, strip joints, jazz venues, and comedy clubs in North Beach. By that time, *Ramparts* magazine had established itself as a prominent voice against the war in Vietnam. Robert Scheer, a former graduate student at Cal who also had worked at City Lights, was the magazine's resident expert on that conflict. With financial support from Paul Krassner, publisher of a satirical magazine called *The Realist*, Scheer visited Vietnam and returned to challenge mainstream media accounts of the war and its origins. *Ramparts* had not yet collected its Polk Award for investigative reporting, exposed the CIA's infiltration of the National Student Association, or hired Eldridge Cleaver, who was then serving time in state prison. Nevertheless, the magazine was already reaching a large and relatively sophisticated audience. One survey indicated that its average readers were 25 to 30 years old, registered Democrats, married with two children, and living in apartments in large eastern cities. They worked as teachers or other professionals, and their household incomes were $14,000 per year (about $137,000 in 2025). They bought 20 to 30 books and a dozen records per year, and they also read the *Saturday Review*, *The New Republic*, *The New York Review of Books*, *Time*, *Newsweek*, *Psychology Today*, and *Look*.

During his first week on the job, Wenner met Jane Schindelheim, the magazine's receptionist. A recent arrival from Pittsburgh, where she studied drawing at the Carnegie Institute of Technology, Schindelheim was living with her sister, who also worked for *Ramparts*. They grew up in New York, where their father headed the bureau of dentistry at the city's Department of Health. Jane quietly stood out in San Francisco. "She wasn't a hippie," Wenner said later. "She was the Bloomingdale's girl." Recalling her signature trench coat and black turtleneck, one classmate compared her to "some babe that would have walked off a Godard movie." Attracted by Jane's beauty and poise, Wenner turned on the charm and was soon living with her on Potrero Hill. She accompanied him to concerts, got along well with his friends, and helped him recover from his breakup with Kaufman.

Wenner enjoyed his work at the magazine's spinoff newspaper, where he wrote short reviews for the entertainment section, edited the calendar listings, and produced several feature articles. He also tried to interest Hinckle in the counterculture, but the *Ramparts* editor was in many ways a throwback. Working out of a nearby cop bar, Hinckle identified with the nineteenth-century journalists who created San Francisco's rowdy bohemian scene. His world, like theirs, consisted of paper, type, ink, and the drinking press who knew how to combine them. Wenner fared no better with Scheer, who was a decade older than Wenner, preferred jazz to rock and roll, and was focused on Vietnam, Cuba, and the New Left. "They were oblivious to the cultural changes in San Francisco," Wenner recalled. "Warren ridiculed it, and Scheer had no use for it."

The gap between the politicos and freaks was especially evident in 1966, when Scheer ran for Congress in the East Bay. His campaign speeches called for an end to the war in Vietnam, more attention to poverty and racism in the East Bay, and the legalization of abortion and marijuana. His friendship with Bill Graham afforded him access to hippies, but Gleason was adamant about the mismatch between Scheer and the counterculture. "I don't think there is any possibility whatsoever of Bob Scheer ever becoming a leader of the hippies," Gleason wrote to one colleague. "These kids will not listen to political speeches, and Bob Scheer doesn't swing and he doesn't move and he doesn't get to them." Trying to politicize the hippies, Gleason believed, was "discussing them in the wrong framework." After running a surprisingly strong race, Scheer lost to the incumbent in the Democratic primary.

Although Wenner didn't convert the *Ramparts* brass to his cause, his time at the newspaper was well spent. He admired the art direction of Dugald Stermer, who created a stylish design for the magazine and spinoff newspaper. Wenner also appreciated Hinckle's showmanship, which frequently induced *The New York Times* to run the magazine's major stories on its front page. Adam Hochschild, a *Ramparts* staff writer who later cofounded *Mother Jones* magazine, described Hinckle's winning formula: "Find an exposé that major newspapers are afraid to touch, publish it with a big enough splash so they can't afford to ignore it, and then publicize it in a way that plays the press off against each other." Both *Rolling Stone* and *Mother Jones* would master that recipe, and Wenner later acknowledged his magazine's debt to *Ramparts*. "It was a breakthrough magazine of its time. And in addition it was elegant," he told biographer Joe Hagan. "The mix was highly unusual. And that mix moved into *Rolling Stone*."

The high concept for the new magazine emerged when Wenner met with Gleason to discuss his future. Gleason recounted that exchange in a 1973 documentary film.

> And finally Jann came over one day and said, "How about a magazine like *Melody Maker* or [*New*] *Musical Express*, but an American one that would be different and better, that would cover not just records and music, but the whole culture?" As soon as he said it, we both agreed it was a hell of an idea, and that was it.

It seemed simple, but Wenner's idea—and its professional execution—would distinguish the new magazine from practically every other media outlet.

In March, Wenner attended the symposium in Oakland that featured Gleason, Tom Donahue, Bill Graham, and legendary music producer Phil Spector. There he met Baron Wolman, a 30-year-old freelance photographer whose clients included Mills College, the venue for the symposium. Wenner told Wolman about their plans for a new magazine and emphasized the need for excellent photography. He recounted the exchange in his memoir: "I felt that rock and roll was also about imagery—looks, sex, and attitude—good or bad. I didn't want public-relations portraits or performance shots with microphones in everyone's face. I needed a photographer, not a rock fan with a hobby." The obvious choice for that position was Jim Marshall, who lived in San Francisco. Like Gleason, Marshall was ubiquitous. He was present at Dylan's press conference in 1965, backstage with the Beatles at Candlestick Park, and on hand at the Monterey Pop Festival. The only problem with Marshall, Wenner said later, was that he was "a full-time hothead who usually packed heat. I wasn't up for dealing with that." If Marshall was difficult and obsessed with guns, Wolman was interested, available, and less likely to brandish a pistol.

Shortly after the Mills College symposium, Hinckle shut down the *Sunday Ramparts.* The unemployed Wenner turned to what he and Gleason called Plan B, the rock magazine that still lacked a title. Gleason suggested *Rolling Stone*, a phrase that was top of mind as he drafted his essay for *The American Scholar.* Wenner accepted the suggestion, and Wolman agreed to serve as chief photographer. He didn't receive a salary, but the magazine covered his film and developing costs, let him retain the rights to his photographs, and gave him stock in the company. The magazine's goal was to fill an empty niche in the media ecology. "There was nothing that gave Bob Dylan his due gravitas nor spoke to what amazing musicians and writers the Beatles and the Stones were," Wenner wrote later. "Nothing showed any awareness of the cultural revolution under way."

In fact, Paul Williams launched *Crawdaddy!* magazine in February 1966 with similar goals. (It soon dropped the exclamation mark in the title.) As a 17-year-old freshman at Swarthmore College, Williams filled his mimeographed fanzine with his own rock reviews. The total budget for his first issue, with its print run of 500 copies, was less than $40. Although Williams didn't pay his contributors, they soon included Jon Landau, Richard Meltzer, and Peter Guralnick. Williams identified even more strongly with the counterculture than Wenner did. "I was a hippy, I was taking LSD and marching in peace demonstrations and everything that went along with that," Williams recalled.

Crawdaddy quickly reached a circulation of 25,000, but Williams was already pondering his next move. In 1968, he left the magazine and moved to a cabin in Mendocino County, 100 miles north of San Francisco. He had already concluded that readers wanted something more like what Wenner had in mind. "I recognized from the beginning that Jann would leave me in the dust, but that was fine," he said. "I didn't even try to compete." In his view, *Crawdaddy* had already served its purpose. "The *New York Times* was reviewing the new Beatles album when it came out, and there was no longer any need for the crusade which I had been on, to get people to try to take this stuff seriously," Williams said. "I had a lot of fun with it, but by then it was obvious that people were taking this stuff far *too* seriously."

Rolling Stone's origins were fancier than *Crawdaddy*'s but still quite modest. "We created *Rolling Stone* in Ralph's living room," Wenner recalled, "sitting in his green, cracked-leather armchairs." For seed money, they collected $2,000 from Gleason, the same amount from the Schindelheim family, and $1,500 from Wenner. Other friends and family brought the first round of fundraising to $7,500. For the new corporation's name, Wenner used the one Chet Helms had chosen for the magazine he wished to create. *Rolling Stone* would be owned by Straight Arrow Publishers Inc. Wenner later said he liked the name because it captured the magazine's no-bullshit approach.

·   ·   ·   ·   ·

At the Monterey Pop Festival that summer, Wenner and Gleason ran into Michael and Susan Lydon. Michael was covering the festival for *Newsweek*, a sister publication of *The Washington Post*. He grew up in a large Irish-Catholic family near Boston and attended Roxbury Latin School, where he befriended fellow student Peter Guralnick. At Yale, Lydon wrote for the campus newspaper, which was headed by the future U.S. senator and vice-presidential candidate Joe Lieberman. Both Lydon and Lieberman were Kennedy supporters who didn't identify with radical students. "I was headed to a shirt, tie, and jacket professional career working for a major media company," Lydon wrote later. "I didn't want to be a bearded protestor carrying a hand-painted sign in the rain. Why leave the mainstream? There wasn't anything wrong with America that the Democratic Party couldn't fix."

Lydon also resented the Beatles and urged his fellow students to focus on the American music that he loved. "Much of this was tongue in cheek," he recalled later, "but in ways I barely recognized, I was dead serious. The Beatles did unsettle me; I did hear their music as a raucous challenge to American rock and roll." After graduating, Lydon covered Freedom Summer in Mississippi for *The Boston Globe* and joined *Newsweek* as an intern in London. By that time, he had come to appreciate the Beatles and eventually interviewed John Lennon and Paul McCartney. In 1967, *Newsweek* transferred him to its bureau in San Francisco, where the Summer of Love was in full swing.

Originally from the Bronx, Susan Lydon studied at Vassar and didn't share her husband's political views. "He was from Boston and a family of staunch Kennedy Democrats," Susan recalled. "He wanted to work in the mainstream of American politics. 'Not me,' I said. 'I hate the mainstream. I'm strictly a lunatic fringe kind of girl.'" After she sent him a long, amphetamine-fueled letter about their political differences, he encouraged her to write. In England, she contributed to *London Life*, and when they moved to San Francisco, she wrote freelance pieces for the *Sunday Ramparts*, where Wenner was her editor. Although she later described him as "young, brash, and a little on the pompous side," she appreciated the opportunity to write for the newspaper. "At the time," she recalled, "there were only a handful of journalists writing seriously about rock music, including Richard Goldstein, Bob Christgau, and Ellen Willis on the East Coast, and Michael and me on the West, and we all knew each other."

When Wenner encountered the Lydons in Monterey, he mentioned his magazine idea. The couple listened politely but expressed little interest. Two months later, Wenner met them at Enrico's, a North Beach bistro. After praising Michael's recently published *Esquire* story about the underground press, Wenner again described his new magazine. According to Susan Lydon, Wenner said his ambition was to become "the Henry Luce of the counterculture." After offering Michael Lydon a job, Wenner asked Susan what she did all day, adding that he needed someone to address labels and mail out dummies. "Go fuck yourself, Jann," she replied. "I'm a writer, not a typist." Nevertheless, Susan signed on as an editorial assistant.

Michael Lydon later described the Monterey Pop Festival as "one of those signal events that set me on my adult path." Tempted by the chance to work outside the mainstream media, he accepted Wenner's offer but didn't resign from *Newsweek*. Under the impression that he was *Rolling Stone*'s managing editor, Lydon offered to waive his salary, but when the first issue appeared, he learned that Wenner's former editor at the *Sunday Ramparts* occupied that position. But with his Ivy League credentials, *Newsweek* experience, curiosity about the counterculture, and fondness for the Kennedys, Lydon seemed to be a good fit with the new magazine.

.   .   .   .   .

Wenner wanted a professional look for *Rolling Stone*, but his design experience was limited to laying out his prep school yearbook. He turned to Dugald Stermer, who was too busy to help out on a regular basis, but his production director at *Ramparts* agreed to assist during his free time. Wenner also asked Stermer if *Rolling Stone* could use the design he had created for the *Sunday Ramparts*. When Stermer agreed, Wenner asked if he could borrow the newspaper's pasteup flats as well. Lacking his own stationery, he drew up budgets on the back of *Ramparts* memos.

Wenner asked psychedelic poster artist Rick Griffin to create the new magazine's logo. Perhaps more than any other design element, Griffin's lush lettering reflected *Rolling Stone*'s link with the San Francisco counterculture. As for a printer, Gleason recommended Garrett Press, which had printed the *Sunday Ramparts*. Gleason also told Wenner that printers, if asked, sometimes furnished free storage space. Located in the city's warehouse district, Garrett Press agreed to print the magazine and offered its loft as a free workspace. When the press was running downstairs, it filled the loft with burning odors, but free office space was exactly what the upstart magazine needed.

The union workers at Garrett Press enjoyed watching the youngsters toil away but strongly suspected that their magazine was doomed.

According to Michael Lydon, Wenner was a bulldog when it came to selling advertisements.

> He'd sit there at that corner desk of his, get some record guy on the phone and not ask him for an ad—Jann would demand it. "You've just *gotta* give us a page," he would say. "We need that page. You've just *gotta* put it in." You couldn't believe his balls, but the incredible thing was, it worked. They put in the ads.

For the first issue, Wenner sold a full-page advertisement to KFRC, a Top 40 radio station in San Francisco. KMPX bought another, as did Atlantic Records, and Buddah Records purchased a two-page ad to promote Captain Beefheart's new record.

Wenner was also lining up contributors. In late September, he wrote to Jonathan Cott. On Gleason's recommendation, Cott had written about *A Hard Day's Night* for *Ramparts* and contributed book and film reviews to the *Sunday Ramparts*. But by the time Wenner contacted him, Cott was continuing his graduate studies at the University of Essex. "Ralph and I have done it—started a rock-and-roll newspaper called *Rolling Stone*," Wenner wrote.

> I hereby authorize you to be our feature writer in Merrie Olde. Don't bother with the news and gossip, as we already have *Melody Maker*. Instead, give us your impression of the scene and profiles or extensive interviews with the Beatles, the Stones, Andrew Loog Oldham, Peter Townshend, Donovan, and such like that you can get to.

The timing was propitious. Cott's interest in poetry was waning, but he was impressed by a Cal professor's claim that the lyrics for "Paint It, Black," "Eight Miles High," and "Eleanor Rigby" were better than many published poems. In short order, Cott embraced his role as *Rolling Stone*'s first European editor.

The same month he contacted Cott, Wenner wrote to Jon Landau, whose work he had read in *Crawdaddy*. The son of a blacklisted history teacher and jazz lover in Boston, Landau played in a series of rock bands and wrote his first article, about Woody Guthrie, for a local handout while he was still in high school. By the time he met Paul Williams in Cambridge, Landau was studying at Brandeis University and working at a record store on Harvard Square. When Williams stopped by the store to leave a pile of *Crawdaddy* magazines, he and Landau argued the merits of specific bands. After telling Williams how awful his magazine was, Landau wrote a substantial fraction of the fifth issue.

Landau's pieces, which resembled college essays, expressed strong views about what new music was worthwhile. "At the age of 19, my objectives were messianic, not literary," he said later. During his sophomore year, Landau received an unexpected telephone call from Jerry Wexler, the legendary record producer at Atlantic Records who had once worked at *Billboard* magazine. Landau heard loud music playing in the background. "Can you turn that down?" Wexler asked a colleague. "Can't you see I'm trying to talk to this important young man?" Impressed by Landau's work for *Crawdaddy*, Wexler sent him a package with every Atlantic Records release.

In his letter to Landau, Wenner offered $25 per piece, which was $25 more than Landau received for his articles in *Crawdaddy*. "Looking forward to a long and mutually profitable relationship," Wenner wrote. He also sent the dummy for *Rolling Stone*'s first issue to Landau, who was impressed. In his reply to Wenner, Landau admitted that *Crawdaddy* wasn't a good fit for him. More of a critic than a reporter, he wanted to write about Motown, Atlantic, and Stax/Volt performers as well as English groups. Adding that he wasn't "a tremendous fan" of West Coast music, he wanted a guarantee that his criticisms would be printed along with his praise. "I too look forward to a long and mutually profitable relationship," Landau said in closing.

Wenner welcomed the coverage Landau had in mind. He assured Landau that he wouldn't need to write about the West Coast bands, as the magazine was "fairly well covered in that direction." He also affirmed Landau's misgivings about *Crawdaddy*. "The only thing I ever enjoyed in *Crawdaddy* was your stuff," he wrote. "Paul's piece on SF was a mile wide of the mark . . . as a music critic, as a social critic, as a reporter. After reading the article, you still have no idea of what's going on here."

Negative reviews were fine, Wenner wrote, and he offered more information about *Rolling Stone*'s origins.

> When I left *Ramparts*, I was offered the job of editor of a magazine for rock and roll and hippies with a $200,000 bankroll. Chet Helms of the Family Dog was the publisher, but it fell through because of his inability to get the funds. I figured the only way that would get done is to do it myself. . . . Gleason is involved as well—good for business— mainly as a sort of father and teacher to me over the last three years.

Wenner added that he and Gleason were impressed by Landau's taste in music. Later, Landau reflected on his decision to join forces with Wenner. "I wrote for *Rolling Stone* for ten years," he said. "That's where I got my Ph.D. in life."

Meanwhile, Wenner and Gleason were finalizing their agreement. Gleason would serve as consulting editor and share veto power with Wenner on any matter of policy, content, news, and editorial practice. In cases where they didn't agree, both would have the option of writing about the disputed matter in the magazine. Meanwhile, Wenner was working feverishly on the premier issue. "Flashes," which included snippets about the rock world, mentioned a new group called Blood, Sweat and Tears as well as Bob Dylan, Mick Jagger, the Bee Gees, Eric Burdon and the Animals, the Hollies, and Procol Harum. The column also offered updates on a slew of Bay Area groups, including Big Brother and the Holding Company, Quicksilver Messenger Service, Electric Flag, Blue Cheer, and Mother Earth.

After finishing his daily work at *Newsweek*, Michael Lydon turned to his *Rolling Stone* assignments, including the lead story about the Monterey Pop Festival. The festival was billed as a charity event, but Lydon found that much of the revenue never made it to the beneficiaries. Susan Lydon edited Jon Landau's piece, which compared the latest albums by Jimi Hendrix and Eric Clapton, giving Hendrix the nod. Nevertheless, Landau claimed that Hendrix's *Are You Experienced* was "unrelentingly violent, and, lyrically, inartistically violent at that." He concluded, "Dig it if you can, but as for me, I'd rather hear Jimi play the blues." Susan Lydon reviewed a British film called *Privilege*, which concerned a pop singer whom the government uses to distract the masses from their woes.

On the front page, which doubled as the magazine's cover for the first issues, readers saw a photograph of John Lennon in a vintage army helmet. It was from the set of *How I Won the War* (1967), in which Lennon played his first nonmusical film role. Directed by Richard Lester, whose other credits included *Hard Day's Night* (1964) and *Help!* (1965), the new film was a critical and commercial failure, but Lennon's immense appeal turned the black comedy into grist for *Rolling Stone*'s mill. Inside the magazine, the Beatles' wives were featured in a fashion story, and another piece recounted the police raid on the Grateful Dead house in the Haight. The bust happened just as Wenner was closing the first issue, and he regarded that coincidence as a cosmic twist of fate. The piece summarized the Dead's press conference the day after the bust and included Baron Wolman's photographs. Yet another article, "Hippies: Death on a Sunny Afternoon," discussed the "Death of Hippie" ceremony. Wenner handled the record reviews: Arlo Guthrie's *Alice's Restaurant, Chuck Berry Live at the Fillmore*, and singles by Electric Flag, Traffic, and other bands.

Gleason's first column for the magazine, "Sound Is Without Color," railed against racist double standards in the media. Gleason noted that the BBC filmed Otis Redding in Georgia and that French national radio aired a program from Stax/Volt in Memphis. Gleason asked, "Why has there never been a similar broadcast on U.S. TV or radio of Otis Redding (or James Brown or Wilson Pickett or Jackie Wilson or Ray Charles or Chuck Berry or even Nat Cole or Sam Cooke)?" The answer, he wrote, was race: "They are black, and in

America in the echelons of power which controls these things, color is a handicap."

Gleason rounded out the issue in other ways as well. He advised Wenner to trade copy with *Melody Maker*, an arrangement that landed *Rolling Stone* a Nick Jones article on the London scene. For a short time, Wenner listed Jones, whose father edited *Melody Maker*, as the magazine's London correspondent. Gleason also persuaded John Carpenter to contribute an exclusive interview with Donovan, which *Rolling Stone* ran in two parts. The Scottish singer had missed the Monterey Pop Festival due to drug charges against him, but he was touring again behind several hits, including "Sunshine Superman," "Season of the Witch," and "Mellow Yellow."

On page 2, Wenner ran "A Letter from the Editor." It was his first and best chance to articulate the magazine's goals to its intended audience.

> We have begun a new publication reflecting what we see are the changes in rock and roll and the changes related to rock and roll. Because the trade papers have become so inaccurate and irrelevant, and because the fan magazines are an anachronism, fashioned in the mold of myth and nonsense, we hope we have something here for the artists and the industry, and every person who "believes in the magic that can set you free."

Having quoted the Lovin' Spoonful, Wenner turned to the magazine's broader scope. His tone was hip and earthy.

> *Rolling Stone* is not just about the music, but also about the things and attitudes that the music embraces. We've been working quite hard on it and hope you can dig it. To describe it any further would be difficult without sounding like bullshit, and bullshit is like gathering moss.

Wenner sensed that anything beyond a short description risked the charge of bullshit, which he wished to avoid at all costs. Hippie nonchalance and authenticity, not a wordy justification for the new magazine, were paramount.

Printed on oversize newsprint stock, the first issue cost 25 cents and was dated November 9, 1967. Its 24 pages were packed with rock news and gossip, but its coverage of the Monterey festival's finances, high-profile drug arrests, and charges of systemic racism in the media showed that *Rolling Stone* wasn't a trade or teen magazine. When Greil Marcus saw a stack of magazines at Whelan's Smoke Shop on the corner of Telegraph and Bancroft, he bought a copy. "I hadn't read a paragraph of it before I realized: This is Jann's," he recalled. "I could tell by the design, the voice, and I flipped over to the masthead, and I was right. It made perfect sense."

 Flashes

 Early Days

If Greil Marcus was *Rolling Stone*'s ideal reader, he wasn't the only one. Joel Selvin also recalled buying his first issue on the south side of the Cal campus. Not yet 18 years old, Selvin had dropped out of Berkeley High School and was working as a copyboy at the *San Francisco Chronicle*. At a nearby charbroiler, he ingested the magazine's articles along with a chicken sandwich and french fries. Before that purchase, Selvin learned about musicians by reading liner notes in the aisles of record stores. As he pored over the new magazine, he was astonished by Jon Landau's article about Sam & Dave, whose hit records were produced by Stax Records in Memphis. "This was vital information," Selvin said. "It so hit my sweet spot." He converted that pleasure into action. After placing his first album review in *Rolling Stone*, Selvin became a popular music columnist at the *San Francisco Chronicle*, where he remained for decades.

Gene Sculatti also noticed the first issue of *Rolling Stone*. A student at San Francisco State College, Sculatti was already contributing to *Crawdaddy* and the *Mojo-Navigator Rock & Roll News*, a low-budget fanzine based in the Bay Area. "I walked into a Frisco record store near Kezar Stadium that week and saw a stack of these [*Rolling Stone* magazines] on the floor," he recalled. He immediately noticed the resemblance to the *Sunday Ramparts* and realized that *Rolling Stone* was raising the stakes for rock publications. "It was so pro-looking," he said. "I knew the end was approaching for *Crawdaddy* and the *Mojo-Navigator Rock & Roll News.*" Sculatti later became editorial director at Warner Bros. Records and *Billboard* magazine.

Robin Green saw her first issue of *Rolling Stone* while waiting for the light to change at Fifth Avenue and Fifty-Seventh Street in Manhattan. "It was the issue with Eric Clapton on the cover, handsome, with a mustache and full head of hair then, in jeans shirt and bead necklace," she recalled. "And there I was, waiting for the light in midtown in a sea of men in suits and ties and briefcases, women in heels and pencil skirts." The Brown graduate was working as a secretary at Marvel Comics; three years later, she became the first woman to appear on *Rolling Stone*'s masthead as a contributing editor.

The son of a truck driver, Lester Bangs was an 18-year-old Jehovah's Witness when he purchased the first issue of *Rolling Stone*. Bangs grew up in El Cajon, an agricultural city east of San Diego, where he eagerly consumed Beat literature, jazz, science fiction, comic books, and cough syrup. For him, *Rolling Stone* was a revelation. "I bought the very first issue, and it wasn't long before I was waiting for it with even more enthusiasm," Bangs recalled. "I can remember when my biggest dream was that someday I would be on the staff of that magazine."

When he glimpsed his first issue of *Rolling Stone*, Bruce Springsteen was using a pay telephone on Main Street in Freehold, New Jersey. He and Stevie Van Zandt had discovered *Crawdaddy* on their weekend trips to Greenwich Village, but the new entry claimed his full attention. "These were your lifelines," Springsteen told Wenner biographer Joe Hagan. "You can't explain to someone today how unique and essential those things were to the fiber of your being in those days."

Michael Goldberg saw the first issue of *Rolling Stone* at Tides Book Store in Sausalito. Even at age 14, he knew it differed from other rock publications. "It treated rock and roll *seriously*, like this stuff *mattered*," he said later. Goldberg, who was already reading Ralph Gleason in *Ramparts* and the *San Francisco Chronicle*, also collected the psychedelic posters and handbills that were distributed weekly to Sausalito bookstores, art stores, and other outlets. At 17, Goldberg copublished *Hard Road*, a magazine whose only issue included an interview with Jerry Garcia. Although he went on to write for other outlets, Goldberg claimed that all his work was designed for *Rolling Stone*, where he eventually became a senior editor and contributed more than 350 articles.

Much of the magazine's impact revolved around its design. Jon Carroll, who would later appear on the masthead, noted that *Rolling Stone* didn't look like it was "thrown together in the back of a station wagon." The editorial formula also distinguished it from underground newspapers. "The *Barb* was exciting, the *Oracle* was peculiar," Wenner said later. "But the pieces I was choosing from in assembling *Rolling Stone—Melody Maker, Ramparts, DownBeat,* the London *Times* a little, maybe a little *New Yorker*—had nothing to do with the underground press." Greil Marcus later affirmed Wenner's position on underground newspapers. "He didn't like the prose. He didn't like the look. He didn't like the people. He didn't like the way it was done," Marcus said. "So he never for a minute wanted to be considered part of the underground press. And *Rolling Stone* never was." Although Wenner and Marcus strongly distinguished the magazine from the underground press, historian John McMillian noted that at least some readers regarded *Rolling Stone* "as a slightly upscale underground newspaper."

The magazine quickly attracted more writers. In January 1968, *Crawdaddy* contributor Richard Meltzer told Wenner he wanted to write regularly for *Rolling Stone*. Later that month, however, Meltzer's colleague Jon Landau sent Wenner a seething letter. Landau was irate that Wenner might cut his negative remarks about West Coast bands.

> If you touched the stuff about the Byrds, Grape, Airplane, or Doors, I will really be burned because I really wanted to get those things said. . . . And don't give me this crap about how it's not because you disagree with me because I know that. I also know that every time I get cut it's because what's being cut is going to offend the fucking West Coast audience. I thought *Rolling Stone* was supposed to have balls. I will tell you up front: as bad as *Crawdaddy* may be, I never had to go through this shit with them, and I warn you: Never again.

Although his reviews focused on the musical deficiencies of the West Coast bands, Landau was also averse to "dope culture" and what he called the magazine's "San Francisco nationalism." Yet his dissonant voice, East Coast perspective, and focus on black artists strengthened *Rolling Stone* and broadened its appeal.

Eye magazine, a new Hearst publication whose supervising editor was Helen Gurley Brown, soon asked Landau to produce a music column. Wenner openly disparaged his rival. "I just finished looking at the latest *Eye* magazine," he wrote to Landau.

> It is a cover-to-cover BORE. Even your own level of writing is brought down. You made a mistake becoming *Eye*'s rock columnist. Why don't you wait, instead of grabbing the first thing up. It'll pay off in the long run both in money and prestige.

Eye folded after 15 issues, and though Landau continued to write for other outlets, most notably *The Boston Phoenix* and *The Real Paper*, he remained in the *Rolling Stone* fold.

After several months at *Rolling Stone*, Michael Lydon called it quits. "Jann wanted a big, popular, successful magazine," Lydon said later. "He didn't want it to be an underground newspaper. He wanted to meet the Beatles. . . . I guess I had a more idealistic view. Anyway,

I just split." Shortly after that, Lydon also resigned from *Newsweek* and began freelancing for *Rolling Stone*, *Ramparts*, and other outlets. Susan Lydon continued at *Rolling Stone* for six months, after which she separated from Michael and wrote for *Ramparts*.

. . . . .

Gleason's reputation gave *Rolling Stone* instant credibility in the record business, but the magazine's main virtue in that world was its readership. The rock labels and *Rolling Stone* were riding the same demographic wave. Between 1950 and 1960, the number of college students doubled, then doubled again by 1966, when half the American population was under 25. Meanwhile, record sales were skyrocketing. In 1968, gross sales from records climbed to $1 billion and doubled again within five years. Wenner began corresponding with record industry executives and flying weekly to Los Angeles to solicit advertising. The connections he forged further distinguished *Rolling Stone* from its competitors, including the underground press. Yet even as he built those relationships, Wenner later maintained, the magazine's San Francisco location helped it resist pressure from the major labels to produce favorable reviews.

During this time, Wenner contacted Jerry Wexler. "I wanted to take the opportunity to solicit your opinion of *Rolling Stone*," Wenner wrote. "I am especially curious to know what you don't like and in what areas we could improve. Are there any features or stories not currently in the paper that you would like to see or read?" Wexler typed his reply on the original letter.

> Briefly: First issue was strong; the Monterey finances, Gleason. Second one seemed weak. To be avoided: the milksop fatuity of the *Crawdaddy* approach.
>
> Giant: Ralph Gleason, ever.
>
> Great Promise: Jon Landau. Boy is out of sight; most brilliant, cogent new critic in years. Incredible grasp of R&B.

> Believe *Rolling Stone* needs a more specific orientation and point of
> view. For God's sake, avoid the GROUPIE syndrome, and let's not be
> wide-eyed about hashcapades or pot busts of the venerated. Need pro-
> fessionalism and detachment. Need identity. Are you a trade paper,
> critical journal, combined fan-and-trade a la [*New Musical Express*],
> fan thing like *16*? What?

Wenner knew the second issue was weak. The first one took months
to assemble and used all the quality material they had on hand. Nevertheless, they pulled together a cover story on Ike and Tina Turner
(which referred to her as "an incredible chick") and ran the second
part of the Donovan interview. Michael Lydon wrote about Jefferson
Airplane's *After Bathing at Baxter's*, Tom Donahue described Top 40
radio as "a rotting corpse" that was "stinking up the airwaves," and
shorter items detailed the drug arrest of Canned Heat in Denver,
Joan Baez's arrest for blocking the U.S. Army induction center in
Oakland, and Jonathan Cott on James Brown's performance in
Paris. To fill out the issue, Wenner also ran a transcript of Dylan's
1965 press conference in San Francisco.

Wexler's feedback wasn't lost on Wenner. Writing to a CBS
Records executive, he defined *Rolling Stone*'s identity and mission.

> We are operating on at least four premises: 1) The only thing that the
> ten million people between the ages of 16 and 25 have in common is
> that they listen to rock and roll; 2) The great portion of them, espe-
> cially those who are fans of Bob Dylan and the Beatles, are interested
> in rock and roll as a lifestyle; 3) At this time, there does not exist a
> single publication in the music field which in any way reflects the
> changes which have occurred in rock and roll during the past three
> years; 4) Being "hip" or young does not involve going around telling
> everyone that you are hip or young.

The earliest and most favorable response to *Rolling Stone*, Wenner
added, didn't come from its own promotions, but rather from
KMPX, which attracted the largest nighttime radio audience of
young adults in Northern California.

Wenner shaped *Rolling Stone*'s identity in other ways as well. Writing to Stan Cornyn at Warner Bros. Records, he maintained that the magazine shouldn't be mistaken for an underground publication, especially when it came to advertising. Small ads in the underground press were common, he noted, whereas *Billboard* favored full-page ads. The five-inch ad Warner Bros. bought for the new Jimi Hendrix album was fine for underground papers, Wenner told Cornyn, but it would be wasted in *Rolling Stone*, which was designed for full-page advertisements. "The back page of our next issue is still open and I would earnestly suggest using that with a second color," he wrote. "I hope I haven't hurt our cause, but I think it makes sense and is important both to us and Warner Brothers."

Clive Davis of Columbia Records was an especially important ally. His company controlled a quarter of the record market but had been slow to sign rock acts. (Columbia's key talent scout, Mitch Miller, thought rock and roll was a fad.) Beginning his career as a corporate lawyer, Davis knew little about rock music, but after Los Angeles record executive Lou Adler persuaded him to attend the Monterey Pop Festival, Davis signed Janis Joplin and went on to enlist Moby Grape, Electric Flag, Santana, and other emerging acts. Columbia's sales doubled in three years, making the label almost as large as its next two competitors combined.

Columbia began running ads in *Rolling Stone*'s eighth issue, but when the magazine needed cash that same year, Davis advanced it $20,000 against planned advertising. "I was anxious to help *Rolling Stone*," Davis said later. "What was good for them was good for the business, and what was good for the business was good for Columbia." Davis also had his sales representatives distribute *Rolling Stone* through record stores, a move that accounted for 15 percent of the magazine's newsstand sales.

Although Davis supported *Rolling Stone* financially, he resented its negative reviews of Columbia's records. "I always took it personally when the paper made a snide comment about Columbia or took one of its artists to task," Davis wrote in his first memoir. "Despite my anger, I recognized that *Rolling Stone* did this as a service of sorts to its allegedly anti-establishment readership. I occasionally wondered how they could accept consulting and advertising assistance from Columbia—and then poke fun at us . . . or say downright nasty things." Yet Davis tried to remain calm and consider Wenner's larger purpose.

> Then I'd cool down and realize that this was part of the game. Jann knew his readership, and his first loyalty obviously had to be to them. Nice notices for Columbia made him vulnerable to charges of "selling out." I began to realize that he blasted us occasionally just to protect himself against this kind of problem. Also, we were so successful that we could withstand the barbs and still come up strong.

Running critical reviews might have pleased the magazine's "allegedly anti-establishment readership," but Wenner also had his writers to consider. They would have objected strenuously if either he or the magazine's advertisers openly influenced record reviews.

Not every label was on board with *Rolling Stone*'s program. Stax Records was a holdout, and Wenner was dissatisfied with Atlantic Records' advertising. "I am feeling very frustrated in this regard about getting Atlantic's advertising and moral support," he wrote to Wexler in 1968. Wenner pleaded with Wexler to advertise in every issue: "I hate to beg, but it keeps us going and it makes financial sense for Atlantic. *Rolling Stone* is the best medium available today for this sort of advertising; we're the only publication with this kind of influential and taste-making audience. Can you help?" Even compared to Clive Davis, however, Wexler was prickly about negative reviews. After praising Landau lavishly in a letter to the editor in March, Wexler was furious about Landau's review of a new Aretha Franklin record. Writing to Wenner, he said Landau was trying to be "a surrogate A&R man, and that's not the place of a critic." Two years later, Wenner was still trying to placate Wexler. "As I explained to you on the phone," Wenner wrote, "*Rolling Stone* is not on a vendetta against Atlantic Records, and never has been."

Meanwhile, Wenner was jealously tracking where labels spent their advertising money. "I was shocked to see a Carole King ad in *Circus*, and none yet in *Rolling Stone*," Wenner wrote to record executive Lou Adler. He also chided Jac Holzman of Elektra Records for advertising his albums elsewhere. "The decision was made to promote and advertise in print media these artists, and the decision was also made not to advertise them in *Rolling Stone*," he wrote to Holzman. "That's what I was wondering about." Nevertheless, Wenner developed a strong connection with Holzman, who wrote complimentary letters to the editor and hosted Wenner on a ski trip to Aspen in November 1968. Wenner's ease in that social milieu was another asset. It was difficult to imagine hippie impresario Chet Helms, for example, joining a record executive on the slopes.

When they weren't complaining about negative reviews, many record executives objected to *Rolling Stone*'s advertising rates. "Three grand for an ad?" a Capitol Records executive wrote to Wenner. "I'm stunned! I can't believe that this is the same righteous publication that only recently denounced the record industry in general, and Capitol in particular, for its shameless pricing practices!" An executive at Decca Records combined the two major themes in a single letter. When Wenner said he couldn't believe Decca was taking only a half-page ad to promote *Tommy*, the executive fired back: "It's nice to see your concern for The Who . . . since it wasn't too long ago that you voted *Tommy* the most overrated album of the year." He then took a stroll down memory lane: "Ah, for the good old days—like a year ago—before *Rolling Stone*'s rates skyrocketed and full-pages were still within our reach."

The zestiest letters came from Saul Zaentz of Fantasy Records, a small label based in Berkeley. In March 1969, Wenner told Zaentz that he regretted *Rolling Stone*'s "foolish" review of a Creedence Clearwater Revival album. He also offered to help Fantasy design an ad. After noticing that Wenner's letter was addressed to Sol Zaentz, Gleason scrawled on the carbon in large letters, "HIS NAME IS SAUL." Zaentz had already written a letter to the editor about the negative review, but when Wenner cut it significantly to run in the magazine, he added insult to injury. Zaentz's next missive was pithier: "Dear Jann: Go fuck yourself. Warmest personal regards, Saul Zaentz." Zaentz also responded to a *Rolling Stone* communication about the magazine's reprint policy. Returning the memo to *Rolling Stone*, Zaentz scribbled, "Who would want to reprint the shit in your paper?"

Wenner's journalistic peers could also be short with him. Rock critic Robert Christgau submitted a review to *Rolling Stone* whose opening sentence was, "When I began to write my column for *Esquire* in January of 1967, I decided to do a brief survey of what I thought of as California music." In his reply, Wenner wrote that a record review should be about the record, not the reviewer. Christgau was having none of it.

> Let me tell you, Jann, as we're in the same critical fraternity, yuk-yuk, that I think you're bright and earnest and have the worst case of San Francisco pompousness I've ever observed. I have no desire to answer your letter beyond that because for the most part it's beneath contempt. I think you should teach in college, it would be a good life for you, and you could disseminate your ideas about art from there without hurting anyone seriously. Your aesthetic assumptions are hopelessly outdated.

"Do you always write letters when you're high?" Christgau wondered. "Or have you merely developed the faculty of sounding that way when you're straight?"

Wenner could dish out the criticism as well, especially when it came to his magazine's competition. "I just saw the latest issue of *Eye*; they have missed it so badly, just incredibly badly, and yet get worse and worse with each issue," he told Memphis-based writer Stanley Booth. "Soon we shall have something far better than they could even hope for."

.   .   .   .   .

As *Rolling Stone* built its business, Haight-Ashbury hit a rough patch. Hard drugs, street crime, and other forms of urban blight afflicted the neighborhood as the Summer of Love wound down. Street urchins were more vulnerable than usual to predators, including Charles Manson, the ex-convict who lived with his followers at 636 Cole Street. But as Haight-Ashbury collapsed, even Manson didn't feel safe. Describing the neighborhood as ugly and mean, he loaded up the family's black bus, his answer to Kesey's brightly painted one. He and the family headed to Southern California, where Manson's goal was to break into the music business. They stayed wherever they could, but their softest berth was the home of Beach Boys drummer Dennis Wilson. During their extended stay there, Manson met Terry Melcher, who produced the Byrds' first two albums.

Meanwhile, many San Francisco hippies migrated to California's northern counties to fashion simpler lifestyles. The hippie diaspora, which was part of the larger back-to-the-land movement, was as utopian as the Haight-Ashbury scene that preceded it. Poet Gary Snyder had urged hippies to form tribes, purchase land, and live communally in remote areas, and many prominent figures were heading for the hills. After serving time in San Mateo County for marijuana possession, Kesey retreated to his family's dairy farm in Oregon. Hunter S. Thompson moved to a small town outside of Aspen, Colorado. Paul Williams and Michael Lydon landed in rural Mendocino County, and Lou Gottlieb of the Limeliters bought a 32-acre spread in Sonoma County that he described as a utopian community without hierarchy or government. Peter Coyote, a member of the Diggers and San Francisco Mime Troupe, helped organize communes in the rugged and sparsely populated counties of Northern California. Some of the communards planted marijuana, first on a small scale and then in substantial quantities. Despite a series of crackdowns and eradication efforts, cannabis became a major California cash crop.

Janis Joplin, Bill Graham, and the Grateful Dead resettled in the bucolic Marin County communities immediately north of San

Francisco. That mini-migration reflected the back-to-the-land impulse, but it also responded to the drug crackdown in San Francisco following the Summer of Love. In 1970, *Rolling Stone* reported that Marin County was "where all good San Francisco musicians go when they've made it, or even before." The article also claimed hyperbolically that the concentration of musicians had become demographically significant: "Maybe half of Mill Valley is composed of rock musicians and the dope dealers they support, and the lawyers they support, and the attendant narcs and politicians."

A key figure in the Bay Area's back-to-the-land movement was Stewart Brand, who studied biology at Stanford University and was influenced by the work of Ayn Rand. But his libertarian impulses were tempered by the teachings of Paul Ehrlich, the Stanford biologist who emphasized the need for collective action in the face of the planet's ecological limits. Brand was also drawn to the Beat scene in nearby San Francisco, ingested Aldous Huxley's work on psychedelic drugs, and was connected to the human potential movement centered in Big Sur. After attending the Acid Tests, Brand helped organize the Trips Festival, which he envisioned as a showcase for avant-garde efforts, including his own multimedia presentation on American Indians. He later admitted that the Trips Festival was the beginning of the Grateful Dead and the end of everybody else.

Even as reporters descended on San Francisco during the Summer of Love, Brand was moving on to his next big idea. While tripping on the roof of his North Beach apartment building, he wondered why he hadn't seen a photograph of Earth from outer space. Such a photograph, he believed, would incite a new form of planetary consciousness. During this time, he also realized that his rusticating friends would need new tools to live off the grid. He loaded his pickup truck and plied his wares at communes across the West. Brand sold very little merchandise, but when he published his catalog in 1968, it became his most popular product. With its cover photograph of Earth from outer space, the *Whole Earth Catalog* expressed a distinctively American blend of utopian aspiration and pragmatism. "We are as gods," the catalog claimed in its opening sentence, "and might as well get good at it." Most of its readers would never live off the grid, but the catalog quickly became a symbol of the back-to-the-land movement.

The catalog's success sparked a correspondence between Brand and Wenner. Brand noted that the *Whole Earth Catalog* had received many reviews but nothing very critical. He asked Wenner to write "a good mean itchy impatient critique of its flaws." Instead, the magazine ran Thomas Albright's "The Environmentalists: The *Whole Earth Catalog* Gets Down to Business." The magazine's art critic quoted Brand on the catalog and its success. It was "strictly an outgrowth of the commune movement," Brand said, and paralleled that movement's phenomenal growth. Albright also nested the *Whole Earth Catalog* in two philosophical traditions.

> From one point of view, the Catalog represents a use of Marxist assumptions toward the ideals of anarchism, an attempt to spread control over the means of production—and education—so widely that anyone who wants to can be the locus of his own economic and political power. From another, the Catalog reflects an updating of the 19th-century crafts movement to electronic-age technology, and of New England transcendentalism to an earthy, peyote-vision mysticism in which the most visionary ideas are eminently practical, and the most prosaic implements are sacred.

It was heady stuff for a rock magazine, but Albright, who later served as the *San Francisco Chronicle*'s art critic, was on point. In a letter to Wenner, Brand praised the article and Baron Wolman's photographs.

Meanwhile, Brand updated his catalog and built the franchise. In 1971, the *Last Whole Earth Catalog* swelled to 448 pages, sold 1.2 million copies, and landed a National Book Award. But once again, Brand was ready for something new. The next time he appeared in the pages of *Rolling Stone,* it would be in a very different context.

•   •   •   •   •

As *Rolling Stone* found its footing, Gleason used his column to develop his favorite themes. "If rock can change the business world, what can't it do?" Gleason wrote in February 1968. "This society works on money. Change the way the moneychangers change money and you change the society. Rock is doing that." But Gleason's optimism was tempered by the news from Vietnam. Launched on January 30, 1968, the Tet Offensive shattered the illusion of progress that helped maintain public support for the war. After Tet, almost half of Americans polled said that the United States shouldn't have intervened in Vietnam in the first place. In March, Senator Eugene McCarthy nearly defeated President Johnson in the New Hampshire primary, and four days after that, Senator Robert Kennedy entered the race. On March 31, President Johnson announced he would not seek reelection. The announcement upended the presidential race, the Democratic Party, and the anti-war movement, which had targeted Johnson.

Appearing in the wake of LBJ's announcement, another Gleason column cited a litany of urgent problems. Nevertheless, he repeated his claim that music might redeem the nation. "Music, if Plato was right, may save us yet," Gleason wrote. "Certainly no hippie, no folk singer, no long-haired guitar playing rock musician is going to fry us with napalm or blow us all up with the bomb." True as far as it went, Gleason's point failed to explain rock's superpowers over the nation's most intractable problems. When Dr. Martin Luther King Jr. was assassinated in Memphis the same week, redemption seemed more remote than ever.

In May, Wenner showcased his political views in a signed piece called "Musicians Reject New Political Exploiters: Groups Drop Out from Chicago Yip-In." In that article, Wenner noted that a very small, recently organized, and media-savvy group of activists was encouraging young people to attend a music festival that summer in Chicago. Although the Youth International Party, whose members were called Yippies, wished to sponsor a music festival, their main purpose was to attract several hundred thousand young people to

Chicago, where the Yippies would enlist them in their anti-war protest at the Democratic National Convention, which was also scheduled for that summer.

Most of the Yippies were well-known in Berkeley circles. Abbie Hoffman was a Cal graduate student before he joined the civil rights and anti-war movements. In addition to publishing *The Realist,* Paul Krassner lived in San Francisco, funded Robert Scheer's first trip to Vietnam, and served as *Ramparts* magazine's "society editor." Jerry Rubin was a graduate student at Cal before dropping out to become a full-time activist. As a leader of the Vietnam Day Committee in Berkeley, Rubin spoke at the Human Be-In. Jerry Garcia later derided his style. "I remember once being at a be-in or one of those things, and the Berkeley contingent—Jerry Rubin and those guys—got up on stage and started haranguing the crowd," Garcia said. "All of a sudden it was like everyone who had ever harangued a crowd. It was every asshole who told people what to do. The words didn't matter. It was that angry tone. It scared me; it made me sick to my stomach."

Although Rubin specialized in media stunts, casting himself as the P. T. Barnum of the revolution, it wasn't all fun and games. "A movement that isn't willing to risk injuries, even deaths, isn't for shit," he insisted. After running a distant second in Berkeley's mayoral race, Rubin also renounced electoral politics. "I learned the hard way that you can't build a new society while scrounging for votes in elections," he said. For him, the lesson was simple: "Fuck electoral politics. *Live* the revolution." Like Wenner, Rubin believed that rock music and the Free Speech Movement marked the beginning of that revolution. Yet Wenner was no fan of Rubin. "I had disliked Jerry Rubin when he organized two bloody antiwar protests in Berkeley," Wenner recalled in his memoir. "Nothing about him struck me as genuine. I thought he was a hustler who saw protest primarily as a way to become famous."

That view was clear from the opening lines of Wenner's Yippie story.

A self-appointed coterie of political "radicals" without a legitimate constituency has formed itself into a "Youth International Party," opened up offices in New York City, and begun a blitzkrieg campaign to organize a "hip" protest at the 1968 Democratic National Convention in Chicago during August. Their techniques are as old fashioned as those of any city-boss politician, as up-to-date as the cleverest Madison Avenue "media buyer," and as brassy as any show biz promotion man. It looks like a shuck.

The attempt to exploit rock music for political purposes rankled Wenner. "What makes this otherwise transparent event worthy of notice," Wenner claimed, "is that these left-over radical politicos will rise and fall on their ability to exploit the image and popularity of rock and roll." Having struck the note of hippie authenticity in *Rolling Stone*'s first issue, Wenner now positioned himself as the defender of rock's image and popularity. In doing so, he compared Yippies to the least authentic figures imaginable: old-school political bosses, clever advertisers, and brassy show-biz publicists.

In the course of discrediting the Yippies, Wenner explained how the media worked. "If an event is not covered and reported in the newspapers or on television, it simply did not happen." Conversely, he added, something that didn't happen "can be made to have happened." As an example, Wenner cited the Gulf of Tonkin incident, which was used as the basis for escalating the war in Vietnam. Wenner then extended the analysis to Dr. King's assassination. "In a similar way, in the last few weeks, the television networks and the newspapers have manufactured a period of national mourning for Martin Luther King, Jr.," Wenner wrote. "Shattering though this tragedy was, I am convinced that it meant little or nothing to the majority of American people."

That bruising claim and its timing no doubt reflected the magazine's overwhelmingly white perspective, but it also figured in Wenner's larger rhetorical objective. Later in the piece, Wenner identified what young (presumably white) people did care about.

Rock and roll is the *only* way in which the vast but formless power of youth is structured, the only way in which it can be defined or inspected. The style and meaning of it has caught the imagination, the financial power, and the spiritual interest of millions of young people.

Rock's success, he continued, "means that ten million middle-class white kids are relating to the Negro, through his music, in a way that all the dignitaries who finally had some kind words about Dr. King never had and never will." Yet the question of how middle-class white kids related to black music was more problematic than Wenner's claim suggested. Indeed, that question remains at the center of a complex critical debate. Wenner acknowledged that complexity before restating his claim. "To be sure, the answer is not as simple as that," he wrote, "but there is a great body of evidence that points that way, and it may be that it is indeed where the only possible solution lies." Rock's appeal to young people, Wenner implied, might be the only path to improved race relations. More Lovin' Spoonful than Plato, it was the strongest version yet of Gleason's idea that politics was downstream from culture.

Wenner then returned to the Yippies and their misbegotten project.

> The style they have been desperately trying to become adept in is the style of the musicians, the style of rock and roll, because they want the power and the audience which it represents. But what they do not understand is that as surely as the Beatles, Bob Dylan, the Grateful Dead, and scores of other rock and roll people have changed the face of popular music, become the de facto spokesman [*sic*] of youth, as surely as all this has happened, they have also brought with them new ideas, new approaches, new means, and new goals.

Although many activists and journalists shared Wenner's concerns about the Yippies, his article revealed a massive projection on his part. Yippies weren't the only ones who wanted to exploit the image and popularity of rock music. It was Wenner, after all, who reportedly told the Lydons that he wanted to become the Henry Luce of the counterculture.

Wenner's article was predictably controversial, and Abbie Hoffman later called Wenner "the Benedict Arnold of the Sixties." *SunDance* magazine, a leftist publication based in San Francisco, later singled out Wenner for criticism. Editor Craig Pyes wondered who, exactly, was exploiting rock and roll—the Yippies or hip capitalists like Wenner? It was a legitimate question, especially for those who fantasized about political revolution, but Wenner had no intention of allowing Yippies to become the voice of their generation. For him, that role was reserved for *Rolling Stone* and the musicians it venerated.

It would not be the last time *Rolling Stone* distanced itself from radical politics while claiming to speak for the younger generation. According to historian John McMillian, the magazine was "generally favorable toward the cultural and commodifiable aspects of the youth rebellion—especially rock and roll—while thumbing its nose at New Left activism." Although Wenner and *Rolling Stone* were pilloried in the underground press and elsewhere, the magazine's positioning was commercially astute. In the late 1960s, rock advertising in the underground outlets dried up, while *Rolling Stone* continued to lure advertisers and readers who might be apprehensive about the New Left's growing militancy. In this sense, McMillian noted, Wenner's approach was "both genius and cunning."

·　·　·　·　·

In June, Robert Kennedy won the Democratic primary in California but was assassinated immediately after his victory speech in Los Angeles. Although the war had weakened Wenner's identification with the Democratic Party, he favored Robert Kennedy and once again mourned the loss of a charismatic leader. Meanwhile, Hunter S. Thompson traveled to New Hampshire to cover the Nixon campaign for *Pageant* magazine. Thompson had detested Nixon for years, but now he was targeting the GOP candidate openly in his magazine work. When the article appeared in July, the illustrations showed Nixon as a smiling wind-up doll. Thompson called him "a plastic man in a plastic bag, surrounded by wizards so cautious as to seem almost plastic themselves." Nixon, he concluded, had "the integrity of a hyena and the style of a poison toad." It was strong language for a magazine whose other stories included "How to Avoid Bedroom Boredom," "Warn Your Kids About Homosexuals," and "Finally—a Safe Diet Pill That Works."

In August, Thompson attended the 1968 Democratic National Convention in Chicago, where the managing editor at *Ramparts* assured him that all hell would break loose. Sure enough, thousands of demonstrators flooded Chicago's streets and public parks while police officers attacked provocateurs, protestors, and observers. The violence shocked Thompson. "I witnessed at least ten beatings in Chicago that were worse than anything I ever saw the Hells Angels do," he told his editor at Random House. Thompson held Democratic Mayor Richard Daley responsible for the bloodshed, but most Americans blamed the demonstrators.

Thompson's experience in Chicago was a turning point. Under Tom Wolfe's influence, he had reported on exotic West Coast subcultures, including the Hells Angels and San Francisco hippies. After the convention, however, he began to take direct aim at the political class. The convention was also a turning point for *Ramparts*. Despite its impressive circulation, the magazine never developed a reliable advertising base, and it filed for bankruptcy months after the 1968 election. *Ramparts* reorganized under the leadership of Robert Scheer, and Hinckle departed to cofound *Scanlan's Monthly*, where he would once again make American journalistic history—this time with Thompson.

.   .   .   .   .

That summer, Wenner and Jane Schindelheim exchanged wedding vows at the synagogue next to the Fillmore Auditorium. None of the parents attended the brief ceremony, but Wenner's mother gave the couple her 2,000 shares of Straight Arrow stock as a wedding present. It was, Wenner later said, "the cheapest thing she could get away with." But the magazine's ownership wasn't a trivial matter. Although Wenner was determined to lead the company, the Schindelheim family owned a significant minority stake, and Jane's interests could not be ignored. She removed her name from the masthead but played an important backstage role, entertaining at their home and informally vetting job candidates. After their stint on Potrero Hill, the newlyweds moved to 38 Ord Court. The neighborhood lay between Haight-Ashbury and the Castro district, which was rapidly becoming a gay mecca. While many hippies were getting back to the land, the Wenners remained in the heart of San Francisco.

In its first anniversary issue, *Rolling Stone* ran Jonathan Cott's interview with John Lennon. It was another coup for *Rolling Stone*, but the issue's most significant feature was its cover photograph. When Gleason learned that Capitol Records refused to feature two nude photographs of Lennon and Ono on the cover of *Two Virgins*, Lennon's first solo album, he suggested that *Rolling Stone* run the photos in the magazine. Wenner contacted Beatles publicist Derek Taylor, whom he had met in Monterey, and acquired the photographs. Wenner used the tamer of the two images on the front cover and ran the other one, with its full-frontal nudity, inside the anniversary issue. The caption on the magazine's cover quoted the book of Genesis: "And they were both naked, the man and his wife, and were not ashamed." The issue made national news and boosted newsstand sales. "This was our first experience with controversy," Wenner said. "We sold out and we reprinted the issue for another, like, 20,000 copies." In a subsequent issue, Wenner announced the moral of the story. "The point is this, print a famous foreskin and the world will beat a path to your door."

  Staffing Up

As *Rolling Stone* entered its second year, Wenner recruited new staff to power its growth. One of the earliest recruits was Charles Perry, another Cal student and SLATE member. Among the magazine's key staff, Perry was the most closely connected to the counterculture. During his senior year at Cal, he lived in North Berkeley with LSD kingpin Owsley Stanley, who later became the Grateful Dead's patron and sound engineer. After graduation, Perry attended dance parties in San Francisco, sampled psychedelic drugs, and tended animals for Cal's psychology department in the hills behind campus. He quit that job to play the shawm in a Tibetan liturgical music group that performed at solstices and other events. He supported himself by dealing weed until another college roommate invited him to share a flat in San Francisco. That roommate landed a job at *Rolling Stone* but entered a treatment center for heroin addiction shortly after that. Perry replaced his friend on the magazine's staff, worked his way up to associate editor, and remained with *Rolling Stone* for the rest of its San Francisco stint.

Known around the office as Smokestack El Ropo, sometimes shortened to Smoke, Perry covered the drug scene and the counterculture's spiritual fringes. In November 1968, he also wrote the magazine's first major feature about a nonmusical topic. In it, Perry claimed that the U.S. military was "directly responsible for turning on probably more than a quarter of a million American innocents by sending them to Vietnam," where drugs were plentiful and cheap. It was Gleason's idea to send a questionnaire to personnel at fifty military posts, and Perry included their responses to support his case. "Most Army jobs are so intellectually easy that it is possible to be stoned all the time, which many of us do for (literally) weeks on end," one serviceman reported.

Perry later reflected on his early years at the magazine as well as his abiding interest in drugs.

> When I started working at *Rolling Stone*, I imagined that I might gain access to some psychedelic wisdom that the Beatles and the Dead et al. had partly encoded in their music. Pretty soon I realized they didn't actually know anything more about psychedelics than I or anybody else did, but by then I was enthralled by the excitement of journalism and proceeded to work 55- and 60-hour weeks for the next eight years.

Perry also recalled a photograph of Timothy Leary on the wall at the Brannan Street office. "Jann was kind of into Leary," Perry said. "Personally, I distrusted the good doctor because of his obviously practiced fake smile, and I had the feeling that to a degree, Jann's interest was just part of his fascination with celebrities."

Wenner also hired Jerry Hopkins, a former newspaper reporter who moved to Los Angeles, worked in television, opened the city's first head shop, and wrote a column for the *Los Angeles Free Press*. His first contribution to *Rolling Stone,* which featured a Doors concert in Los Angeles, ran in February 1968. After he was hired as the magazine's Los Angeles bureau chief, he urged Wenner to report more on "underground" artists, such as Joni Mitchell, Dino Valenti, and Harry Nilsson. It was important, Hopkins maintained, for *Rolling Stone* to run the first major profiles of such figures. Like Landau, Hopkins warned Wenner about his San Francisco bias. "Your provincialism still shows some," he wrote to Wenner in 1968, "but thankfully not as much as earlier. You are, wisely, getting out of the San Francisco bag you were in." In the same letter, Hopkins urged Wenner to swap advertising space with *TeenSet* magazine. Based in Los Angeles and pitched to young women, *TeenSet* enjoyed a paid circulation of 200,000, roughly ten times larger than *Rolling Stone*'s. Wenner was initially leery of associating *Rolling Stone* with a teen magazine, but the two publications swapped ads in 1969. The same year, Hopkins took a leave of absence to write the first major biography of Elvis Presley.

At Gleason's suggestion, Wenner hired John Burks as managing editor. Nine years older than Wenner and a jazz aficionado, Burks edited the campus newspaper at San Francisco State College before logging five years at *Newsweek*'s San Francisco bureau, where he overlapped with Michael Lydon. After taking a year off to travel, Burks returned to Haight-Ashbury and landed at *Rolling Stone*. Five years later, Burks recalled his arrival.

> It was about issue No. 18, I guess. Circulation was at 20,000, they'd had a hell of a hard time meeting deadlines and no success at developing a real news-gathering squad, etc., and were in direst need of [a managing editor] if anything was going to happen. Gleason used to write a column for a San Francisco weekly I put out during 1965, the *Observer*. He liked the way it looked, the way it came out regular as clockwork, my professionalism, thought I was halfway hip, told Wenner so, Wenner hired me. I thought: for $125 a week, I'll give it a try, see if I can get something cooking here. I thought RS was an awful good idea being lamely, if promisingly, executed.

With Wenner spending more time out of the office, Burks's magazine experience was a valuable asset. Burks quickly began professionalizing the newsroom and nudged *Rolling Stone* toward nonmusical topics. "When John was at *Rolling Stone*, he basically used his position to make the magazine more political and current," recalled associate editor Jon Carroll. "It was a rock-and-roll magazine that had caught on with the youth culture, and John saw the power in that."

Once Burks was on board, he began to tap his own network. One of his contacts was Ben Fong-Torres, who was raised in Oakland's Chinatown, worked in the family restaurant, and grew up listening to Top 40 radio. During his family's short stint in West Texas, Fong-Torres was subjected to racial teasing and stereotyping, but he also realized that his interest in rock and roll connected him to many of his peers. After his family returned to the East Bay, he attended San Francisco State College and edited the campus paper. His roommates alerted him to *Rolling Stone*, and he later described the magazine's tone and media niche.

> Those articles were about rock and roll, written in a style that was knowing, critical, good-humored and hip—neither fawning, like teen and fan magazines, nor crude and condescending, like so much of the mainstream press (that is, when it deigned to stoop to cover rock and roll).

Fong-Torres also cast the magazine as "the most effectively targeted new publication since Hugh Hefner founded *Playboy* in 1955."

When one of Fong-Torres's roommates mentioned a free concert to promote a new documentary film about Haight-Ashbury, Fong-Torres pitched that story to *Rolling Stone*. While delivering the piece, he encountered the magazine's bare-bones staff—Wenner, one other editor, the art director, and a secretary. In April 1968, Fong-Torres's item appeared in the "Flashes" column. Even before Wenner hired him, Fong-Torres contributed more items to that column and wrote freelance pieces about Gordon Lightfoot, Dino Valenti, Creedence Clearwater Revival, and Jethro Tull. Once he became a full-time staff writer, Fong-Torres interviewed a long list of diverse artists, including Ray Charles, Joni Mitchell, Bob Dylan, Tina Turner, George Harrison, Marvin Gaye, Roberta Flack, the Jackson 5, Al Green,

Linda Ronstadt, Jim Morrison, Stevie Wonder, Quincy Jones, Elton John, and Carlos Santana. Fong-Torres also reported on the radio business for *Rolling Stone* and hosted a weekend program at KSAN, which under Tom Donahue's leadership had replaced KMPX as the Bay Area's key FM station. That arrangement allowed Fong-Torres to interview his subjects in two different but equally hip outlets.

Surrounded by freaks and radicals, Fong-Torres was neither. "The whole point about *Rolling Stone* magazine is that it was a business, and still is," he said later. "Jann Wenner did not try to start a commune that published a newsletter." Fong-Torres's memoir refers to the occasional toke with college friends, but when asked about his drug use, he later claimed that he didn't indulge when he was working, and added that he was always working. He did, however, pick up on Wenner's aesthetic sensibility. "Jann managed to impart a sense of style, of Victorian chic—hip, but clean and orderly," he recalled. When he started at *Rolling Stone*, Fong-Torres wore white shirts, narrow ties, horn-rimmed glasses, and short hair. He soon grew a mustache, let his hair grow, and favored blue work shirts, jeans, and rimless glasses.

While the counterculture celebrated spontaneity and self-expression, Fong-Torres became famous for his preparation and professionalism. Cameron Crowe, who would later make his own mark at the magazine, described the example Fong-Torres set.

> Ben was my first glimpse of what a professional journalist and editor was like. When I was on an assignment, I would always think, how would Ben carry himself—with the proper amount of distance, but giving the artist the comfort to say what's on their mind? Shockingly, there were many journalists I ran into who were not like Ben. They were kind of there to meet people, hang out, get drunk, or whatever. Ben, to me, was never one of those people that was just really there to hang out. He was there to get the job done and to come back with the goods.

Eventually, Wenner relied on Fong-Torres to direct and edit most of the magazine's music coverage. That included "Random Notes," which replaced "Flashes" and was one of the magazine's most popular features.

Another hire during this period was David Felton, whom Burks edited at the San Francisco State newspaper. The son of a Los Angeles journalist, Felton landed at the *Los Angeles Times* after graduation, but he read *Rolling Stone* and sent story ideas to Burks. The *Los Angeles Times* was establishing a national reputation for the first time, and when the Haight became an important news site, Felton covered hippie culture for the newspaper. When Wenner hired him as the magazine's Los Angeles editor, his presence was another sign that *Rolling Stone* was upgrading its nonmusical coverage and editorial standards.

Burks also encouraged the early work of Lester Bangs, the shoe salesman and cough-syrup addict from El Cajon who saw a house ad soliciting articles. "So I started sending them reviews," Bangs said later.

> The first four reviews I sent said that *Anthem of the Sun* by the Grateful Dead and *Sailor* by Steve Miller were pieces of shit, and *White Light / White Heat* by the Velvet Underground and Nico's *The Marble Index* were masterpieces. And I couldn't figure out why they weren't printing any of these things.

When *Rolling Stone* featured MC5's Rob Tyner on the cover of its twenty-fifth issue, Bangs eagerly bought *Kick Out the Jams*. Disappointed by the album, he submitted a scathing review to *Rolling Stone* along with a cover letter, which he later paraphrased: "Look, fuckheads, I'm as good as any writer you've got in there. You'd better print this or give me the reason why!" Burks ran the review and called Bangs to solicit more. For the next several months, Bangs submitted up to a dozen reviews each week. They were often accompanied by chatty cover letters explaining his views on music and writing.

Jon Carroll also found his way to *Rolling Stone* during this time. After studying at Cal and editing Gleason at the *San Francisco Chronicle*, Carroll served as managing editor at *Earth Times*, the environmental magazine Wenner launched in 1970. Once described as "a catalog of doom," the magazine folded after three months, and Carroll joined *Rolling Stone* as an associate editor. Later he noted the large gap between the magazine's image and the people who worked there. Readers seemed to think that the staff "all worked together in a big house in the Haight, and we were some kind of commune and probably they could crash on our floor if they showed up at our door." The reality was that they were "displaced academics and radio guys and journalists, all of us pedaling rather hard to keep the whole rickety edifice upright." It was another reminder that *Rolling Stone* covered the counterculture and its music but was not itself a hippie operation.

During Burks's tenure, Jon Landau urged him to assign Peter Guralnick a story about Elvis Presley. "Peter is very into the whole Sun, white Memphis thing," Landau added. Burks accepted the recommendation, and Guralnick contributed articles about Presley, Solomon Burke, Carl Perkins, Otis Redding, Jerry Lee Lewis, and Muddy Waters. He later produced critically acclaimed biographies of Presley, record producer Sam Phillips, and soul singer Sam Cooke.

Photographer Annie Leibovitz also began contributing to *Rolling Stone* during this time. The daughter of a career U.S. Air Force officer, Leibovitz later said the photojournalism coming out of Vietnam remained etched in her mind. Although her parents wanted her to attend college in the Philippines, where her father was stationed, she lived with her sister in Berkeley, enrolled at the San Francisco Art Institute (SFAI), and interned at KSAN. Leibovitz left school midway through her program to work on a kibbutz in Israel. Her boyfriend gave her a gift subscription to *Rolling Stone*, her sole source of U.S. news during that time.

After returning to SFAI, Leibovitz changed her major to photography and approached *Rolling Stone* art director Robert Kingsbury with photographs taken at the kibbutz and an anti-war rally. Even at that time, she recalled, her photographs didn't resemble the standard rock images.

[Kingsbury] saw a lot of pictures by people who had gone to a concert and used their camera to get to the front of the stage. It seemed to me that a concert was the least interesting place to photograph a musician. I was interested in how things got done. I liked rehearsals, backroom, hotel rooms—almost any place but the stage.

Burks reportedly claimed that Wenner held female photographers in low regard, but one day he told Wenner that someone in the reception area had photographs he should look at. Impressed with Leibovitz's portfolio, Wenner ran one of her photographs from the anti-war rally on a *Rolling Stone* cover and began giving her more assignments.

In 1970, Baron Wolman sold his Straight Arrow stock and used the proceeds to start *Rags*, a short-lived fashion magazine that targeted the counterculture. San Francisco photographer Robert Altman, who credited Burks for discovering him and changing his life, succeeded Wolman as chief photographer. Meanwhile, Leibovitz was hired as a staff photographer and succeeded Altman as chief photographer in 1973. Her contract required her to be available 24 hours a day, seven days a week, but those terms were fine with her. "I was looking to be adopted, and found Jann and Jane, and it turned into family for me," she recalled. "It was more than a magazine. It was a way of life." Eventually, Leibovitz shot 142 covers for *Rolling Stone*. "Annie was one of the closest editorial collaborations I've ever had with anybody," Wenner said later. "And she helped define the look and style of *Rolling Stone*."

.   .   .   .   .

As Burks upgraded the news operation, Wenner hired Greil Marcus to edit the record review section. Wenner and Marcus had lost touch after meeting at Cal, but Marcus was writing a music column for the *San Francisco Express-Times*, pursuing a graduate degree in political science, and assembling an edited volume called *Rock and Roll Will Stand* (1969). In that book, Marcus claimed that rock music was a foundational experience for his generation. Most listeners over the age of thirty couldn't share that experience, he argued, because they were never immersed in rock music the way younger listeners were. He didn't believe that rock and roll was "a message as to what is to be done and who is to be fought," all of which Marcus associated with folk music. Nevertheless, rock and roll had a political dimension. It was "a way to get a feeling for the political spaces we might happen to occupy at any particular time" as well as a method for keeping those spaces open. If listeners could keep moving in that space, Marcus added, they might muster "an honest response to the coldly serious New Left and to fascism of the old guard." Although Marcus placed Gleason on the other side of the generational divide, he joined Gleason in scorning both the unhip left and paleoconservatives.

Even before Marcus began contributing album reviews to *Rolling Stone*, he noticed that the magazine didn't seem to censor its writers. He tested that theory in his first submission, which grew out of pique with an album he purchased. Marcus found *Magic Bus: The Who on Tour* in a Telegraph Avenue record store and assumed it was a live album. He quickly discovered, however, that it was a random collection of tracks, including three repeats from earlier albums. Feeling cheated, he submitted a scathing review to *Rolling Stone*. "And two weeks later, I pick up the next issue, and it's there," he recalled. "And a week after that, I get a check for actual money, for $12.50. And I think, this is easy, this is fun, I should do this more often." Even more surprising was the critical response from Paul Williams, who described Marcus as a naive amateur in the *San Francisco Express-Times*. "That felt kind of weird," Marcus said. "But I realized, also, I wrote something and people read it."

When Marcus met Charles Perry the following year at a party, he complained about the overall quality of the record reviews in *Rolling Stone*. "All anybody ever does is write about lyrics," Marcus told Perry. "It's like a bunch of folk-music reviews." Days later, he received a call from Wenner, who asked him to edit that section for $35 a week. Marcus accepted the offer and claimed his territory. "When I became record reviews editor, I made it clear to [Wenner] after a few months—nobody had done the job before me—that the record review section was an independent republic within the country of *Rolling Stone*," he said later. "That meant that nobody else could tell me what to review or what a writer could say. They could argue with me, but ultimately it was my decision. And that worked well."

·   ·   ·   ·   ·

In the fall of 1969, Wenner offered to fly Lester Bangs to the Bay Area to visit the office. Assuming the visit was a job interview, Bangs wore a brown suit and tie. "I don't know whether Lester was fried from whatever pharmaceutical combination or just freaked out about being there," Burks said later. "But he certainly seemed weird." Bangs stayed with Marcus, who suggested he move to Langdon Winner's place after two days. "Lester was the all-time oblivious, obnoxious houseguest," Marcus recalled.

> Lester thought he wasn't good enough to stay at my house, and he would write about that over the years to various people—how badly I had treated him. But the thing that really got to him, and that he really felt betrayed by, was that he thought we were flying him up to see whether or not we should hire him at *Rolling Stone*, and that had never occurred to any of us. We just wanted to meet him, and we thought he would want to meet us.

Bangs was also put off by Gleason. After submitting an interview with jazz artist Charles Mingus, Bangs received a telephone call from Gleason. "I got the feeling I was being totally condescended to," Bangs wrote later, and the Mingus interview never ran in *Rolling Stone*. Bangs endured another insult when he sent his novel-in-progress, *Drug Punks*, to Wenner, who returned it without comment. For these and other reasons, Marcus maintained that *Rolling Stone* was never Bangs's "place of freedom," and Bangs would later claim that the magazine was "crammed with the most predictable portraits of uninteresting people. In fact, the literature of the counterculture could well be the most boring of all."

Although Bangs continued to write for *Rolling Stone*, he began contributing to *Creem* and other outlets. Calling itself "America's Only Rock 'n' Roll Magazine," *Creem* distanced itself from *Rolling Stone* and the San Francisco counterculture in favor of the grittier urban rock culture in and around Detroit. It was *Creem*, Marcus wrote later, that "gave Lester space for the farthest reaches of invective, scorn, fantasy, rage, and glee." Bangs became "rock's essential wild man, a one-man orgy of abandon, excess, wisdom, satire, parody—the bad conscience, acted out or written out, of every band he reviewed or interviewed." That image, Bangs later realized, didn't serve him well. "One thing that really fucked me up at *Creem* was that I got caught up in the whole idea that Lester Bangs was this thing, this idea," he said later. "I call it, like, Hunter Thompsonism. It's when you pay more attention to your image than you do to your work. And that destroys your writing."

In 1970, Marcus recruited Ed Ward to replace him as the record review editor. Raised in Eastchester, New York, Ward attended Antioch College in Ohio and first visited San Francisco in 1967 at age 18. Almost by chance, he bunked at 1836 Pine Street, home of the Family Dog. He heard Big Brother and the Holding Company at the Avalon Ballroom and chatted with Janis Joplin on the street the next day. When he complimented her performance, she planted a kiss on his cheek. "I was on Cloud 9," he recalled. After his San Francisco visit, Ward met Paul Williams at a concert in New York and began contributing to *Crawdaddy*. He also helped out in its New York office, but that arrangement ended after Williams left the magazine. When Ward saw a solicitation for writers in *Rolling Stone*, he began submitting record reviews.

Ward revered Burks for turning his recruits into a crack news team. "I've always thought of John as my journalism school," Ward said later. But he never clicked with Wenner. As Ward settled into his new job,

Wenner asked him to arrange an interview with Bill Graham. Ward later described his exchange with the rock impresario.

> I called and got right through to Graham. "You're new. You don't know how things are around here. But let me just say this about your boss," upon which he started one of the most virtuoso displays of malediction I've ever been privileged to witness. While he was doing this—it was about 15 minutes—Wenner came back to my cubicle and stood there giggling, fully aware of what was going on.

Ward concluded that Wenner had submitted him to "a kind of hazing ritual." He also resented the editorial pressure Wenner applied to record reviewers. When Dylan's *New Morning* (1970) appeared, Wenner made it clear to Ward that the review should be positive. Ward wasn't planning to pan the record, but he decided to close his review on an unenthusiastic note. Ward and Wenner failed to jibe in other ways as well. Ward's work area was messy, and Wenner dropped several hints before ordering him to clean up his "pig sty." That directive sparked a confrontation, during which Ward chased Wenner around the office with a broom. Ward's six-month tenure at *Rolling Stone* was over.

Rolling Stone panned several important albums during this period, but there was no denying the critical talent that the magazine had assembled. Landau, Marcus, Bangs, Ward, Guralnick, and others would all leave their mark on rock criticism, history, and biography.

·   ·   ·   ·   ·

As the magazine achieved liftoff, Wenner formed an editorial board that consisted of himself, Gleason, Burks, and Marcus. The meetings, which were held at Marcus's house, focused on personnel decisions, editorial matters, and planning. Each board member held strong opinions and expressed them openly. After one meeting, Marcus's wife wondered how long Wenner would tolerate their criticisms, but Marcus thought their points were well taken. The editorial board was also struggling with a clear pattern. When the magazine featured black musicians on the cover, which it did six times in 1969, newsstand sales dropped significantly. It was another reminder, if any were needed, that the magazine was produced largely by and for young white men with specific musical interests.

There were notable exceptions to that pattern. One was Sheila Weller's 1969 piece about Jimi Hendrix, with whom Weller spent a quiet weekend not far from Woodstock. It was the first contribution from Weller, who grew up in Los Angeles, studied sociology at Cal, and was also writing for *Eye* and other outlets. Another Weller article for *Rolling Stone* profiled a famous Moroccan hash dealer. That piece, which Wenner relished, appeared in a section called "The Dope Pages." Weller also reviewed Nikki Giovanni's autobiographical *Gemini* (1972) and several other titles that were written by, intended for, or primarily about women. Later she interviewed Gil Scott-Heron, the first artist Clive Davis signed to Arista after leaving Columbia. When asked about her experience as a *Rolling Stone* contributor during this period, Weller said she didn't feel she had to overcome any gender barriers. She added, however, that she was glad the magazine rarely explored the personal lives of female artists. That omission allowed her to recount the experiences of Carly Simon, Carole King, and Joni Mitchell in her 2008 book *Girls Like Us*.

In March 1969, Wenner learned more about his magazine's readership. The Field Research Corporation found that 80 percent of the magazine's readers were age 25 or under, that nine out of ten subscribers were male, and that seven in ten had at least some college education. About half were employed; of those, most were in professional or technical occupations. About 25 percent were affiliated with the music industry, and about half of those readers were musicians. On average, subscribers purchased five records per month and said that radio play and *Rolling Stone* magazine were the two most important factors in their purchases.

That audience was ideal for attracting advertising from record labels, but the staff also wanted to cover politics and current affairs, especially as they pertained to the counterculture. In April 1969, *Rolling Stone* published "American Revolution 1969," a special issue that focused on campus activism. It featured Wenner's short introduction about the urgency of the political moment and included articles by Gleason, FSM activist Michael Rossman, and George Mason Murray, a graduate student and member of the Black Student Union at San Francisco State College.

Murray was a controversial figure. In 1967, he was given probation for assaulting the editor of the campus newspaper in his office. As minister of education for the Black Panther Party, Murray also published a manifesto in the party newspaper calling for revolutionary violence. After he repeated those calls on campus, the chancellor of the California State College system insisted that San Francisco State College suspend Murray from teaching. Civil libertarians cast that decision as a violation of a teacher's First Amendment rights. Meanwhile, the Black Student Union pledged to strike until the college met its demands, which included more black and ethnic studies classes and instructors. The student strike, which lasted five months, was the longest in American history. When it was over, San Francisco State College established the nation's first school of ethnic studies.

Murray's essay in "American Revolution 1969" combined cultural commentary with violent exhortation. "We have to drive the racist dog police out of communities or kill them," he maintained. But mostly the essay was an attack on cultural nationalists, whom Murray dismissed as "sissies." He also described their position as the last stage before oppressed people "pick up the gun, fire bomb, and dynamite in an organized manner in order to make the revolution."

> Once one realizes his human worth, his intrinsic value, then he knows that he must not tolerate slavery, oppression, capitalist exploitation any longer. It is at this point that the slave picks up his tools of liberation, sharpens his razor, steals a gun, shoots a police [*sic*], robs a

bank, seizes control of a school, assaults a job foreman, runs a racist landlord off, burns up a cotton field, or grape field, shoots down a helicopter.

Murray pledged to "make the revolution by fighting with the basic tool, the people organized and armed with the correct ideology and guns."

The next article in that issue, written by Gleason, was titled "Is There a Death Wish in the U.S.?" In it, Gleason charged that political activism was failing to achieve its ends. He singled out Students for a Democratic Society (SDS), which by that time had 300,000 members and was a major force in the New Left. "Nothing I have read by the SDS and the rest is as relevant as Allen Ginsberg's poems," Gleason wrote. "None of it says as much to me as Bob Dylan, and none of it inspires like the simple thing of the Beatles singing 'Hey Jude' on TV." Having started something that was beyond politics, Gleason claimed, Dylan and the Beatles were "changing the heads of the world." That transformation, he continued, would lead inexorably to positive political outcomes. "Out of it will come the programs," Gleason said. "Out of it will come the plans. When the time is right." In a letter to the editor, Elektra founder Jac Holzman supported Gleason's position.

> Ralph's column "Perspectives: Is There a Death Wish in the U.S.?" is the best piece of writing on the subject of "the revolution" that I have yet encountered. It is apt, incisive, and intensely human. Where it's really at, as Gleason so perceptively points out, is not politics but poetics. Certainly Dylan will do more to change the course of future history than all the SDS chapters combined.

Holzman's letter suggested that the social revolution not only trumped political activism, but also made that activism unnecessary.

Wenner sent proofs of the special issue to Goddard Lieberson, president of the CBS/Columbia Group, who expressed doubts about campus activism.

Thanks for sending on the proofs of "The American Revolution, 1969."
I was very interested in it. But a lot of things worry me about students,
the SDS, and the blacks, because I don't see any real program except
the use of violence as a *modus operandi* with confusion or anarchy as
an objective.

Lieberson predicted that the campus unrest would result in suppression, and that the labor movement would refuse to form a larger
coalition with students and black activists. He found the political
options, if not the issue itself, dispiriting.

So I am rather depressed by the whole thing since the American
Revolution 1969 is moving like an uncontrolled blob in an old-
fashioned horror movie with no apparent program or direction and
using, for the most part, the methods of the people they are fighting
against.

Lieberson acknowledged that campus activism should be covered,
but he found it hard not to laugh when black militants at Duke University pushed successfully for separate living quarters. "All the institutions in the South will be very glad to accede to their requests in
this regard," he told Wenner.

Other readers also had misgivings about "American Revolution
1969." One letter to the editor criticized the issue's leftist slant.

It is truly unfortunate that *Rolling Stone* should devote its pages to the
delirious propaganda and rancorous political diatribes of Messrs.
Rossman, Williams, Berlandt, and Murray. What was once essentially
a well-written rock magazine, I hope, has not turned into an open
forum for political extremists.

Under Burks's direction, *Rolling Stone* was speaking out about politics and current affairs, but some advertisers and readers openly
wondered about the magazine's tone and coverage.

6 Wild West

In 1969, an enterprise called Woodstock Ventures was formed in New York. Its purpose was to sponsor a music festival in the upstate town of the same name, but when residents resisted the company's proposal, the firm chose a 300-acre farm in nearby Bethel as its festival site. Scheduled for mid-August, the Woodstock Music and Art Fair featured 32 acts, including many Bay Area bands and headliners from the Monterey Pop Festival. Despite the stellar lineup, *Rolling Stone* devoted little attention to Woodstock in the weeks leading up to it.

When the festival began, even the musicians were taken aback by its scale. Sly Stone described that feeling as he arrived at the venue by helicopter.

> As I flew in, I couldn't see the whole crowd, but you could see enough people dotting the landscape that it was hard to believe that there were even more. *Goddamn,* I said to myself. *Goddamn. What the fuck is this?* So many people, an ocean of them without any land for miles.

Sly and the Family Stone went on at 3:30 a.m., but when they played "I Want to Take You Higher," Stone orchestrated a thunderous call-and-response with the audience. It was one of many memorable performances, most of them captured on film. The sheer size of the event, its anarchic spirit, and its relatively peaceful execution made Woodstock an important countercultural landmark.

Rolling Stone ran Greil Marcus's lengthy cover story and Baron Wolman's photographs one month after the festival's conclusion. Meanwhile, the magazine focused on a local event that was also slated for mid-August. By that time, the San Francisco music scene had enough clout to earn a proclamation from Mayor Joseph Alioto, who declared that the city "was in the midst of a cultural renaissance centering around the vitality and freedom of expression of music and art." Noting that a new entity called the San Francisco Music Council was planning a festival, Alioto proclaimed that August 18–24 would be Wild West Week in San Francisco.

The festival's backstory began in March, when Ron Polte, who managed Quicksilver Messenger Service, invited Donahue, Graham, Gleason, and Wenner to breakfast at Jefferson Airplane's mansion on the northern edge of Golden Gate Park. Record producer David Rubinson, LSD mogul Owsley Stanley, Berkeley Folk Music Festival organizer Barry Olivier, Grateful Dead manager Rock Scully, and Jefferson Airplane manager Bill Thompson also attended. Polte proposed a music festival that would express the counterculture's core values of community and peaceful cooperation. The council considered calling the event "Get Together," echoing the hit song written by Dino Valenti and famously recorded by the Youngbloods. In the end, however, the council settled on the Wild West Festival and appointed Barry Olivier to direct it.

The San Francisco Music Council set lofty expectations for the festival. Olivier predicted that it would be "both a party and spiritual statement," and Gleason told his fellow council members they had "the potential to change the world." Under Olivier's direction, the council rented Kezar Stadium in Golden Gate Park, published a newsletter, and lined up financial support from banks and other businesses, including *Rolling Stone*. Even at that stage, the council alternated between its democratic vision and the organizational discipline required to fund and promote the festival. In its public-facing announcements, the council stressed its inclusive philosophy; privately, it assured backers that it was running a tight ship.

In the meantime, *Time* ran a story on *Rolling Stone*. "Rock and roll is now the energy core of change in American life," Wenner told the newsweekly. "But capitalism is what allows us the incredible indulgence of this music." A similar feature ran in *Newsweek,* whose closing paragraph put an even finer point on Wenner's entrepreneurial outlook.

> As for Wenner, he remains, for the moment, straddling two worlds, a swinging capitalist marching profitably to the big beat of rock. He has already turned down a couple of $500,000 offers for *Rolling Stone*, but, he says: "If a real lot of money came along, I'd sell it and get out. Things don't last forever."

It was good publicity for the magazine, but Wenner's hip capitalism alienated parts of the San Francisco counterculture.

When the San Francisco Music Council called a public meeting at Glide Memorial Church in July, the San Francisco Mime Troupe noted that the big magazines, rock promoters, and record companies were profiting handsomely off the counterculture. It urged everyone else to withhold their free labor from the festival organizers. Arnold Townsend, a representative of the Neighborhood Arts Council and veteran of the San Francisco State College strike, noted the council's lack of diversity and maintained that residents of the Mission, Fillmore, and Chinatown neighborhoods would effectively be left out of the festival. Bill Graham challenged Townsend, and the exchange devolved into a screaming match. Shortly after that meeting, a group calling itself the Haight Commune claimed that the festival was an attempt to exploit the labor and culture of local artists. It called for an expanded San Francisco Music Council and wanted to shut down the festival. That position was endorsed by the San Francisco Mime Troupe, the local chapter of the White Panthers, the Liberation News Service, the local chapter of SDS, and the staff at the *Berkeley Tribe*, an underground newspaper.

Other signs of strife also began to surface. The Light Artists Guild picketed a Grateful Dead show hosted by the Family Dog, leading to protracted negotiations. During one public meeting, hippie guru Stephen Gaskin took Graham to task. "You can't ask for both our money and our love," Gaskin said. "You've got our money, so you can't have our love. You are a good manager, a good promoter, but still you've fucked over many heads with your emotional trips." Graham flew into a rage.

> I apologize, motherfucker, that I'm a human being! I fucking apologize. Emotional, you're fucking right. Fuck you! You stupid prick. Do you know what emotions are? Stand up and have emotions! Get up and work, get up and sing, get up and act. . . . You're full of shit, man, I have more fucking emotions and balls than you'll ever see. You want to challenge me in any way about emotions? You slimy little man. . . . You slimy . . . little . . . man! Fuck you! Fuck you!

As Graham left the forum, a hippie tried to soothe him. "Don't get peaceful with me!" Graham yelled. *"Don't touch me!"* Dennis McNally, the Grateful Dead publicist and historian, later rated the diatribe among the top five in Graham's lifetime.

When Polte and Donahue met with the Haight Commune, they offered to expand the San Francisco Music Council, but one commune member charged that the council was aligned with the establishment instead of the hip, black, and Third World communities. Publicly, Donahue remained optimistic. "I want the festival council to be expanded to whatever number is necessary to involve a total participation of the community," he said. But he wondered whether the protestors would "trust us enough to sit down with us and get this festival on." Olivier organized an "Expanded Council Committee Meeting" but argued that the original council should proceed with its planning. On August 12, Polte cited death threats against him and resigned from the council. At a press conference the next day, the San Francisco Music Council canceled the festival.

In a flyer titled "The Natives Were Restless," the San Francisco Mime Troupe declared victory. The *Berkeley Barb* headline struck a different note: "Wild West Falls in Class Struggle." A *Daily Cal* article concluded that the festival failed because "some segments of the radical community couldn't relax enough to enjoy a festival which had the blessings of the straight world." However one parsed the event's collapse, it revealed the friction between some parts of the San Francisco counterculture and the hip capitalists who were packaging and promoting its music.

Rolling Stone had covered the Wild West story from the first public announcement in July. The following month, Ben Fong-Torres previewed the upcoming event and stressed its audacity: "The Wild West Show, the kind of venture only madmen would try to pull off, is being pulled off. And businessmen and bankers and city officials—along with artisans from every sector of San Francisco—are helping them to do it." In his account, the event and its planning were as participatory as the council hoped it would be. "At this point, it appears that everyone wants to get in on the celebration," Fong-Torres reported. The talent included the Grateful Dead, Big Brother and the Holding Company, Sly and the Family Stone, Creedence Clearwater Revival, Janis Joplin, Santana, Quicksilver Messenger Service, the Sons of Champlin, and the Ace of Cups, the all-female band that included Denise Kaufman. Passing over the protests in silence, Fong-Torres's article ended with a quote from Tom Donahue: "Wild West can make a statement: that San Francisco is a beginning for so many groovy things and attitudes."

The event fizzled days after that issue's publication date, and the next *Rolling Stone* story didn't appear until September 6. This time, the tone was much sharper. According to an unsigned story, "The Wild West Festival, the glorious dream of the San Francisco music scene, has died, the stillborn child of incompetence, paranoia, and half-baked political speed-freaks." For the first time, *Rolling Stone* mentioned the Haight Commune's leadership and claims, which it submitted to a withering critique. It singled out Ronnie Davis, "the hate-filled, politically anachronistic leader of the San Francisco Mime Troupe," and recounted how Polte, "the main target of the truculent scream-troupers," decided to resign. The dream of providing 200 hours of free music to the community "ended not with a bang, but a whimper."

In the same issue, Gleason got in his licks. In "Perspectives: Festival Paranoia," he argued that the festival was "viciously and bitterly and irrationally attacked by so-called street people, elements of the underground so-called press, and agents provocateurs." Repeating his claim that rock music was transforming the social landscape, he charged that attacks on the festival came from "hardcore politicos" who were "musical parasites attempting to steal the power of the music." He recalled a fruitless conversation with one activist who wondered how they could hold a festival when people were dying in Vietnam. He also quoted novelist Henry Miller, who maintained that it was silly to fight the status quo. "The thing to do is to create," Gleason wrote. "The thing *not* to do is destroy." Gleason's response resembled Wenner's depiction of the Yippies in 1968, but this time the conflict was more personal. Before it was derailed, the Wild West Festival promised to support his claim that the rock revolution was an engine for social progress.

Letters to the editor lamented the demise of the festival, but some *Rolling Stone* readers wondered about Gleason's arguments. One called bullshit on his assertion that "rock music in America has been the single most potent social force for change."

> *What* change? Rock music hasn't stopped the slaughter in Vietnam. It hasn't made the pigs any nicer. It hasn't stopped any racism or war or poverty that I know of. It *has* made some corporations a lot of bread. On the plus side, about all it has done is make pop music a lot more fun and a great deal easier to listen to—and everything else considered, what else *can* it do?

Rock music could play a role in the revolution, the letter continued, but it was "*not* the revolution and by itself can do nothing to stop all the shit that's going down these days. That will be up to those people whom Gleason despises and fears precisely because they *are* what really makes a revolution—the politicos."

If Woodstock was a peak moment for the counterculture, the Wild West Festival was an absurd defeat. But what lay ahead for the Bay Area rock community was even more dispiriting.

·   ·   ·   ·   ·

For its second anniversary issue, *Rolling Stone* ran a long interview with Bob Dylan. Although the earliest Rolling Stone Interviews were sometimes fashioned from found materials, Wenner wanted them to resemble the lengthy interviews in established outlets, especially *Playboy* and *The Paris Review*. Yet some subjects subverted attempts to take their music seriously. Dylan deflected Wenner's questions about the lyrics for "Leopard-Skin Pill-Box Hat": "It's just about that. . . . There's really no more to it than that," he said. "Just a leopard-skin pill-box hat. That's *all*." Likewise, Mick Jagger told Jonathan Cott that his band's lyrics were "just the Rolling Stones sort of rambling on about what they feel." When Cott claimed that some of the lyrics were very good, Jagger replied, "Oh, they're not, they're crap." Similarly, Jagger rejected the premise behind Cott's questions about *Their Satanic Majesties Request* (1967). "What were your original ideas about putting it together?" Cott asked. "None at all," Jagger replied. "Absolutely no idea behind it." He also dismissed the idea that rock concerts repaid analysis. "Pop concerts are just gatherings of people who want to have a good time, and I don't think they have any higher meaning," Jagger said.

In 1969, Mick Jagger announced that the band's U.S. tour would conclude with a free concert in the Bay Area. The idea reflected changes on the ground since the group's tour three years earlier. The counterculture's profile had risen dramatically during that interval, and Woodstock had already achieved landmark status. The Rolling Stones missed that festival but hoped to score some hip cachet in San Francisco. The original concept was a relatively modest event in Golden Gate Park, but the Rolling Stones, who commissioned a documentary film about their tour, had something grander in mind. After promoters billed the event as "Woodstock West," San Francisco officials refused to issue a permit. The Sears Point Raceway in Sonoma County was the second option, but time was short, and logistics were only part of the problem. The Rolling Stones created ill will by canceling a Los Angeles show that would have been put on by the raceway's sister company. When the parent company asked for a $100,000 fee or the distribution rights for any film made at the racetrack, Jagger refused to negotiate, effectively nixing Sears Point as a venue. As Gleason reported in the *Chronicle*, the Stones still lacked a site only days before the scheduled event.

Meanwhile, key figures in the San Francisco counterculture were repeating the routines that doomed the Wild West Festival. The San Francisco Mime Troupe declined to participate in any capitalist venture, and a meeting held at Grateful Dead headquarters led to hours of discussion and little progress. On hand were Chet Helms, Digger cofounder Emmett Grogan, Rolling Stones road manager Sam Cutler, Grateful Dead manager Rock Scully, and several Hells Angels. At Scully's suggestion, Cutler wanted to invite the Hells Angels to sit by the stage, which was barely one meter high, to prevent fans from mounting it. John Burks, who was covering the meeting for *Rolling Stone*, broke from his journalistic role to oppose that idea, but Cutler overrode his objection.

·   ·   ·   ·   ·

Days before the concert's scheduled date, a major news story emerged from Southern California: Charles Manson and his followers were arrested for murder. Shortly after visiting the Esalen Institute in Big Sur that summer, Manson directed some of his followers to Terry Melcher's home. Melcher had declined to produce Manson's album, and film director Roman Polanski and his pregnant wife, actress Sharon Tate, were renting Melcher's former residence. "Leave a sign," Manson instructed his minions. "You girls know what to do. Something witchy." Four Manson Family members entered the house at night and butchered Tate and her friends. Using Tate's blood, one of the assailants wrote "PIG" on the wall. After police examined the crime scene the next day, one officer said the victims were wearing "hippie-type clothing." Another said the crime looked like "a typical fag murder." But there was nothing typical about the Manson Family or its violence.

The next night, Manson's followers broke into the Los Feliz home of Leno and Rosemary LaBianca. The LaBiancas didn't know their attackers, but their next-door neighbors had served the Manson Family peyote fruit punch the previous year. The intruders tied up the LaBiancas, bayoneted them to death, and carved the word "WAR" into Leno LaBianca's abdomen. They also used Rosemary LaBianca's blood to write "RISE" and "DEATH TO PIGS" on the walls and "HEALTER SKELTER," misspelling the title of the Beatles song, on the refrigerator. The murderers then fed the couple's dogs, rifled through the refrigerator, ate a snack, and drank chocolate milk. Law enforcement was tracking the Manson Family for a rash of auto thefts, one of which was connected to the murder of a Manson associate. A suspect's jailhouse conversation tied the group to the Tate–LaBianca murders, and a motorcycle gang member told law enforcement that Manson had mentioned the homicides to him.

More a product of the penal system than the counterculture, Manson was nevertheless cast as a hippie in much of the media coverage. Roman Polanski took that association for granted. "Prior to the murders," he recalled in his memoir, "I'd never thought of hippies as potentially dangerous. On the contrary, I'd found them an attractive social phenomenon—that had influenced us all and affected our outlook on life." But the murders changed his outlook.

Clearly I'd underestimated the dangers latent in the hippie lifestyle, for which Sharon and I both had felt a certain admiration, seeing only its absence of cant, its freedom from hang-ups and hypocrisy. "I want a hippie wife," I remember telling Sharon on one occasion. I had not expected that she would lose her life because of this obscene inversion of hippie values.

As the Manson story shaped up, what Polanski called "the dangers inherent in the hippie lifestyle" became a major theme. In effect, the media coverage that year put the counterculture on trial along with the Manson Family.

The same week Manson was arrested, police officers in Chicago killed Black Panther leader Fred Hampton. Weeks before that, while the 21-year-old Hampton was out of town, his comrades had exchanged gunfire with police officers, leaving two Black Panthers and one officer dead. Now fourteen plainclothes officers entered Hampton's building at 4:00 a.m., kicked down his front door, and opened fire. A grand jury concluded that police sprayed between 82 and 99 gunshots through doors, walls, and windows. Only one shot appeared to have been fired by anyone else. Hampton and a fellow Panther were killed, and several others were seriously injured. Later investigation revealed that the FBI coordinated the raid. It also ran a secret program to destroy the Black Panther Party, which FBI Director J. Edgar Hoover considered the greatest threat to the internal security of the country.

Members of Weatherman, the revolutionary faction of SDS that derived its name from a Bob Dylan lyric, were outraged by what they considered a political assassination. Their anger was compounded by photographs of the My Lai massacre in Vietnam, which appeared in the December 1 issue of *Life* magazine. At its so-called War Council later that month, Weatherman leader Bernardine Dohrn called on the group to begin the armed struggle against the U.S. government. Weatherman's other goals were to destroy U.S. imperialism, support international liberation movements, and usher in world communism. Along the way, Weatherman also meant to smash white privilege, bourgeois individualism, and monogamy. It was a tall order for a small group, but its members were nothing if not determined. After the War Council, Weatherman leaders began to plan potentially lethal operations for the first time.

.   .   .   .   .

Back in the Bay Area, and at the very last second, the owner of the Altamont Speedway in eastern Alameda County offered that property as a concert venue. Although the venue lacked the necessary facilities for a large event, planners hoped that good vibes would overcome bad logistics. The talent was certainly impressive. Santana, Jefferson Airplane, the Flying Burrito Brothers, and Crosby, Stills, Nash & Young were all scheduled to play. After the Grateful Dead's set, the Rolling Stones would furnish the climax for their documentary film.

When the concert began, Hells Angels arrived on their motorcycles, parted the immense crowd, parked in front of the low stage, and took up their positions. Members of the Oakland and San Francisco chapters, whom Hunter S. Thompson had featured in his bestselling book, were in attendance along with members of the San Jose chapter. As the crowd surged forward, Hells Angels retaliated with pool cues, bottles, and fists, threatening both spectators and musicians alike. One San Jose member cold-cocked Jefferson Airplane's Marty Balin during its set. Another spectator threw a full beer bottle that struck Denise Kaufman, Wenner's former girlfriend. Six months pregnant at the time, Kaufman suffered a fractured skull. She sought medical care, but the first-aid facilities were inadequate for an event of that size. Dismayed by the violence, the Grateful Dead chose not to play.

When the music resumed after nightfall, the mayhem intensified. As the Rolling Stones began their seventh number, a young black man from Berkeley named Meredith Hunter rushed the stage and was rebuffed. Hunter brandished a gun and was immediately swarmed, stomped, and stabbed by Hells Angels. Many in the audience had no idea what transpired in front of the stage, but the documentary footage caught much of the violence on film. Police used that footage to identify the killer, a Hells Angel from San Jose who was eventually acquitted on grounds of self-defense.

Many mainstream outlets missed or downplayed the violence, but Ralph Gleason pondered the disaster in his *Chronicle* column. "Is this the new community? Is this what Woodstock promised?" he asked rhetorically. "Gathered together AS a tribe, what happened? Brutality, murder, despoliation, you name it." Gleason saw Altamont as the death knell of hippie utopianism. "If the name 'Woodstock' has come to denote the flowering of one phase of the youth culture," he wrote for *Esquire*, "'Altamont' has come to mean the end of it." Gleason couldn't point the finger at political activists, as he had when the Wild West Festival was canceled. Instead, he blamed the entire community for what transpired. "There are no specific guilty parties for Altamont," he wrote in a 1971 review of *Gimme Shelter*, the documentary film commissioned by the Rolling Stones. "We were all guilty, myself included."

Wenner expected Stanley Booth, who was writing a book about the Rolling Stones, to cover the tour for *Rolling Stone*. Shortly after the Altamont debacle, however, Booth wrote to Wenner with his apologies.

> Sorry I didn't stay to see you after the Stones' free fiasco, but it was really—well, I'd had just about all I could handle, after two months without sleep, living on cocaine, grass, and bourbon, all of it building up to an insane crescendo which I watch helpless like in a scene from one of those legs-heavy anxiety dreams as a gang of motorcycle outlaws kill a n***** in a green suit. I had to come home.

The black man in the green suit wasn't a figment of Booth's addled imagination. It was Meredith Hunter, who died on his way to the hospital. When Booth's book finally appeared in 1984, *Rolling Stone* excerpted his Altamont account, which described how one Hells

Angel grabbed the microphone and addressed the crowd: "Hey, if you don't cool it, you ain't gonna hear no more music! Now you wanna all go home or what?" As Booth wrote, "It was like blaming the pigs in a slaughterhouse for bleeding on the floor." In addition to witnessing the attack on Hunter, Booth watched his killers carry his limp body behind a stack of speakers.

Booth apologized to Wenner for failing to submit a story. "If you knew how hard it was simply to survive the tour, you'd understand," Booth wrote. "If I could possibly have done it for you, I would've." He also spoke for Michael Lydon, who was covering the tour for *The New York Times*. "Michael can tell you the same thing, I'm sure," Booth told Wenner. In fact, Lydon was finishing his article at a Berkeley commune. It was too long for *The New York Times*, but *Ramparts* agreed to run it in full. When Wenner heard about that, he tried to outbid his former employer. Lydon seemed to take satisfaction in declining the offer.

Wenner wasn't ready to concede the Altamont story. Burks reminded him that no one had nailed it, and Gleason maintained that *Rolling Stone* should either cover Altamont like it was World War II or close up shop. When Greil Marcus endorsed that course of action, Wenner recalled, he gave his staff the green light. Marcus remembered that episode differently, noting that the editorial meeting after the concert produced no consensus on how to cover it. At the end of the meeting, Wenner announced, "We are going to cover this from top to bottom. And we are going to lay the blame."

Burks found an eyewitness to Meredith Hunter's death, and Marcus interviewed Hunter's family. Nine other writers, including Lester Bangs and Langdon Winner, contributed to the lengthy cover story, which Burks lashed together. Marcus recommended John Morthland, a friend of his and Langdon Winner's, to help with the issue, and Burks subsequently offered Morthland a full-time job. Some contributors were unhappy that their work didn't appear separately with their bylines, and the coverage showed signs of haste, but "The Rolling Stones Disaster at Altamont: Let It Bleed" was extensive, detailed, and unstinting in its judgment. It opened with the eyewitness account of Hunter's death and went on to describe "the blueprint for disaster" that was Altamont. "Let It Bleed" concluded that Altamont was "the product of diabolical egotism, hype, ineptitude, money, manipulation, and, at base, a fundamental lack of concern for humanity."

The story drew a compliment from *San Francisco Chronicle* columnist Herb Caen. "Again, congratulations on the Altamont coverage," Caen wrote to Wenner. "If there isn't a Pulitzer Prize for rock publications, how about a Wurlitzer, dad?" Wenner wanted to sponsor a book about Altamont, but he suspected that New York publishers would underestimate the story's importance. When he contacted an editor at Bantam Books, Wenner addressed that issue directly: "I know you may think that it's not big enough—although there is a story in *Newsweek* where they just copped our coverage, blow by blow, again—but this story and the interest in it is much bigger than you can see from New York." The Altamont book idea never panned out, but "Let It Bleed" showed that *Rolling Stone* could break an important story that other outlets couldn't or wouldn't take on. Moreover, it showed that the magazine, a creature of the San Francisco counterculture, was also one of its sharpest observers.

·   ·   ·   ·   ·

One month after "Let It Bleed" ran, Ellen Willis, the popular music columnist at *The New Yorker,* replied to a letter from Ralph Gleason. Although her interests ranged far beyond music, her column established Willis as a leading voice in the male-dominated field of rock criticism. In her reply to Gleason, Willis began by complimenting *Rolling Stone.* "Though I think *Rolling Stone* is the best rock magazine going, and I read it all the time, I don't feel I can write for it," she wrote. She then cited several objections to the magazine's editorial slant. Her primary problem with the magazine was its sexism. "The main thing that bugs me about Rolling Stone is that it is viciously anti-woman," she charged. "RS habitually refers to women as chicks and treats us as chicks, i.e., interchangeable cute fucking machines."

Sexism was part of the larger rock culture, Willis acknowledged, but that fact created an even greater obligation to flag the problem.

> I realize that the whole rock subculture and most of the music is very male supremacist, and a magazine about that subculture can't ignore that fact, but it seems to me it's the responsibility of RS, just for that reason, to be critical, to admit the fact that there's some rottenness going on, instead of helping to perpetuate it.

By that time, *Rolling Stone* had published "The Groupies and Other Girls," a lengthy packet of stories about the subculture of (mostly) female rock fans, not all of whom identified as groupies. Conceding that the stories contained "a lot of good information," Willis described them as "uncomprehending and offensive."

Willis also disliked the magazine's "anti-political, pro-cultural revolutionary bias," which Gleason himself had promulgated.

> When it comes to changing the basic conditions of my life, the women's liberation movement has done more for me in the few short years of its existence than the so-called cultural revolution will ever do. To me, when a bunch of snotty upper-middle class white males start telling me that politics isn't where it's at, that is simply an attempt to defend their privileges. What they want is more bread and circuses; I like to have fun, too, but what I really want is an end to my oppression.

Willis later admitted to her daughter that she, too, had credited the notion of cultural revolution, but when it failed to produce political change, she stopped writing about rock and roll.

Finally, Willis told Gleason that the dearth of female contributors at *Rolling Stone* was problematic for her.

> Also, in the years I've been reading *Rolling Stone*, I can't remember having read one article by a woman. There are plenty of women writers—more women journalists, percentage-wise, than women in

anything else, so scarcity isn't the reason. And I feel strongly that I don't want to be a token woman writer for a magazine that doesn't print women in general.

In her postscript, Willis encouraged Gleason to reconsider the magazine's diction: "P.S. In case I didn't make it clear, the word 'chick' is just as bad as 'n*****.' Which you wouldn't use—would you??"

Willis's trenchant letter showed how carefully she was reading *Rolling Stone* and the larger cultural scene. Although women had written for the magazine, her sense that she might become a token female writer was well-founded. So was her claim that *Rolling Stone* was perpetuating the sexist nature of rock culture. Finally, her point about "snotty upper-middle class white males" diverting attention from politics wouldn't have been lost on Gleason, who consistently emphasized cultural rather than political revolution. Willis's critique of *Rolling Stone* was on point, but the magazine was still evolving. Five years after her exchange with Gleason, Willis began contributing to *Rolling Stone* and left *The New Yorker*.

Figure 1. Music journalist Ralph J. Gleason (*right*) with John Lennon backstage at Candlestick Park. Gleason mentored Jann Wenner, cofounded *Rolling Stone*, and gave the fledgling magazine instant credibility. Photo: Jim Marshall.

Figure 2. In the wake of the Trips Festival, promoter Bill Graham gave San Francisco hippies a platform for reinventing rock music and its live performance. Photo: Jim Marshall.

Figure 3. Timothy Leary, who touted LSD at the Human Be-In in Golden Gate Park, corresponded with Wenner from jail, prison, and Algeria, where he stayed with fellow exile Eldridge Cleaver. Once opposed to political activism, Leary later described Black Panther Party cofounder Huey P. Newton as "a complete turned-on holy man, a golden black Aquarius tuned into the central energy." Photo: Jim Marshall.

Figure 4. At Gleason's home in Berkeley, *Rolling Stone* cofounder Jann Wenner articulated the high concept for a new magazine. He remained the magazine's driving force for five decades. Photo: Annie Leibovitz (Getty Images).

Figure 5. Wenner recruited Boston-based writer Jon Landau, whose work he had seen in *Crawdaddy*. Landau had little use for the San Francisco counterculture, but he made significant contributions to *Rolling Stone* before serving as Bruce Springsteen's manager. Photo: Leni Sinclair (Getty Images).

ROLLING STONE

NOVEMBER 9, 1967
VOL. I, NO. 1

OUR PRICE:
TWENTY-FIVE CENTS

MFP

Recognize Private Gripeweed? He's actually John Lennon in Richard Lester's new film, How I Won the War. An illustrated special preview of the movie begins on page 16.

Tom Rounds Quits KFRC

Tom Rounds, KFRC Program Director, has resigned. No immediate date has been set for his departure from the station. Rounds quit to assume the direction of Charlatan Productions, an L.A. based film company experimenting in the contemporary pop film.

Rounds spent seven years as Program Director of KPOI in Hawaii before coming to San Francisco in 1966. He successfully effected the tight format which made KFRC the number one station in San Francisco.

Les Turpin, former program director of KGB in San Diego will replace Tom Rounds at KFRC. Turpin has spent the last year as a consultant in the Drake-Chenault programming service.

The new appointment could mean a tightening up of programming policies. Rounds liberalization of KFRC's play-list may well become more restricted.

THE HIGH COST OF MUSIC AND LOVE: WHERE'S THE MONEY FROM MONTEREY?

BY MICHAEL LYDON

A weekend of "music, love, and flowers" can be done for a song (plus cost) or can be done at a cost (plus songs). The Monterey International Pop Festival, a non-profit, charity event, was, despite its own protestations, of the second sort: a damn extravagant three days.

The Festival's net profit at the end of August, the last date of accounting, was $211,451. The costs of the weekend were $290,-233. Had it not been for the profit from the sale of television rights to ABC-TV of $288,843, the whole operation would have ended up a neat $77,392 in the red.

The Festival planned to have all the artists, while in Monterey, submit ideas for use of the proceeds.

In the confusion the plan miscarried and the decision on where the profits should go has still not been finally made.

So far only $50,000 has definitely been been allocated to anyone: to a unit of the New York City Youth Board which will set up classes for many ghetto children to learn music on guitars donated by Fender. Paul Simon, a Festival governor, will personally over see the program.

Plans to give more money to the Negro College Fund for college scholarships is now being discussed; another idea is a sum between ten and twenty thousand for the Monterey Symphony.

However worthy these plans, they are considerably less daring and innovative than the projects mentioned in the spring: the Diggers, pop conferences, and any project which would "tend to further national interest in and knowledge and enjoyment of popular music." The present plans suggest that the Board of Governors, unable or unwilling to make their grandiose schemes reality, fell back on traditional charity.

The Board of Governors did decide that the money would be given out in a small number of large sums. This has meant, for instance, that the John Edwards Memorial Foundation, a folk music archive at the University of California at Los Angeles, had its small request overlooked.

In ironic fact, what happened at the Festival and its financial affairs looks in many ways like the traditional Charity Ball in hippie drag.

The overhead was high and the net was low. "For every dollar spent, there was a reason," says Derek Taylor, the Festival's PR man and one of its original officers.

Yet many of the Festival's expenses, however reasonable to Taylor, seem out of keeping with its announced spirit. The Festival management, with amateurish good will, lavished generosity on their friends.

• Producer Lou Adler was able to find a spot in the show for his own property, Johnny Rivers; Paul Simon for his friend, English folk singer Beverly; John Phillips for the Group Without A Name and Scott MacKenzie. None of them had the musical status for an international pop music festival.

It is ironic that the Rivers and the rest appeared "free," but the money it cost the Festival to get them to Monterey and back, feed them, put them up (Beverly

—Continued on Page 7

Airplane high, but no new LP release

Jefferson Airplane has been taking more than a month to record their new album for RCA Victor. In a recording period of five weeks only five sides have been completed. No definite release date has been set.

Their usual recording schedule in Los Angeles begins at 11:00 p.m. in the evening and extends through six or seven in the morning. When they're not in the studios, they stay at a fabulous pink mansion which rents for $5,000 a month. The Beatles stayed at the house on their last American tour.

The house has two swimming pools and a variety of recreational facilities. It's a small small little paradise in the hills above Hollywood. Maybe suntans and guitars don't make it together.

Figure 6. Rolling Stone's debut issue impressed readers with its high production values and unique editorial mix. It would not be mistaken for a teen magazine, trade publication, or underground newspaper, though it incorporated some of their elements. Courtesy of Rolling Stone.

Figure 7. John Burks in his *Rolling Stone* office. Gleason urged Wenner to hire Burks as managing editor. In his short stint with the magazine, Burks professionalized the newsroom and pushed *Rolling Stone* toward more political coverage. Photo: Jim Marshall.

Figure 8. The magazine's *Two Virgins* cover created a sensation. "The point is this," Wenner wrote. "Print a famous foreskin and the world will beat a path to your door." Courtesy of *Rolling Stone*.

Figure 9. While the counterculture celebrated spontaneity and self-expression, Ben Fong-Torres became famous for his preparation and professionalism. He eventually directed the magazine's music coverage as well as "Random Notes," one of the magazine's most popular features. Photo courtesy of Annie Leibovitz.

Figure 11. In a 1970 letter to Gleason, Ellen Willis declined to write for *Rolling Stone*, citing its sexist tone and lack of female writers. After Marianne Partridge became a senior editor, however, Willis contributed important pieces on rape, Janis Joplin, and other topics. Photo courtesy of the Willis family.

Figure 12. In its third year, *Rolling Stone* earned a National Magazine Award for its coverage of Altamont and the Manson Family murder trial. The awards committee cited the magazine's willingness to probe the counterculture's dark side. Courtesy of *Rolling Stone.*

Figure 13. The untimely deaths of Jimi Hendrix, Janis Joplin, and Jim Morrison dramatized drug abuse in the rock world and the counterculture more generally. Courtesy of *Rolling Stone*

Figure 14. Annie Leibovitz became *Rolling Stone*'s chief photographer in 1973 and eventually shot more than 140 cover images. "Annie was one of the closest editorial collaborations I've ever had with anybody," Wenner said later. "And she helped define the look and style of *Rolling Stone*." Photo: Allan Tannenbaum.

Figure 15. John Lennon's Rolling Stone Interview in 1971 was another turning point in rock journalism, but Wenner's decision to publish the book version effectively ended his relationship with the former Beatle. Courtesy of *Rolling Stone*.

Figure 16. Hunter S. Thompson (*left*) and Oscar Zeta Acosta at Caesar's Palace in Las Vegas. Their trips to Nevada informed Thompson's "Fear and Loathing in Las Vegas," which *Rolling Stone* ran in November 1971. Its success relaunched Gonzo journalism and made *Rolling Stone* its new home. Photo: Cashman Photo Enterprises.

Figure 17. Wenner (*right*) and Yale law professor Charles Reich interviewed Jerry Garcia (*left*) at the musician's home in Stinson Beach. Reich saw Garcia as a symbol of the social revolution he described in his best-selling book *The Greening of America*. Photo courtesy of Annie Leibovitz.

▲ *Figure 18.* Hunter S. Thompson (*left*) and George McGovern during the senator's 1972 presidential campaign. Thompson covered the campaign for *Rolling Stone*. Mixing invective, satire, and hallucination with insightful reporting, Thompson produced what was later described as the least factual and most accurate account of the campaign. Photo courtesy of Annie Leibovitz.

◀ *Figure 19.* Annie Leibovitz persuaded teen idol David Cassidy to pose nude for Robin Green's 1972 profile. "Naked Lunch Box" parodied the sexual currents roiling beneath teen celebrity even as it exploited their power. Courtesy of *Rolling Stone*.

Figure 20. Cameron Crowe's youthful enthusiasm helped the magazine heal rifts with rock stars it had alienated. By the mid-1970s, *Rolling Stone* was more focused on establishing the rock pantheon than on the social revolution heralded by rock music. Photo: Fin Costello (Getty Images).

Figure 21. Marianne Partridge (*standing*), the first woman senior editor at *Rolling Stone*, with staff members Sarah Lazin (*left*), Barbara Downey, Christine Doudna, Harriet Fier, and David Young (*right*). After joining the magazine's editorial staff, Partridge recruited Ellen Willis and offered female staffers new career paths. Photo: Max Aguilera Hellweg.

Figure 22. Ellen Willis's story about Janis Joplin was drawn from her essay in *The Rolling Stone Illustrated History of Rock & Roll*, a benchmark in rock historiography. This issue's cover also demonstrates the evolution of the magazine's design. Courtesy of *Rolling Stone*.

Figure 23. Howard Kohn (*right*) and David Weir wrote the blockbuster story about Patricia Hearst's underground exploits, which Wenner called "the scoop of the seventies." It was the first time an issue of *Rolling Stone* sold one million copies. Photo: Alison Weir.

Figure 24. Wenner's star-studded party in New York during the 1976 Democratic National Convention signaled his magazine's arrival on the national political stage. Here Wenner visits with Sally Quinn of *The Washington Post*. Photo: Allan Tannenbaum.

 You Must Do More!

7   Keep Growing

The magazine's Altamont coverage impressed the journalist most closely associated with the Hells Angels. "Did you read the coverage in *Rolling Stone*?" Hunter S. Thompson asked his editor at Random House. "That scene at the Altamont rock festival shames my worst fantasies; the sharks finally came home to roost." The story prompted Thompson to write his first letter to Wenner. "Your Altamont coverage comes close to being the best journalism I can remember reading, by anybody," he told Wenner. Wenner's reply was equally complimentary. "Having once read your Angels book in galley proof forms (stole them when I worked at *Ramparts*) and having really dug it in its pre-cut form, I've been a fan of yours," Wenner wrote. "Glad you are now a fan of ours." He invited Thompson to contribute something to *Rolling Stone*, and when Thompson mentioned that he was running for sheriff of Pitkin County, Colorado, Wenner said his campaign would be a suitable topic for a 2,500-word article.

At the time, Thompson's primary outlet was *Scanlan's Monthly*, which Warren Hinckle had cofounded after leaving *Ramparts*. Its debut issue included Thompson's profile of Olympic skier Jean-Claude Killy. The piece was originally commissioned by *Playboy*, but when its editors saw that Thompson ridiculed the rituals of American marketing, they spiked the story. Although Thompson was pleased that *Scanlan's* ran the Killy article, he was unhappy with the illustrations and layout. "Graphically, it was a fucking horror show," he wrote to Hinckle. "It looks like it was put together by a compositor's apprentice with a head full of Seconal."

When Thompson visited *Rolling Stone's* office for the first time, he met with Wenner and editor John Lombardi. Years before, Lombardi had run one of Thompson's articles in an underground newspaper, but the two men had never met. When Thompson arrived late for the appointment, Lombardi described him as "a bizarre sight." Thompson was wearing a cheap lady's wig that he frequently took off, straightened, and replaced while he pulled out random items from his bag. Sporting his cigarette holder and aviator sunglasses, which he never removed, he drank from his six-pack of beer and held forth for the entire meeting, pausing only to relieve himself. During one of those breaks, Wenner said to Lombardi, "I know I am supposed to be the youth representative in this culture . . . but what the fuck is that?" It was a good question. Almost a decade older than Wenner, Thompson was an air force veteran who never finished college, lived in the Rocky Mountains, and didn't write about music. Nevertheless, Wenner thought Thompson's iconoclasm might click with his readers.

Thompson kept in touch with Wenner throughout 1970, but he produced a career-altering story that year for Hinckle's new magazine. The idea arose at an Aspen dinner party hosted by novelist James Salter. After learning that Thompson was from Louisville, Salter suggested that he write about the Kentucky Derby, the city's signature event. Thompson pitched the idea to Hinckle, who paired Thompson with illustrator Ralph Steadman. The two men met in Louisville and prepared to skewer the spectacle at Churchill Downs.

The same week, President Nixon announced U.S. attacks on North Vietnamese strongholds in Cambodia, a neutral nation. He also urged Americans to remain vigilant against international and domestic enemies.

> My fellow Americans, we live in an age of anarchy, both abroad and at home. We see mindless attacks on all the great institutions which have been created by free civilizations in the last 500 years. Even here in the United States, great universities are being systematically destroyed.
>
> Small nations all over the world find themselves under attack from within and from without. If, when the chips are down, the world's most powerful nation—the United States of America—acts like a pitiful, helpless giant, the forces of totalitarianism and anarchy will threaten free nations and free institutions throughout the world.

The main problem, Nixon maintained, wasn't the unlawful use of American power in Southeast Asia, but rather the anarchy that would be unleashed if the U.S. government failed to exercise that power. His remark about universities was meant to discredit campus protests against the war and its expansion into Cambodia. One such protest erupted that week at Kent State University in Ohio, where students surrounded the ROTC building and eventually lit it on fire. The governor called in National Guard troops, whom some students pelted with rocks. Without warning, the troops shot at a cluster of students in a nearby parking lot. Within seconds, thirteen students were down, most of them bystanders. One was paralyzed, and four were dead.

Still brooding over the bloodshed at Kent State, Thompson finished his Kentucky Derby piece in New York. His first-person account made almost no mention of the race, focusing instead on the drunken debauchery that surrounded it. With his deadline looming, Thompson reportedly tore pages out of his notebook and fed them into the telecopier. Back in San Francisco, Hinckle received those fragments and assembled the text. Thompson hoped Steadman's drawings would redeem the story, which he privately described as "lame bullshit" that might end his career. But Hinckle was elated. When Steadman's illustrations arrived, he knew he had a "game-changer."

"The Kentucky Derby Is Decadent and Depraved" wasn't the disaster that Thompson feared. To the contrary, he received congratulatory letters and calls as soon as it appeared. Thompson compared the experience to "falling down an elevator shaft and landing in a pool full of mermaids." Journalist Bill Cardoso, who had appeared in the Killy piece, described the Kentucky Derby article as "totally Gonzo." Thompson liked that description and soon applied it to a strain of his work. Although Gonzo journalism developed fitfully over the next several years, it eventually transformed Thompson's public image, model of authorship, and critical fortunes.

.   .   .   .   .

One year after the Democratic National Convention, the Chicago conspiracy trial was making national headlines. The Department of Justice charged eight defendants—including Tom Hayden, Jerry Rubin, Abbie Hoffman, and Bobby Seale—with conspiracy, crossing state lines to incite a riot, and other crimes. Seale, who had cofounded the Black Panther Party three years earlier, was represented by Bay Area attorney Charles Garry at the arraignment. But Garry was recovering from surgery when the trial began, and Judge Julius Hoffman wouldn't permit Seale to represent himself. When Seale called the judge a bigot, a racist, and a fascist, Hoffman ordered him bound, gagged, and chained to his chair. A week later, Hoffman declared a mistrial and ordered Seale to be tried separately at a later date. He also cited the Black Panther leader on 16 charges of contempt. In all, Judge Hoffman cited the defendants and their lawyers more than 150 times for the same offense.

The jury acquitted all seven defendants of conspiracy but found five defendants guilty of crossing state lines to incite a riot. On appeal, the criminal convictions were reversed, many contempt citations were dismissed, and the Justice Department decided not to try Seale or to retry the other defendants. The outcome indicated that the legal establishment was struggling to control the narrative about its own conduct and legitimacy.

Rolling Stone ran a long article about the Chicago trial by Gene Marine, a senior editor at *Ramparts* whom Wenner cast as his special correspondent. Marine addressed readers in the second person and called attention to his own authorial decisions in recounting the tumultuous trial. That style reflected the influence of New Journalism, and Wenner was sufficiently proud of the article to take out a full-page ad in *The New York Times*. Even so, Hendrick Hertzberg of *The New Yorker* was unimpressed. "The Gene Marine thing was kind of a disappointment," Hertzberg told Burks, his former colleague at *Newsweek*'s San Francisco bureau. "Too much rhetoric. RS should develop its own political writers, cover politics the way it covers rock, i.e., straight, no jargon."

Jean Genet was also unimpressed by *Rolling Stone*, but for a different reason. The 60-year-old French novelist, playwright, and poet was touring the United States in support of the Black Panthers. When Genet scheduled a press conference at the party's headquarters in Oakland, Marcus asked Langdon Winner to attend. Genet's first words were, "Is there anyone here from *Rolling Stone* magazine?" Winner raised his hand, and Genet addressed him directly. "Your efforts to make your readers political won't succeed if whites do not want to understand that you must go beyond racism and reach a solidarity with the blacks." Genet then referred to Marine's article about the Chicago conspiracy trial. "You bring out the most emotional attitudes of whites concerning the Chicago trial and Bobby Seale," Genet said. "But after what I read and what was translated for me, there was no political or revolutionary argument used." Moreover, he criticized *Rolling Stone* for "paternalistic attitudes towards blacks characteristic of all liberals."

Genet then issued a request to Winner and his colleagues: "I am asking you to think politically more and more so that you can make the readers of *Rolling Stone* political." That couldn't be done, he maintained, by sandwiching the Black Panther coverage between stories about drugs and sex. Winner tried to explain the magazine's predicament to Genet. "There is a group among the writers and editors who are trying to include more political coverage in *Rolling Stone*, including stories about the Vietnam War and the Black Panthers," Winner said. "But given the editorial constraints of what's basically a rock-and-roll publication, it's an uphill battle." Genet was unimpressed. "Those are *only words*," he told Winner. "You must do more!"

·   ·   ·   ·   ·

In June, *Rolling Stone* did more. It ran a packet of stories on Kent State and Jackson State College in Mississippi, where two black students were killed 11 days after the bloodshed in Ohio. "Jann was out of town," Greil Marcus recalled, "so John Burks and I put together a really fabulous issue called 'The Pitiful Helpless Giant.'" Annie Leibovitz contributed her first cover photograph, and the title was drawn from President Nixon's televised speech. For Burks, the political stakes were too high to ignore. "It was literally a life-and-death matter for our generation," he said later, "and if we hadn't moved on it right away, we'd have lost the moment."

Wenner didn't think the issue was fabulous, and he worried about *Rolling Stone*'s direction, especially after the staff drew up a list of "principles to be affirmed" while he was out of the office. He wasn't prepared to alter the magazine's editorial formula, especially if that meant radicalizing the political coverage. Nor was he willing to cede more power to his staff. After Wenner called a meeting to clarify his position, Burks tendered his resignation. "Wenner thought he was training me," Burks wrote in a 1974 letter to Chet Flippo. "I thought I was training him, and we were both right in some ways."

Describing Wenner as "about the most difficult cat I've ever worked with and one of the most complicated," Burks later recounted the incidents that led to his departure.

It all came to a head at midsummer when he'd wasted an outrageous amount of money that *Rolling Stone* had made and had to go back to New York to float a loan from the Kinney Corp. (owners of WB-Reprise,

Atlantic, etc.) to keep the trip going. A hundred thousand dollar loan. Then not long after his return he "decided" that RS should do a lot more interviews with the stars and all the Random Notes ought to be rock and roll and a lot of other bullshit that added up to a magazine that would—well, it sounded like it was going to be a tastefully executed fan magazine, but nothing more than that. It was going to stick with the rock-and-roll trip, and not get into all this troublesome political shit.

Even this brief passage throws the editorial conflict into sharp relief. Burks thought Wenner was too attached to "rock and roll and a lot of other bullshit," which would consign *Rolling Stone* to a "tastefully executed fan magazine" at best. Moreover, Burks questioned Wenner's ability to make key editorial decisions and cast his flawed leadership as a wasted opportunity to do serious journalism.

In the same letter, Burks suggested that advertisers shared Wenner's concern about the magazine's political coverage.

The advertisers (I learned from our ad side) had complained that with the repression that's coming they weren't sure whether they could get behind a paper that didn't do just about a hundred per cent rock and roll, and besides, you know, we got to look out for our asses and not get caught up in some political trip if you can dig what I mean, Jann, baby.

Cash-strapped again, *Rolling Stone* missed an issue for the first time since its earliest days, but Wenner received advances against future advertising from A&M, Columbia, and Elektra. Many record executives disapproved of Nixon and the war, but selling records, not saving the world, was their top priority. Elektra Records ran a full-page advertisement in *Rolling Stone* asserting that violence wounded everyone, and that contemporary music was perhaps the only medium through which a troubled world could be understood. The clear message, which Jac Holzman sounded many times, was that poetics trumped political activism. If the magazine's editorial line reversed those priorities, it would presumably do so without Elektra's support.

During this time, Wenner also sought a major investor. He contacted venture capitalist Arthur Rock, who had backed Max Palevsky's company, Scientific Data Systems. When Xerox bought that company in 1969, it was the largest acquisition in American history. Rock introduced Wenner to Palevsky, who sent Wenner a check for $200,000. Later, Wenner claimed that he didn't need those funds because the loans from the labels solved the magazine's cash problems.

After Burks resigned, Wenner named Jon Carroll managing editor and fired him two weeks later. Burks and Carroll migrated to *Rags*, Baron Wolman's new countercultural fashion magazine. Its paid circulation reached 50,000, but it folded after twelve issues. Burks and Carroll then moved to *Flash*, where they were joined by John Morthland, Ed Ward, *Rolling Stone* film critic Michael Goodwin, and chief photographer Robert Altman. The goal was a countercultural version of *Life* magazine, but after the pilot issue was distributed to potential writers and advertisers, the idea collapsed. Meanwhile, John Lombardi accepted a position at *Esquire*, and Langdon Winner began teaching at MIT.

When asked about the editorial turnover during this period, Wenner attributed it to the normal sifting that occurs at every magazine. Yet elsewhere he acknowledged the conflict over *Rolling Stone*'s mission. "Our core mission was the purpose of the music," Wenner told his biographer. "I didn't like their politics, and I wanted to do what I wanted to do, which was about music." That claim must be weighed carefully. In fact, Wenner was actively courting Hunter S. Thompson, who was increasingly attuned to politics and didn't write about music. The question wasn't whether *Rolling Stone* would cover national affairs, but how much and what kind of political coverage and commentary made the most sense for its audience.

Later, Marcus reflected on Wenner's concerns.

When Jann got back, I think he found that the paper—we didn't call it a magazine then—was being taken away from him. It wasn't that he did or didn't like what we had done, but what we had done was something major: a firm and strong political stand just through what we'd published. The paper was slipping away from him. He was losing his moral authority by having ceded so much of it to other people.

As it turned out, the most protracted debate between Marcus and Wenner was about music, not the magazine's political coverage. It revolved around the magazine's review of *McCartney,* the artist's first solo album, whose publicity packet contained dismissive remarks about the Beatles. Wenner maintained that Langdon Winner's review should be revised to acknowledge the dissolution of rock's most important group. Wenner and Marcus argued the point for several hours, including over dinner with their wives. Wenner finally convinced Marcus, who then argued with Winner for three more hours. Winner agreed to rewrite the review, which noted the "tawdry propaganda" accompanying the release. In Marcus's view, his debates with Wenner and Winner were entirely appropriate, for they showed that Wenner was honoring his original agreement to respect that section's autonomy. To alter a record review, Wenner still had to persuade Marcus or replace him.

Shortly after Marcus criticized Dylan's *Self-Portrait* (1970), Wenner asked to meet with him. "I really want to talk about what you're going to be doing here," Wenner said. Marcus thought their conversation was meant to expand the scope of his work. "I came away from this long conversation really feeling great: it was a new role at the magazine, with more freedom," he said. When Marcus detailed the conversation for his wife, however, she informed him he had been fired. When Marcus sought clarification, Wenner told Marcus he could still contribute to the magazine, but that he no longer had an actual job. "Now to this day," Marcus said, "Jann will probably say that I quit, and I will say I was fired. But it was that subtle. It was pretty slick." After his split with the magazine, Marcus was supposed to coauthor a book about Altamont with John Burks. Straight Arrow Books, which Wenner formed in 1970, would publish it, but when the project fizzled, Marcus remained on the outs with Wenner and *Rolling Stone* for years.

For Marcus, all was not lost. He was delighted when Cal offered him a chance to teach the American Studies seminar that had inspired him as an undergraduate. But the class went poorly, and Marcus made two fateful decisions: He dropped out of graduate school and began to write *Mystery Train*. He didn't plan to argue that rock and roll clarified "the reality of what's happening today," as Gleason claimed in 1967. For him, the stakes were higher and more specific than that. Rock and roll revealed, often with unexpected power, what it was to be American at any one time—not only its possibilities, but also its limits and traps. The music showed whose America they were living in, where that version of America came from, and how artists were continuously reworking or inventing it. How he would put across those ideas wasn't clear, but after leaving *Rolling Stone*, he poured himself into the project.

As Burks, Marcus, and others left *Rolling Stone*, several stalwarts remained on the masthead, most notably Ben Fong-Torres, Jon Landau, David Felton, and Charles Perry. Landau took over the record review section, retained many reviewers, and added several new ones to the mix. Meanwhile, Wenner recruited a new set of writers and editors. They included Hunter S. Thompson, whose name appeared on the masthead after his first story; Grover Lewis, formerly of *The Village Voice*; Joe Eszterhas, a newspaper reporter from Cleveland; Timothy Ferris from the *New York Post*; and Tim Cahill, who studied creative writing at San Francisco State College. The editorial turnover didn't damage the magazine's brand; indeed, a *New York Times* business story the following year sang the magazine's praises for attracting young readers, many of whom scorned the offerings of larger publishers.

·   ·   ·   ·   ·

The magazine's next major story appeared in June 1970, when it ran a 30,000-word piece by David Felton and David Dalton. Divided into six parts, the story explored the Manson Family saga and its aftermath.

The first section described the murders but also criticized the *Los Angeles Times*, Felton's former employer. Before the trial, the newspaper ran a confession by Susan Atkins, which a promoter had obtained from her attorney with the understanding that it would run only in foreign outlets. But the promoter hired two *Times* journalists to rewrite the piece, and once the confession was scheduled to appear abroad, the *Times* decided not to let another domestic outlet scoop it. By running the confession, which Atkins later retracted, the *Los Angeles Times* made it more difficult for the defendants to receive a fair trial.

The Manson piece also critiqued the underground press's coverage. The *Los Angeles Free Press* refused to run an advertisement for Manson's hastily released album, but it published several lurid headlines and a weekly column written by Manson from jail. Another alternative paper, *Tuesday's Child*, named Manson "Man of the Year" and ran a front-page cartoon that showed him nailed to a cross. The plaque above his head read "HIPPIE." The question that divided the underground press, Felton and Dalton maintained, was whether Manson was part of the counterculture. It was further evidence of that movement's importance, but the *Rolling Stone* article also described the underground coverage as a hypersensitive reaction to "the relentless gloating of the cops, who, after a five-year search, finally found a longhaired devil you could love to hate."

The rest of the Manson story included a prosecutor's lengthy account of the court case, a long jailhouse interview with Manson, a preview of the trial, and remarks from Manson's friends about his personality and state of mind. The final section described the squalid scene at Spahn Ranch. Like the Altamont story, the Manson piece revealed the dark side of the counterculture, if that term could be stretched to accommodate the Manson Family. In this case, hippies didn't stand for peace, love, and understanding, but rather for drugs, orgies, senseless murders, and a crackpot spirituality that converted vice into virtue.

The Manson Family story dominated that issue of *Rolling Stone*, but a Lester Bangs book review reinforced the magazine's take on the counterculture. Bangs delighted in Jerry Rubin's memoir, especially its humor and anarchic energy, but he recoiled from Rubin's glorification of violence, especially when Rubin declared that "Amerika's children should start killing and dying for themselves." Bangs was having none of it.

> Jerry's razzing and his pipe-dreams of an inspired Looney Tune cultural revolution hit like a healthy dose of laughing gas. But just as it remains to be seen whether Woodstock or Altamont more truly represents the sense of community in the "counter-culture," it also remains to be seen whether the deaths of even four Ohio students will be worth all these pipe-dreams.

The scare quotes around *counter-culture* were a nod to social critic Theodore Roszak's recent coinage, and Bangs's references to Altamont and Kent State recalled the violence there. In the weeks leading up to the shootings at Kent State, Rubin had given a speech on campus urging students to kill their parents. "And I mean that quite literally," Rubin said, "because until you're ready to kill your parents, you're not ready to change this country. Our parents are our first oppressors." Even for Bangs, Rubin's exhortations were over the top, and his review reaffirmed the magazine's aversion to radical politics and slogans.

If *Rolling Stone* distanced itself from radical politics, it included many hippie-friendly elements, including an astrology column written by Ambrose Hollingsworth. (His actual surname omitted the *s*.) Hollingworth, who managed Quicksilver Messenger Service and the Ace of Cups before a disabling automobile crash in 1966, also applied his astrological expertise to select the day for the Human Be-In. When Wenner formed Straight Arrow Books in 1970, he hoped that Hollingworth's columns could be fashioned into a profitable anthology. Hollingworth noted that the stars were aligned for success, but when he asked for a $2,000 advance, Wenner didn't bite. Hollingworth then sent Wenner a snippier letter. "Now and then I'll send you a column which will cost you nothing whether you publish it or not," he wrote. He also corrected Wenner's description of him: "I am not an astrologer, I am an occultist and a nature-mystic."

Rolling Stone ran Hollingworth's final column shortly after the "Let It Bleed" issue appeared, but the magazine's staff didn't abandon astrology as such. The job interview paperwork, for example, asked for an applicant's sun, moon, and rising signs. "I didn't know the difference, so I wrote Gemini on all three," one applicant recalled, but the employee who took her form was astonished. "Triple Gemini!" she said. "How do you cope?" When Ed Ward asked why he needed to specify the day and time of his birth, Wenner's assistant explained her purpose. "Jann wants to make sure the staff is astrologically compatible," she replied. "So you're a Scorpio. Hmmm. We'll have to see how this balances out."

·   ·   ·   ·   ·

The planets were also beginning to align for Hunter S. Thompson. After the Kentucky Derby piece was well received, Thompson contacted Hinckle about a series of Gonzo-style stories for *Scanlan's*. He proposed that the "Thompson–Steadman Report" cover the Super Bowl, Mardi Gras, America's Cup, and other spectacles. The idea, Thompson explained to Steadman, would be to "rape them all, quite systematically, and then we could sell it as a book: *Amerikan Dreams*." The pair would "travel around the country and shit on *everything*." Thompson considered the "Rape Series on Amerikan Institutions" a "king-bitch dog-fucker of an idea." They would turn out articles "so weird & frightful as to stagger every mind in journalism." Hinckle approved, and Thompson and Steadman set their sights on the America's Cup regatta in September.

Meanwhile, Thompson continued to work on his first article for *Rolling Stone*. After his unsuccessful bid for sheriff, he sent Wenner "The Battle of Aspen." He began by noting that he decided to run only after witnessing the street violence outside the Democratic National Convention.

> For me, that week in Chicago was far worse than the worst bad acid trip I'd even heard rumors about. It permanently altered my brain chemistry, and my first new idea—when I finally calmed down—was an absolute conviction there was no possibility for any personal truce, for me, in a nation that could hatch and be proud of a malignant monster like Chicago.

Thompson's key campaign issue was drug enforcement, but he also opposed Aspen's rapid growth and everything President Nixon stood for. Convinced that many young voters shared his disdain for conventional politics, Thompson framed the election as a local race with national significance. On election day, Thompson received most of the votes in Aspen but lost the county. In his concession speech, he channeled Richard Nixon after his loss to Pat Brown in 1962: "This is my last press conference. You won't have Hunter Thompson to kick around anymore, you motherfuckers."

Despite his theatrics, Thompson's piece avoided the Gonzo pyrotechnics of the Kentucky Derby article. Still hoping that his Aspen story could pull together the nonfiction book he owed Random House, Thompson was struggling with his major theme, the death of the American Dream. The following year, however, Thompson delivered the manuscript to Random House. It was set in the Nevada desert, not the Rocky Mountains, and it was Gonzo from start to finish.

·　　·　　·　　·　　·

In the fall of 1970, Jimi Hendrix and Janis Joplin died unexpectedly, and *Rolling Stone* ran a cover story on each. Hendrix choked on his own vomit after taking barbiturates in London, while Joplin overdosed on heroin at her hotel in Hollywood. The year before Hendrix's death, *Rolling Stone* named him Performer of the Year, but he was playing relentlessly, his personal affairs were messy, and he was arrested for possession of narcotics in Toronto. The Joplin story focused on her state of mind, the personal challenges she faced, and the circumstances of her death. The article also documented her split with Big Brother and the Holding Company, the troubles she had with her subsequent band, and the spirit-crushing review that Gleason penned for the *Chronicle* following a March 1969 performance at Winterland. That same month, she appeared on the cover of *Rolling Stone* with the caption, "A Report on Janis Joplin: The Judy Garland of Rock?"

That question reflected Joplin's rocky relationship with the magazine. When Burks contacted her in December 1968, he met with stiff resistance. "Talked to Janis Joplin, sort of, for about 41 seconds," Burks told Wenner. "Doesn't want to tell us the lineup of her new band, her plans or anything, because 'I don't like the way your paper has treated me and I don't see why I should do you any favors.' Doesn't want to talk with us about anything, period, finis, end of story." Her feelings about *Rolling Stone* were no mystery. A month earlier, an article claimed that Joplin screamed, moaned, and cooed lyrics onstage, "stomping and posing like an imperious whore." The sexual double standard was difficult to miss. Jimi Hendrix could hump his speaker at the Monterey Pop Festival, but Joplin's onstage persona was considered slutty.

Hendrix and Joplin weren't the only rock casualties. The Rolling Stones' Brian Jones drowned in his swimming pool the month before Woodstock, and the Doors' Jim Morrison, the subject of a Rolling Stone Interview in 1969, would perish in the bathtub of his Paris apartment two years later. The counterculture was losing its heroes at a rapid clip.

.   .   .   .   .

In December 1970, Timothy Leary wrote to Wenner, not for the first time. He addressed Wenner as "Comrade Jann" and offered encouragement. "Keep growing," Leary wrote. "It's beautiful to watch you do it."

Much had changed since the two men first met. While working for the *Sunday Ramparts*, Wenner accompanied Leary on an all-day drive to a college where Leary was scheduled to speak. "I fancied myself his wingman," Wenner recalled, "an accomplice on his mission to convert the next audience." Leary, he said, "was a magician with words and had the spirit of a leprechaun. He was Irish to the core, talkative and charming." But all was not well in Leary's world. When they stopped at the home of Leary's ex-wife, Wenner heard the couple screaming at each other. "He was some kind of visionary or saint, a holy man or a fool, or all of them together," Wenner said later. "I liked him."

Even before Wenner met him, Leary had been arrested for marijuana possession in Texas. Leary's lawyers argued for dismissing the charges on constitutional grounds. As that case made its way to the Supreme Court, Leary wrote two books, *High Priest* and *The Politics of Ecstasy*, which received respectful reviews in *Rolling Stone*. Leary also consorted with the Brotherhood of Eternal Love, an Orange County drug network that purchased property in the mountains above Palm Springs. Before a lecture tour in 1968, Leary drove from their ranch to Berkeley, where he still owned a home. Along the way, he was arrested again for marijuana possession, this time in Laguna Beach.

While awaiting trial, Leary decided to run for governor of California and attended John Lennon and Yoko Ono's Bed-In for Peace in Montreal. By that time, Leary's influence on Lennon was plain. The lyric for "Tomorrow Never Knows," the final track on *Revolver* (1966), borrowed directly from *Psychedelic Experience* (1964), which Leary coauthored and Lennon read with interest. In Montreal, Leary sang along with "Give Peace a Chance," which name-checked him, and asked Lennon to write a campaign song for him. When Lennon asked what the theme should be, Leary replied that his campaign slogan was "Come Together—Join the Party!" Lennon liked the slogan, worked out a few verses, and handed Leary a tape recording. Lennon continued to develop the lyric, and that fall, the Beatles released "Come Together," a hit single and the opening track on *Abbey Road*.

Leary also testified for the defense in the Chicago conspiracy trial and attended Altamont. Shortly after that concert, his Texas trial began. When he was convicted, *Rolling Stone* quoted Leary's attorney, who said the government was conducting a coordinated effort to incarcerate, murder, or exile public figures who were addressing social issues. As Leary awaited sentencing in that case, the Orange County trial began. Convicted again, he was sentenced to ten years, denied bail, and placed in solitary confinement. When the Texas sentence came down, it added ten more years and a $10,000 fine. "I hope you will write more stuff for us from jail," Wenner wrote to Leary, "and I hope all goes as well as possible for you there. Love, Jann."

While incarcerated in San Luis Obispo, Leary awaited yet another trial. In 1966, police raided the Hitchcock Estate in Dutchess County, New York, and arrested Leary for possession of marijuana and LSD. But Leary didn't stay in prison long. The Brotherhood of Eternal Love paid Weatherman to spring him from the California Men's Colony. Leary was driven to Oakland, where he spent the night, and then to the Sierra Nevada mountains, where he met Weatherman leaders Bernardine Dohrn, Mark Rudd, Bill Ayers, and Jeff Jones. From there, he drove to Seattle to reunite with his wife, Rosemary. After they watched the Woodstock documentary at a local theater, the Learys flew to Chicago in disguise. The next stop was Paris and finally Algiers. Delighted to hear about Leary's prison break, Charles Manson wrote an open letter to the *Los Angeles Free Press* that named Leary as his successor.

In a letter to Wenner, Leary asked that his subscription be forwarded from his prison address (which he listed as "P.O.W. Concentration Camp, San Luis Obispo") to Algiers. He and his wife were staying with Eldridge Cleaver, who had jumped bail in Oakland after being charged with attempted murder. Leary also mentioned his own escape from prison. "Thanks to the noble protection of the Black Panthers and the bravery of their allies, the beautiful

Weathermen, we are safe and free in the Third World of the future," he told Wenner. Two months later, Leary wrote to Wenner again: "All is perfect here. New life. New reincarnation. You can be any nationality this time around. Why stay hooked to old nasty national habits?" Leary also wanted to write for *Rolling Stone*: "Great level of literary productivity these days. If you are interested." Instead of asking Leary for an article, Wenner dispatched London-based staff writer Robert Greenfield to interview him. Only three years earlier, Leary had denounced political movements in favor of the spiritual path. Now he shared his opinions on a broad range of topics, including the U.S. Constitution, prisoners' rights, the Middle East, and the Black Panthers.

Leary also wrote an open letter to Allen Ginsberg calling for armed self-defense, and Ken Kesey's reply ran in *Rolling Stone* and other outlets. Kesey congratulated Leary on his escape but wondered about his position on firearms. "We don't need another nut with a gun," Kesey maintained before closing with a quotation from Leary himself: "The revolution is over, and we have won." When Greenfield asked about Kesey's letter, Leary justified his position. "We're not in favor of violence," he said, "only self-defense against gun-carrying robots who are looking to wipe us out." He added that Kesey should read Frantz Fanon, George Jackson's *Letters from Soledad,* and Huey Newton, who was convicted of killing an Oakland police officer and was Leary's fellow inmate in San Luis Obispo. "Read the writings of Huey P. Newton or look into his eyes when you see him," Leary told Greenfield. "He's a complete turned-on holy man, a golden black Aquarius tuned into the central energy."

Soon after that, Leary was on the run again. His relationship with Cleaver, whom he described as his political guru, had deteriorated. The Learys departed for Switzerland, where he was detained, but Swiss officials refused to extradite him to the United States. He was eventually captured in Kabul, returned to the United States, and sent to Folsom State Prison near Sacramento. Placed in solitary confinement and unable to see other inmates, Leary was nevertheless able to chat with the voluble prisoner in the next cell. "I've been waiting to talk to you for years," Charles Manson said.

·   ·   ·   ·   ·

As 1970 drew to a close, Wenner received a note from Jon Landau. "A matter has come up about which I don't know what [the] policy is," Landau wrote. "Namely, Lester Bangs has lost his straight job at a shoe store and is desperate for cash." Could Wenner advance Bangs $75 against the six album reviews that Landau had accepted?

While Bangs was struggling, the magazine was hitting its stride. For its work that year, *Rolling Stone* received the National Magazine Award for Specialized Journalism. The awards committee credited the magazine's "freshness of presentation and effective formula-free journalism as reflected in its exhaustive reporting on the Charles Manson case and the tragedy of the Altamont rock festival." The judges particularly admired "the integrity and courage of the magazine in presenting material that challenged many of the shared attitudes of its readers." In effect, the committee was rewarding the magazine for its critical distance from the counterculture, but it also implied that *Rolling Stone* was telling the truth as it understood it.

Less than three years old, *Rolling Stone* joined the world of credible journalism. As Ed Ward noted later, however, no one who worked on the Altamont story was still employed by the magazine. For the ceremony at the Plaza Hotel, Wenner was accompanied by record executive Clive Davis.

  New Morning

As *Rolling Stone* became an award-winning magazine, the Beatles underwent a painful dissolution. It began in September 1969, when John Lennon said he was withdrawing from the group, but his decision was kept private for business reasons. Paul McCartney retreated to Scotland, worked on his solo album, and refused to delay its release in deference to *Let It Be* (1970), the band's final studio album. When *McCartney* appeared in April, it received mixed reviews, and McCartney was vilified for breaking up the band.

In the meantime, Lennon and Yoko Ono began working with therapist Arthur Janov, author of *The Primal Scream* (1970). Their first sessions took place at Lennon's home in England, but Janov suggested they continue the therapy in Los Angeles, which they did for four months. Janov described his therapeutic approach as "the most important discovery of the twentieth century," but few experts now credit that claim or even the therapy's effectiveness. It was founded on the belief that repressive social strictures inflicted psychological wounds beginning in early childhood. For Janov, it followed that loosening these strictures would cure mental illness. His logic chimed well with countercultural views of Western civilization and its discontents, and Lennon threw himself into the therapy. Janov encouraged the couple to strip away all forms of artifice. "We were just becoming stark-naked real," Ono recalled. "We both kind of exposed ourselves."

During their time in California, Lennon and Yoko Ono visited *Rolling Stone*'s new office on Third Street. It was a peak moment for Wenner, who had worshipped Lennon since watching *A Hard Day's Night* six years earlier. Lennon presented Wenner with an inscribed copy of Janov's book.

> Dear Jann,
>
> After many years of searching—tobacco–pot–acid–meditation–brown rice–you name it—I am finally on the road to freedom and being REAL + STRAIGHT. I hope this book helps you as much as it did for Yoko + me. I'll tell you the "true story" when we're finished.
>
> Love, John + Yoko

The inscription reflected Lennon's emphasis on authenticity, a hallmark of the counterculture. Wenner later noted how Lennon absorbed and eventually discarded new ideas, philosophies, and therapies.

> John was always full of enthusiasms. He was a man who was always searching for some kind of answer, some kind of solution, or something that would bring him peace, or bring the world peace. And he went through enormous numbers of ideas and philosophies and ideologies and fads. . . . And he'd go through them and kind of eat it up, get really over the top about it, and then kind of discover that it wasn't all what it was cracked up to be. And maybe he retained some of it, and kind of reject it and move on to the next thing.

Lennon would reject primal therapy as well, but he was very much in its grip at the time.

After Wenner showed Lennon and Ono around the office, he and Jane took them to Enrico's for lunch. Surprised to learn that Lennon hadn't seen *Let It Be*, the documentary film about the making of that album and the band's disintegration, Wenner suggested they catch the matinee. Lennon sat silently through the film. "When we walked out," Wenner recalled, "the four of us stood on the sidewalk, arms around each other in a huddle. John cried, and then all of us joined in."

The following weekend, the Wenners visited Lennon and Ono in their rented Bel Air mansion, where they lived in "one room hung with weavings, incense burning and candles lit." Lennon again agreed to the post-therapy interview. "He was ready to tell his story of the Beatles," Wenner said later. Returning to England in September, Lennon recorded his solo album, *John Lennon / Plastic Ono Band*, while Ono assembled its companion, *Yoko Ono / Plastic Ono Band*. Lennon wanted to call his album *Primal* and hers *Scream*.

Wenner's interview with Lennon took place in New York and preceded his album's release. Running in two parts one month later, the interview recounted the rock star's experience with the Beatles, but it also touched on Janov's philosophy. "You're born in pain, you know," Lennon said. "And pain is what we're in most of the time. And I think the bigger the pain, the more gods we need." That idea informed the lyric for "God," a track on his new album that began, "God is a concept by which we measure our pain." The lyric repudiated a litany of historical figures, holy scriptures, and popular musicians, including Jesus, the Gita, the I Ching, the Bible, John F. Kennedy, Buddha, Elvis, and Zimmerman (Bob Dylan). "I just believe in me. Yoko and me," the lyric added. The final line, "The dream is over," was considered a comment on the counterculture's futile search for transcendent meaning.

In his exchange with Wenner, Lennon also discussed his drug use, claiming he took LSD as many as one thousand times. "I got a message on acid that I should destroy my ego," Lennon said, "and I did. I was reading that stupid book of Leary's and all that shit." He and Yoko also used heroin "because of what the Beatles and their pals were doing to us." He noted that marijuana, alcohol, and speed had influenced his musical output.

> I was a fuckin' drop-down drunk in art school, I was a pill addict until *Help!*, just before *Help!* when we were turned onto pot and dropped drink. Simple as that. I've always needed a drug to *survive*. The others, too, but I always had *more*. I always took *more* pills and *more* of everything because I'm *more* crazy.

Lennon dismissed recent albums by George Harrison and Bob Dylan, adding that Ringo Starr's second solo album embarrassed him less than the first one did. He described *McCartney* as rubbish and claimed that the documentary film he watched in San Francisco was "a set-up by Paul for Paul." Shots of himself and Ono were "chopped out of the film for no other reason than the people were oriented for Engelbert Humperdinck. I felt sick." That dynamic, he said, was one of the main reasons the Beatles ended. "I can't speak for George, but I pretty damn well know we got fed up of being sidemen for Paul."

"Never before had a rock star given an interview so open and honest," Robert Sam Anson claimed in his history of *Rolling Stone*. Lennon's candor exemplified the hippie authenticity that the magazine sought to exude, but Lennon biographer Tim Riley observed that the interview was also notable for its "frequent exaggerations, false claims, misremembered history, and prickly outbursts." Each paragraph of the interview, Riley added, combined confessional interview with therapeutic gush. Nobody was spared, not even the fans, especially those whom Lennon called the "fucking idiots who don't know anything." Unable to feel, Lennon claimed, those fans lived vicariously through him. Lennon's purpose, it seemed, wasn't to polish his image or even to sell albums, but rather to demythologize himself, the Beatles, and everything and everyone he believed in along the way, with the notable exception of Yoko Ono.

According to Ringo Starr, Lennon's remarks were startling but not unprecedented. "He was always brave," Starr said. "He would put it out there. And the consequences sometimes were very harsh. But he would always put it out there. And that's why you could not *not* like him." Yet Lennon's admissions and dismissals were remarkable even by his own standards. "It was shocking," Wenner said later. After the interview, Tim Riley noted, "nothing about Beatlemania would ever be the same."

Meanwhile, McCartney was filing suit in London to dissolve the Beatles' partnership. After the Lennon interview appeared, *Life* magazine asked him about it. "It was so far out that I enjoyed it, actually," he replied. "I looked at it and dug him for saying what he thought, but to me, short of getting it off his chest, I think he blows it with that kind of thing." McCartney also claimed, unconvincingly, that he ignored the interview and was unaffected by the barbs directed at him: "I know there are elements of truth in what he said. And this open hostility, that didn't hurt me. That's cool. That's John." In his Rolling Stone Interview three years later, McCartney was again asked how he felt about the Lennon interview. "Oh, I hated it. You can imagine, I sat down and pored over every little paragraph, every little sentence," he said. "At the time, I tell you, it hurt me. Whew. Deep."

· · · · ·

Accompanied by Leibovitz's photographs, Wenner's interview with Lennon boosted the magazine's newsstand sales. That surge wasn't lost on Alan Rinzler, whom Wenner had hired as the head of Straight Arrow Books. Raised in a leftist family in New York, Rinzler had already served as a senior editor at two major publishing houses, and at age 31, he was the oldest executive at Wenner's company. *The New York Times* reported that Rinzler would publish "an entire program based on the realities of the youth market." Rinzler was enthusiastic about the company's prospects: "There is a huge market out there— the so-called youth market—that the New York establishment publishers are completely out of touch with."

The Lennon interview was ideal for Straight Arrow Books, but Lennon didn't want it published anywhere but in *Rolling Stone*. It was one thing to spout off during an interview, quite another for his hurtful remarks to be enshrined in book form. Lennon repeated his position at least two more times in writing and called Rinzler to prevent the book's publication. Back in the office, however, Rinzler argued for its importance. On June 30, he told Wenner they were "going ahead full-speed on the Lennon book as you know." It would reach readers who hadn't seen the interview in *Rolling Stone*, had never heard of the magazine, or might be willing to pay five dollars for a permanent book and handsome gift. "This is a bloody important book," Rinzler wrote. "There's no need to apologize for it, as you will soon realize."

Lennon felt betrayed by Wenner's decision to release the book. "By then, we felt that Jann was our ally, and we could trust him, so John had a big surprise," said Ono. "There was a phone call from Jann to our hotel room. He said something like 'We're putting out this book, and I'm gonna send you six copies.' So John just hung up on him. He was furious." The Beatles' label temporarily withdrew its advertising from *Rolling Stone*, and Lennon never spoke to Wenner again. Lennon and Ono later supported the short-lived *SunDance* magazine, whose contributors included Abbie Hoffman, Robert Scheer, John Burks, and Paul Krassner. (Two other journalists associated with *SunDance*, David Weir and Howard Kohn, would eventually make major contributions at *Rolling Stone*.) Wenner regretted publishing the Lennon book but was proud of the interview. When the book was reissued in 2000, this time with Ono's permission and foreword, Wenner wrote that it was "the first time that any of the Beatles, let alone the man who had founded the group and was their leader, finally stepped outside of that protected, beloved fairy tale and told the truth."

Yet another alumnus of San Francisco State College helped edit that interview. After working on the campus newspaper with Ben Fong-Torres, Paul Scanlon began reading *Rolling Stone* while stationed at Fort Ord, the U.S. Army base near Monterey. After his discharge, Scanlon caught on with the *Palo Alto Times*, but with Fong-Torres's recommendation, he joined *Rolling Stone* toward the end of 1970. His first day on the job was unexpectedly quiet.

> Accustomed to a daily afternoon newspaper schedule, I showed up around 8:00 a.m., which I felt would be fashionably late. The place was deserted. Nobody. Jann Wenner, who had hired me a few weeks earlier, was in [New York] interviewing John and Yoko. Annie Leibovitz was there, too. I wandered into my cubicle, had a seat, and stared at the blank cork board. What, I thought, was I doing here?

Not long after that, however, Scanlon was planted at the large round table in the editorial bullpen, working with Charles Perry and John Lombardi on raw transcripts of the Lennon/Ono interview.

·   ·   ·   ·   ·

The same month Wenner interviewed Lennon, the Weather Underground Organization issued a communique called "New Morning—Changing Weather," which quoted the title of a new Bob Dylan record. After three of its members perished while assembling a bomb in a Greenwich Village townhouse, the leaders went underground and changed the outfit's name. During that time, the Weather Underground praised black militant Jonathan Jackson, who had taken over a Marin County courtroom at gunpoint and kidnapped a judge, prosecutor, and three jurors. The abduction led to a shootout that left the prosecutor paralyzed and four people dead, including Jackson and the judge. Shortly after that, the Weather Underground called the courthouse attack "heroic." It also blew up a monument to the slain judge and announced a fall offensive that included four more bombings. By that time, the explosions were not meant to kill or injure anyone, but rather to highlight the establishment's vulnerability. With few other options for claiming media attention, the

Weather Underground resorted to what one writer called "exploding press releases."

Issued from a secret meeting in Mendocino County, the "New Morning" communiqué sent a less strident signal. The Weather leadership wanted to express itself "not as military leaders but as tribes in council." It condemned the idea that armed struggle was the only legitimate form of revolutionary action, and it described the use of marijuana and LSD as revolutionary. It claimed that the Weather Underground was part of the counterculture, praised that movement's revolutionary potential, and repudiated Weatherman's original theory of revolution, which called for a militant vanguard. Now the leadership embraced a broader movement that people could participate in "freely and with love." As the Weather Underground moved away from guerrilla tactics and toward larger "families and tribes," it was also claiming a leadership role in a politicized counterculture.

That effort was aided by an unforeseen development. Meeting with intelligence officials in the White House that year, President Nixon called for a coordinated effort to investigate Americans, most of them under age 30, who were "determined to destroy our society." When Nixon pressured the FBI to locate the Weather fugitives, agents contacted Timothy Leary. He agreed to cooperate in exchange for a reduced sentence, but his information was too inconsistent to aid the search. In the end, prosecutors dropped many charges against Weather fugitives when it became clear that the FBI repeatedly broke the law in its attempts to arrest them. High-ranking FBI officials, not the fugitives they were chasing, were eventually prosecuted.

Rolling Stone never condemned the Weather Underground outright during this period, but Greil Marcus turned a gimlet eye to its project. Unlike the Black Panther Party, which was formed to protect Oakland's black neighborhoods from police abuse, Weather began with the notion that America was uniquely evil and must be destroyed so that the world could live. In that sense, Marcus claimed, "the Weathermen were perhaps the first revolutionaries to hate their own country and cut themselves off from its traditions." A decade later,

Rolling Stone ran a lengthy story about the Weather Underground by David Horowitz and Peter Collier, the former *Ramparts* editors who had begun their long march to the right wing. By that time, however, the Weather Underground was politically irrelevant. "The underground had run its course by 1975," one Weather leader said later.

Meanwhile, the Weather Underground's chief adversary had its own problems. While examining FBI records, an investigator discovered evidence of unlawful break-ins and surveillance between 1972 and 1975. Nervous agents from Squad 47, the FBI's black-bag specialists, quickly destroyed thousands of pages of internal documents related to Weatherman. After one FBI agent agreed to talk to prosecutors in return for immunity, others followed suit. One prosecutor said, "Some of us felt that what the Bureau did constituted a far greater danger to society than what the Weathermen ever did."

.   .   .   .   .

Meanwhile, Hunter S. Thompson was considering his options. Instead of following up on "The Battle of Aspen," which he still considered the key to his overdue book for Random House, Thompson pursued a lead that grew out of his friendship with attorney Oscar Acosta. At the time, Acosta was defending Chicano movement leaders and running for sheriff of Los Angeles County. Although his campaign was less theatrical than Thompson's, it was more pointed. Acosta's seven-point program called for the ultimate dissolution of the sheriff's department, its immediate withdrawal from barrios and ghettos, investigations of the department's conduct, and the establishment of community review boards. Despite his defeat at the polls, Acosta harbored dreams of becoming an even more important figure in the Chicano community.

With Acosta's encouragement, Thompson pitched a story to *Scanlan's* about the Chicano movement in Los Angeles. Warren Hinckle's partner eventually spiked the piece, but the story took a dramatic turn. During an anti-war demonstration in East Los

Angeles, a deputy sheriff shot a tear-gas canister into a bar, killing Latino journalist Ruben Salazar instantly. Salazar, who had taken refuge from what many observers called a police riot, was a respected figure at the *Los Angeles Times* and in the Latino community. The sheriff's department denied any responsibility for his death, but the county eventually paid Salazar's family $700,000 to settle a wrongful death lawsuit.

Thompson returned to East Los Angeles and updated his account, this time for *Rolling Stone*. Running more than 19,000 words, "Strange Rumblings in Aztlan" appeared in April 1971. Its title alluded to the mythical homeland of the Aztecs, which Chicano activists said they wished to restore, but Thompson was more interested in the possibility that the Sheriff's Department targeted a troublesome journalist for execution. Sifting through the evidence, Thompson saw no indication of premeditation, but he labeled Salazar's death "a second-degree job" and left no doubt that officials were untruthful about the circumstances surrounding it. He dismissed their public statements as "garbled swill" and documented the official mendacity that had long been a favorite target. Lacking Steadman's illustrations and other Gonzo pyrotechnics, "Strange Rumblings in Aztlan" was neither satirical nor especially participatory. Thompson flouted the norms of journalistic objectivity with his frank personal asides, but he also wove an intricate story and delivered a damning conclusion. The lengthy article was also a deviation for *Rolling Stone*. It had nothing to do with music, drugs, or hippie culture, but its appearance was a clear sign that Thompson had Wenner's confidence.

Scanlan's collapsed before "Strange Rumblings" ran in *Rolling Stone*, depriving Thompson of a key outlet. Later, Hinckle found it difficult to credit *Rolling Stone*, which he described in his 1974 memoir as "one of the leading merchandisers of this counterculture bullshit." Perhaps the sorest point for Hinckle was Wenner's relationship with Thompson. "He inherited Hunter," Hinckle said later, "and fell into it very luckily, because the *Stone* was a piece of shit. It was just there to sell records." As for Gleason, Hinckle said he was sorry he had dumped on "his flower children without giving him a chance to defend the little fascists."

·   ·   ·   ·   ·

In the summer of 1971, Wenner drove to Stinson Beach to interview Grateful Dead guitarist Jerry Garcia. *Rolling Stone* began reporting on the band in its first issue, but the Dead had only recently found a large audience for its studio recordings. Wenner was accompanied by Annie Leibovitz and Charles Reich, a law professor at Yale University who was already famous for *The Greening of America* (1970), his best-selling manifesto. In that book, Reich argued that a social revolution, created by and for the younger generation, was a necessary response to the growth of the corporate state, sweeping technological change, and the threats those developments posed to nature and humanity. The revolution Reich had in mind wasn't a political one, but rather a change in consciousness that would transform politics only as its final act. "It will not require violence to succeed, and it cannot be successfully resisted by violence," Reich predicted. "Its ultimate creation will be a new and enduring wholeness and beauty—a renewed relationship of man to himself, to other men, to society, to nature, and to the land." That claim resembled less flowery formulations advanced by Gleason and others.

Given his book's thesis, Reich was especially eager to meet Garcia, who symbolized the Bay Area youth culture in which Reich placed so much faith. During his visits to San Francisco, Reich discovered LSD and marijuana, and though he acknowledged the dangers of their abuse, he described weed as a "maker of revolution" and "a truth serum that repels false consciousness." A 42-year-old virgin when his book appeared, Reich also began exploring his sexuality after an encounter with a male prostitute in San Francisco.

The interview at Garcia's home, which he shared with Carolyn ("Mountain Girl") Adams, was long and stony. Parking themselves on the lawn overlooking the Pacific Ocean, the three men turned on the tape recorder, fired up some truth serum, and rambled on for five hours while Leibovitz took photographs. The conversation included Adams, the former Merry Prankster who shared a daughter with Ken Kesey. Weeks later, Reich returned for another two-hour session with Garcia, and Wenner followed up with his own four-hour chat. After *Rolling Stone* ran the Garcia interview in two parts in January 1972, Reich returned to Stinson Beach on a foggy Sunday morning in March. Once again, he started the tape recorder, got high with Garcia, and chatted for five hours. Their "stoned Sunday rap" appeared alongside the interviews in *Garcia: A Signpost to New Space*, which Straight Arrow Books published later that year.

In that book's introduction, Reich claimed that the Dead's body of work reflected "a depth of meaning and a distance into new space that I consider to be one of the supreme achievements in American music." Wenner reinforced Reich's endorsement, calling Garcia a "spokesman, teacher, and philosopher." Garcia often disclaimed those roles, but the interview showed why Reich and Wenner thought so highly of him. Hip, irreverent, authentic, and creative, Garcia touched all the countercultural bases.

·　　·　　·　　·　　·

Although the Garcia interview burnished the magazine's image in the counterculture, Wenner continued to feature new writers who broadened the magazine's reach. One was Grover Lewis, whom Wenner lured to *Rolling Stone* from *The Village Voice*. Born in San Antonio to a working-class family, Lewis became an orphan at age eight when his parents reportedly shot each other. After growing up in Fort Worth and Oak Cliff, a scratchy Dallas neighborhood, Lewis received a scholarship at North Texas State University in nearby Denton, which he described as "a kind of gulag operation in the boondocks." The college town was a step up from Lewis's old neighborhood, but not by much. "You could be judged violently nonconformist just by liking jazz," he later wrote. Lewis and his best friend,

Larry McMurtry, studied English literature and clashed with hide-bound faculty and administrators. McMurtry later studied creative writing at Stanford, where he met Ken Kesey. After dropping out of graduate school, Lewis wrote for newspapers and magazines, and his work for *The Village Voice* eventually earned him a reputation as a New Journalist.

Legally blind and partial to speed, Lewis was one of the regulars at Jerry's Inn, *Rolling Stone*'s unofficial watering hole and a busy hub for its many romances and hookups. One longtime friend described Lewis as "a clenched fist in a frail package," but several women described him as courtly. Twelve years older than Wenner, Lewis was a blues fan and film buff who refused to write about rock and roll; indeed, he posted a sign to that effect over his desk. In his jeans, cowboy boots, blazer, and thick glasses, he didn't resemble a hippie. His version of Timothy Leary's famous dictum was less liberating than the original: "Turn on, tune in, drop out, fuck up, crawl back."

During his brief time at *Rolling Stone*, Lewis contributed almost two dozen articles, but two stand out. After he landed a small role in *The Last Picture Show* (1971), which was based on McMurtry's 1966 novel, Lewis enjoyed almost unlimited access to the production. "Splendor in the Short Grass" reported unguarded remarks Lewis heard behind the scenes, some of which were directed at him. "I like your face—it's so *ravaged*," the production designer said. His *Rolling Stone* story included very little pixie dust or star power. To the contrary, it indicated that *The Last Picture Show* was made by human beings with the usual assortment of shortcomings.

Later that year, Lewis spent a week with the Allman Brothers Band on tour. Once again, he pulled the curtain back to reveal an unflattering scene. Channeling the perspective of a horrified flight attendant as the band boarded an airplane, Lewis described the musicians as a scruffy, long-haired horde of Dixie greasers. He also compared Duane Allman to "a skinny orange walrus" and documented his penchant for cocaine, comic books, and hillbilly exclamations, which Lewis's article rendered in dialect. Finally, he quoted

Allman's profane comment about "In Memory of Elizabeth Reed," whose title evoked Dickey Betts's tryst with the wife of another rock star. "Fuck, he wrote that fuckin' song after he fucked this chick on a fuckin' tombstone in a fuckin' cemetery in Macon," Allman exclaimed. "On a fuckin' *tombstone*, my man!" As the week wore on, tensions flared between Allman and Lewis, especially after the band refused to pose for an Annie Leibovitz photograph. When Lewis offered his own view on the matter, Allman threatened to punch him out on the spot.

Shortly after Lewis filed his story, Duane Allman died in a motorcycle crash, and the obituary was the lead story in the same issue that featured Lewis's profile. The band resented both the profile and its timing. Years later, drummer Butch Trucks addressed that matter in a letter to *The New York Times*.

> What [Lewis] wound up writing under the guise of journalism could have been humorous satire, at best, if it weren't for one very tragic fact: it was published within weeks of Duane Allman's death, and the people at *Rolling Stone* had time to pull the article but did nothing.

The band swore off *Rolling Stone*, at least for a while, and Lewis left the magazine shortly after that. The proximate cause for his departure was another book deal gone bad. Wenner commissioned the project, but when Lewis turned his attention to the book, Wenner canceled the contract and refused to pay the large advance. After a legal wrangle, Lewis settled for part of the advance, but he had written his last piece for *Rolling Stone*.

Before Lewis departed, he edited another talented author who never quite clicked at the magazine. Eve Babitz first appeared in *Rolling Stone* not as a writer, but in Thomas Albright's 1969 survey of the Los Angeles art scene. Even by that city's standards, Babitz had a reputation for hedonism. When she was 20, Babitz posed nude for a Julian Wasser photograph in which she and a fully clothed Marcel Duchamp played chess. In an introductory letter to novelist Joseph Heller, she wrote, "I am a stacked 18-year-old blonde on

Sunset Boulevard. I am also a writer." Babitz's lovers eventually included actor Harrison Ford, rock stars Stephen Stills and Jim Morrison, comedian Steve Martin, artist Ed Ruscha, record executive Ahmet Ertegun, art curator Walter Hopps, and writer Dan Wakefield. "In every young man's life, there is an Eve Babitz," record executive Earl McGrath said later. "It's usually Eve Babitz."

After Babitz began writing about her experiences in lightly fictionalized form, Joan Didion recommended one of her pieces to *Rolling Stone*. When Grover Lewis accepted "The Sheik," it became Babitz's first publication there; when he asked her to live with him in San Francisco, she accepted his invitation. "I was almost thirty," she said later, "too old to fuck around, I decided." She and Lewis broke up three months later, and though he offered her other assignments, none of those came to fruition. In the years to come, however, Babitz submitted material to *Rolling Stone* with mixed success. In her recollection, *Rolling Stone* tried and failed to land her as a regular writer. "Joan Didion told the people at *Rolling Stone* to get me, so they tried, and they couldn't," she told her biographer. "I kept dodging out of their orbit."

Although Babitz never became a regular contributor, she maintained personal ties to the magazine. One of her stories, "Bad Day in Palm Springs," featured a lightly fictionalized Jane Wenner and appeared in *Slow Days, Fast Company* (1977). Babitz also remained close with Annie Leibovitz, who shot the cover photograph for *Eve's Hollywood* (1974). Babitz later described her first romantic encounter with *Rolling Stone*'s chief photographer. "She came to my place," Babitz said. "I had this book of Lartigue pictures—Lartigue was how I got everyone in those days—and she looked through it, and that did it. She was in my life. We were on and off again for a long time."

Yet another recruit during this time was Julius Lester, the black writer, folk musician, radio host, and civil rights activist. The son of a Methodist minister, Lester graduated from Fisk University in Nashville before moving to New York, where he taught guitar and banjo. In 1964, Lester played at black churches in Mississippi in support of the civil rights movement. He also wrote several books, recorded two albums, and taught African American history at the New School for Social Research. By the time Wenner contacted him in 1970, Lester was teaching at the University of Massachusetts, Amherst, where he would remain for three decades.

In 1970, Wenner asked Lester for a piece on black radio: "Do you like what's been happening in black pop music in the last two years, the new Motown thing, the new image of the Temptations and all that, Sly Stone, etc.?" In his reply, Lester said he wanted to write for *Rolling Stone* but had no idea what was going on in black radio. He was willing to review Roberta Flack's second album, but he was even more interested in contributing book reviews, political analysis, and cultural commentary. Lester added that *Rolling Stone* was missing something important, especially but not only in its music coverage.

> The perspective on music is almost wholly white, and I think a kind of hype is thereby perpetrated. For example, no major publication had a black review of Eldridge Cleaver. Thus, Cleaver is projected as a spokesman for blacks by whites, and it is assumed that blacks agree (which they don't).

Wenner knew the magazine's perspective was almost wholly white—that was almost certainly why he contacted Lester in the first place—but he wanted musical coverage first and foremost, and when he wrote back to Lester, he asked for a long profile of Aretha Franklin. Instead, Lester offered to review books by Bobby Seale and Eldridge Cleaver, an anthology edited by Ishmael Reed, and Roberta Flack's album. Shortly after the Flack review appeared, Wenner told Lester that Ed Ward would call him about other reviewing assignments. "I've explained to him that I would like to see your byline on a record review in every issue," Wenner said. He also offered ideas for longer pieces, including one on Louis Armstrong.

Lester applauded Ishmael Reed's anthology despite its flaws. He was less enthusiastic about Seale's memoir, *Seize the Time,* which he called "one-dimensional propaganda" that added nothing to the public's understanding of the Black Panthers, America, or revolution. Lester's review of *Conversation with Eldridge Cleaver: Algiers* was likewise negative. In his next contribution, Lester considered jazz critic Frank Kofsky's new book, *Black Nationalism and the Revolution in Music*. Although he credited Kofsky's claims about racism among jazz critics, record company owners, and club owners, he claimed that Kofsky, a friend of Gleason, "insults the music by trying to contain it in the narrow confines of politics." Lester's final article for *Rolling Stone* was a 1971 review of Albert Speer's *Inside the Third Reich* that could have run in any number of magazines.

While Wenner was corresponding with Lester, he was fending off Neil Bogart, president of Buddah Records, who faulted *Rolling Stone* for ignoring Curtis Mayfield's first solo album, *Curtis* (1970). In his reply to Bogart, Wenner explained that it was difficult to find "good R&B reviewers who know anything. Most of the white college kids, etc., aren't into R&B. However, we've just gotten Wendell John and Julius Lester into the picture, and both albums are assigned now for review. I regret the tardiness of this more than anybody." Wendell John wrote only two reviews for *Rolling Stone*, dismissing both *Wilson Pickett in Philadelphia* (1970) and Mayfield's solo effort. Jon Landau also panned *Curtis/Live* (1971) and said it was sad to report that Mayfield's solo career "just ain't happening." The next year, however, Mayfield's soundtrack for *Super Fly*, a blaxploitation drama about a cocaine dealer who longs to go straight, reached number one on the charts. That success seemed to justify Bogart's sentiment, expressed in another letter to Wenner, about Landau's review: "To Mr. Jon Landau, I am sorry for you, that you find you are unable to get into Curtis, but don't worry, the reviewers will catch up to 'the people' sooner or later." Bogart's prediction was fulfilled when *Rolling Stone* ran a positive review of *Super Fly*, featured Mayfield in the next issue, and selected the film's soundtrack as one of the year's top albums.

Although Landau later conceded that the magazine should have done more to recruit black writers, he maintained that *Rolling Stone* treated black artists extensively, respectfully, and with as much integrity as any other national magazine. A substantial fraction of that coverage came from New York critic Vince Aletti, who began contributing to *Rolling Stone* in 1970. Aletti was also writing for *Crawdaddy, Fusion,* and *Rat,* the underground New York newspaper founded in 1968. "All of us were freelancing," Aletti said. "We weren't making much money, but we were dying to talk about the things that we were excited about." His work for local publications was well received, but he noted that writing for *Rolling Stone* offered several practical advantages. The magazine felt established right away, reached a large national audience, and had more cachet with the labels, which made it easier to obtain the records that interested him.

Aletti quickly realized that reviewing the work of black artists was a worthy niche. He was already listening to those records, and fewer writers wanted to review them for *Rolling Stone.* That focus gave him a place at the magazine he could be sure of. Landau considered Aletti "absolutely reliable" and tried to include one of his reviews in every issue. Aletti eventually contributed more than 100 articles featuring Gladys Knight, Aretha Franklin, Jerry Butler, the Jackson 5, Al Green, Stevie Wonder, Little Richard, Chuck Berry, James Brown, Patti LaBelle, Marvin Gaye, Bill Withers, Sly and the Family Stone, Dionne Warwick, the Staple Singers, Wilson Pickett, Roberta Flack, Barry White, the Spinners, Smokey Robinson, and other artists. Aletti also became the house expert on disco, which he began writing about in 1973. At that time, the genre didn't have a name or a chart, but Aletti heard it exploding out of the clubs and recognized its importance. "I started going to The Loft in '71 or '72 with a group of friends," he recalled. "It became a weekly experience for me. Going at midnight, dancing for hours with friends, and realizing that this was one of a number of underground scenes that were generating music that I didn't hear in any other place."

Never a staff writer at *Rolling Stone,* Aletti later wrote a weekly column for *Creem* and became a senior editor at *The Village Voice.* There, he focused on art but also wrote reviews for Robert Christgau, who joined the *Voice* in 1974 to edit the newspaper's music section.

Within six months, Christgau said later, the *Voice* became "the most important music publication in the country except for *Rolling Stone*." Christgau also ran work by Greil Marcus, Lester Bangs, and Stephen Holden, all of whom had written for *Rolling Stone*. Janet Maslin, who at one time was married to Jon Landau, also wrote for *Rolling Stone* and *The Village Voice* and later served for almost four decades as a film and literary critic at *The New York Times*. The traffic ran the other way as well. Grover Lewis left the *Voice* for *Rolling Stone*, and Lucian K. Truscott IV, who covered the Stonewall riot for the *Voice*, later wrote for *Rolling Stone* as a freelancer.

Much like its San Francisco counterpart, *The Village Voice* had ample advertising revenue, but most of it came from classified ads, which helped readers land jobs, find apartments, form bands, and spark romances. "Tuesday nights, people standing on line at the different kiosks, waiting for the earliest copy of the *Voice* to come in," one staff member recalled. "And every single one of them was there because of the apartment ads."

"Strange Rumblings in Aztlan," which ran in April 1971, showcased Hunter S. Thompson's range and style, but it was overshadowed by another work hatched in the middle of that project. After a tense week in East Los Angeles, Thompson accepted an assignment from *Sports Illustrated* to cover an off-road race outside Las Vegas. Claiming he needed a break from the Salazar story, Thompson invited Oscar Acosta to join him. Part of his plan was to separate Acosta from his Chicano colleagues, who had misgivings about his friendship with a white journalist. A road trip would allow the two men to speak openly and at length. Thompson rented a convertible, which he later dubbed the Great Red Shark, and the two men drove to Las Vegas on March 20, 1971.

Although their destination resembled no other city in the United States, it was the most American of places. Founded in 1905 as a railroad town, Las Vegas bloomed in the 1930s, when its cowboy casinos and bordellos became a destination for laborers working on the Hoover Dam. When Los Angeles cracked down on the rackets in the late 1930s, local mobsters saw an opportunity in the desert 250 miles away. A postwar casino boom, fueled by loans from the Teamsters pension fund, drew racketeers from other cities and converted them into pillars of the community. Frank Sinatra and his friends began performing there in the 1950s, and after Elvis Presley's career stalled, he launched his 1969 comeback in Las Vegas. During his residency, Presley sported his signature jumpsuit and cape, and as his weight ballooned, he embodied the city's unhip reputation in the counterculture. For hippies, Las Vegas was proof that the straight world was weirder than they were. Certainly no place was less spiritual, organic, or communal.

When Thompson and Acosta arrived in Las Vegas, they hit several bars and stayed up all night. The next day, Thompson covered the off-road race, returned to the hotel, picked up Acosta, and dropped him off at the airport. Acosta forgot his attaché case in the car, and when Thompson opened it back at the hotel, he found a Colt .357 Magnum, a box of bullets, and a large bag of marijuana. Exhausted by his Dexedrine-fueled weekend, Thompson panicked. Nevada had tough marijuana laws, and Thompson had little cash, an unreliable credit card, and no confirmation that *Sports Illustrated* would cover his expenses. He returned to Southern California without paying his hotel bill.

Thompson submitted his piece to *Sports Illustrated,* but it was much too long for the 250-word slot his editor had created for it. When it was rejected, Thompson decided to draft an even longer version of the story, this time with journalist Raoul Duke and Samoan attorney Dr. Gonzo as the fictional protagonists. "Sooner or later, you'll see what your call (to me) set in motion—a fantastic mushroom," Thompson wrote to his editor at *Sports Illustrated.* "Anyway, your instinct was right. The Lord works in wondrous ways. Your call was the key to a massive freak-out. The result is still up in the air, and still climbing. When you see the final fireball, remember that it was all your fault."

Thompson shared an early draft of the Vegas piece with David Felton. "I was assigned by Jann to edit the Salazar piece," said Felton.

"So Hunter came over to my house to talk about the article—but instead he had these pages in his hand, and he was very excited." Thompson continued to develop the opening section in Wenner's basement in San Francisco. When Paul Scanlon, Charles Perry, and Grover Lewis read it at the office, they couldn't stop laughing. "Everybody was knocked out," Scanlon recalled. "I know Jann was. Nobody expected it."

The road trip with Acosta sufficed for a long article, but Felton alerted Thompson to another event in Las Vegas. The National District Attorneys Association was holding a drug enforcement conference later that month, and Thompson and Acosta decided to attend. In Thompson's article, Raoul Duke notes that he and Dr. Gonzo were mere observers during their first visit to Las Vegas, but this time their very presence would be an outrage. "We would be dealing, from the start, with a crowd that was convened for the stated purpose of putting people like us in jail," Duke remarks. "If the Pigs were gathering in Vegas for a top-level Drug Conference, we felt the drug culture should be represented."

After another chaotic weekend, Thompson returned to Woody Creek to develop the second article. He still didn't know how the Las Vegas pieces would appear in book form or even who would publish it. He assured his editor at Random House that they would have first crack at the material, but he feared it would undermine his reputation as a serious journalist, especially if it was packaged with his other work. He was "a bit leery of making a Public Fool of myself, just to get a book out," he told his editor. A year after he wrote the Kentucky Derby piece, Thompson still didn't realize that Gonzo journalism was his most valuable literary asset.

·   ·   ·   ·   ·

As Thompson labored over the Las Vegas story in the summer of 1971, President Nixon gave a major speech about illegal drugs. "America's public enemy number one in the United States is drug abuse,"

Nixon said. "In order to fight and defeat this enemy, it is necessary to wage a new, all-out offensive." He presented this battle as a bipartisan measure, appointed a drug czar who reported directly to him, and later created the Drug Enforcement Administration. By framing the drug crackdown as a military conflict, the president distinguished it from other social services and set the stage for heavy federal spending. The president's top domestic advisor later acknowledged that the drug war targeted the anti-war left and the black community. "We knew we couldn't make it illegal to be either against the war or black, but by getting the public to associate the hippies with marijuana and blacks with heroin, and then criminalizing both heavily, we could disrupt those communities," John Ehrlichman said. "Did we know we were lying about the drugs? Of course we did."

Nixon's speech, and the so-called War on Drugs that followed, elicited an unexpected letter to the president from Elvis Presley, who offered his services as a federal narcotics officer. "The drug culture, the hippie elements, the SDS, Black Panthers, etc. do *not* consider me their enemy, or as they call it, The Establishment," Presley told Nixon. "I have done an in-depth study of drug abuse and Communist brainwashing techniques, and I am right in the middle of the whole thing, where I can and will do the most good." Presley also paid an unannounced visit to the White House, presented Nixon with a handgun, and posed for photographs. When the drug-addled Presley died in 1977, he still owned an honorary badge from the Bureau of Narcotics and Dangerous Drugs.

Nixon's War on Drugs speech was a milestone, but it was quickly swamped by other news. A week after his address, *The New York Times* began publishing excerpts from the so-called Pentagon Papers, a top-secret government file on U.S. policy in Vietnam. The file was leaked by Daniel Ellsberg, a former marine company commander who served as a Pentagon official and defense consultant at the RAND Corporation. The Pentagon Papers showed, among other things, that the Johnson administration had misled Congress and the American people about the conflict in Vietnam.

When the Pentagon Papers story broke, Nixon aides assembled a covert group called the White House Plumbers. Its name derived from Nixon's desire to prevent leaks, but its primary purpose was to gather illicit information through domestic wiretaps, break-ins, and buggings. The FBI had performed that work in the past, but Nixon believed that J. Edgar Hoover, its elderly director, had lost the will to conduct political warfare. Ehrlichman ordered the White House Plumbers to raid the office of Ellsberg's psychiatrist in search of discrediting information. Ellsberg was arrested and prosecuted under the Espionage Act, but the White House Plumbers, and those who directed them, remained at large.

.   .   .   .   .

Thompson's draft for the Las Vegas story came in clean. Editors checked its facts and constructed timelines to confirm its accuracy, but Thompson told Wenner he would be better off fact-checking a Bob Dylan song or William S. Burroughs's *Naked Lunch*. The generic confusion was understandable. The story was neither a work of New Journalism nor a traditional novel, but rather a hybrid. Thompson later called the Las Vegas book a "nonfiction novel," which only deepened the ambiguity. When it came to editing, Thompson presented his work as fiction, which made fact-checking unnecessary. For his expenses, however, he expected the norms of journalism to prevail.

Ralph Steadman didn't make the trip to Las Vegas, but Thompson made sure his ink-splattered illustrations appeared in the articles and subsequent book. When combined with Thompson's fevered prose, Steadman's illustrations raised Gonzo journalism to a new and more demented level. When the book version appeared, its cover depicted Dr. Gonzo as an amphibious creature and Duke in a full-throated howl as they tear across the desert in their convertible. More than any other image, it laid the foundation for Gonzo journalism's distinctive iconography. By including Steadman and doubling down on the mayhem, Thompson resurrected the Gonzo franchise and made *Rolling Stone* its new home.

Shortly before the first Las Vegas article appeared in *Rolling Stone*, the magazine received a letter from Patrick F. Healy, executive director of the National District Attorneys Association. "It has been called to our attention that Raoul Duke wrote a critique concerning his attendance at our Drug Conference in Las Vegas," Healy wrote. "We would enjoy reviewing a copy of Mr. Duke's critique if one is available. We sincerely hope that he benefited by attending." Using a pseudonym, Thompson replied to Healy on *Rolling Stone* stationery. Adolph Heem, director of sales and promotions, explained that Raoul Duke was semiretired following his unsuccessful experiment in Gonzo journalism. Duke passed his days on his veranda in the Virgin Islands, injecting himself with the local rum. In a shaky hand, Thompson scrawled Heem's signature. Healy played the straight man in Thompson's gag, but he was no joke. Later he served as chair of the Chicago Crime Commission, where he investigated mob murders related to Las Vegas casinos and the Teamster loans that funded them.

.   .   .   .   .

The first installment of "Fear and Loathing in Las Vegas" appeared under Raoul Duke's byline in *Rolling Stone*'s fourth anniversary issue. That issue also included a lengthy letter from the editor. Jann Wenner opened with a reference to Duke, Thompson, and the lead story, but mostly he used that space to mount a defense against Abbie Hoffman's remarks in a previous issue. In September, the magazine ran an article by Izak Haber, who claimed that he conceived and drafted most of *Steal This Book*. That work, which appeared under Hoffman's name in 1971, credits Haber on the title page as a "co-conspirator." After Wenner offered Hoffman the chance to reply to Haber's account, the magazine ran letters to the editor from Anita and Abbie Hoffman. With sly humor, each stressed the other spouse's penury and commitment to the cause. Abbie Hoffman also attached a postscript to his letter: "How about a similar piece on chief *Rolling Stone* stockholder Max Palevsky, who doubles as Chairman of the Board of the Xerox Corporation? I bet he lives in a real shithouse just like us." An editorial note followed that letter and corrected the record. Palevsky was the chief stockholder at Xerox and chairman of the board at Straight Arrow Publishers Inc., not the other way around.

Wenner returned to that exchange in the anniversary issue and moved swiftly to his critique of Hoffman and other countercultural icons.

> Recently we had a go-around with Abbie Hoffman in these pages, a man whom we have always admired for his brilliance as a street and media artist. But like all aspiring political leaders, from Kennedy and Nixon through the Black Panthers, as soon as he began big-time operations, his reality was quickly outstripped by his rhetoric. (For instance, does Jerry Rubin still believe in his "kill your parents" remarks? Has he killed his?)

Quoting Dylan's warning not to follow leaders, Wenner added that the desire to lead was precisely where "so many of our friends have sometimes tripped themselves." Wenner included Hoffman in that group, but he also singled out Ken Kesey, Timothy Leary, Huey Newton, and Eldridge Cleaver for believing their own press releases.

To Hoffman's implied charge that *Rolling Stone* was guilty of capitalism in the first degree, Wenner suggested there was no practical alternative. "If you pay bills, whether for your own family or for your business, you are a capitalist," Wenner claimed. "The choice is whether you are going to be exploitative or whether you will be honest and maintain human dignity." He maintained that as long as printers and writers wanted to buy groceries, raise children, and own homes, *Rolling Stone* would be a capitalist operation. "I always thought that our commercial stance was as plain and obvious as what you read in the paper, as little bullshit and as much honesty as possible," he added. "Simple as that."

But Wenner wasn't finished. He also denounced the rhetoric of revolutionary violence, which he maintained was a losing strategy that generated more violence.

> In the current American situation, talk of some kind of guerrilla insurrection, an armed rebellion, or the destruction of Babylon (Cleaver's phrase) is insane fantasy. The cops have more guns, more training, and more money. They are far better at it. They've won each skirmish so far, and if it ever *really* came down, if we fight it out with their weapons, they're going to win massively.

To call America a fascist military state committed to the genocide of blacks, he continued, did little good. He quoted *New York Times* columnist Anthony Lewis, who maintained that such rhetoric thwarted the very purpose of language, which was communication. Lewis asked, "If one throws the word 'fascist' at the United States, where there is astonishing freedom of expression today, what is there left to say about places where repression is a fact—Greece, for example, or Brazil?"

Wenner's note, like Thompson's article in the same issue, reported on the state of the counterculture, but Wenner was also eager to flag misconceptions about it. "The notion of a coherent 'counter culture' is another myth," he wrote. "The term itself implies mirror culture, and the so-called counter/alternate culture is as fragmented and structured as the other one." Wenner also commented on the counterculture's music and its social consequences.

> Rock and roll obviously will not "save the world," nor is it for everybody "the magic that can set you free"—though I still think that still happens every day to somebody somewhere. We remain basically happy to be called a "rock-and-roll newspaper" and refer back to our first letter from the editor in which we talked of that magic and said *Rolling Stone* would be not only about rock and roll but also "the attitudes and changes the music embraces."

Here Wenner was quietly hedging the convictions that he and Gleason endorsed, beginning in the first issue. Consciously or not, he was also synchronizing his claims with Thompson's sense that the counterculture had peaked several years earlier and was now losing ground to the forces of reaction. Yet even as he did so, Wenner retained his iconoclastic tone and celebrated the magazine's knack for separating rhetoric (in the discredited sense) from reality.

.   .   .   .   .

When it arrived, Raoul Duke's tale jumped off to a quick start. Racing across the desert, Duke is hallucinating wildly.

> We were somewhere around Barstow on the edge of the desert when the drugs began to take hold. I remember saying something like "I feel a bit lightheaded; maybe you should drive. . . ." And suddenly there was a terrible roar all around us and the sky was full of what looked like huge bats, all swooping and screeching and diving around the car, which was going about 100 miles an hour with the top down to Las Vegas. And a voice was screaming: "Holy Jesus! What are these goddamn animals?"

From the outset, readers suspect that Duke's ordeal will be more extreme, more comical, and less transcendent than anything the Beat protagonists experienced.

The opening also plunges readers into one of the work's most fictionalized sections. In fact, the car Thompson drove to Las Vegas contained only alcohol, marijuana, and prescription speed (Dexedrine and Benzedrine). But when Duke pulls over to open the trunk, he compares it to "a mobile police narcotics lab."

> We had two bags of grass, seventy-five pellets of mescaline, five sheets of high-powered blotter acid, a salt shaker half full of cocaine, and a whole galaxy of multi-colored uppers, downers, screamers, laughers . . . and also a quart of tequila, a quart of rum, a case of Budweiser, a pint of raw ether and two dozen amyls.

Duke's inventory prefigures the tale's extravagance. After reading the draft, Thompson's editor at Random House said he didn't believe the characters were on drugs. Thompson urged him to keep that interpretation to himself. The *Rolling Stone* staff, he explained, was convinced that he had spent his expense money on contraband. "Probably we should leave it that way," Thompson suggested.

Thompson was also thinking about the counterculture, which many observers were writing off after Altamont, the Manson Family murders, and other horror shows. Duke frequently refers to the counterculture's failed project and sidelined heroes.

> A very painful experience in every way, a proper end to the sixties: Tim Leary a prisoner of Eldridge Cleaver in Algeria, Bob Dylan clipping coupons in Greenwich Village, both Kennedys murdered by mutants, Owsley folding napkins on Terminal Island, and finally Cassius/Ali belted incredibly off his pedestal by a human hamburger, a man on the verge of death.

By that time, LSD producer Owsley Stanley was serving time in Southern California. Muhammad Ali (formerly Cassius Clay) had refused to appear for military service and lost his court battle, but the Supreme Court overturned Ali's conviction, allowing him to challenge Joe Frazier for the heavyweight championship.

The Ali–Frazier fight was held in Madison Square Garden, and as the ring announcer noted, everyone was there. The politicians included Hubert Humphrey, Ted Kennedy, and New York Mayor John Lindsay. Entertainers Frank Sinatra, Ed Sullivan, Gene Kelly, Woody Allen, Diana Ross, Bill Cosby, James Taylor, and Barbra Streisand were also on hand. So were author Norman Mailer, football star Joe Namath, fast-food icon Colonel Sanders, and three Apollo 14 astronauts, two of whom had landed on the moon the previous month. After taking his seat behind Hugh Hefner, Jann Wenner spotted Bob Dylan. Fifty foreign governments purchased the rights to broadcast the match, and more than 300 million viewers tuned in. For Thompson, the former sportswriter from Ali's hometown, Joe Frazier's victory by unanimous decision was a fitting symbol of the counterculture's plight.

The night of the Ali–Frazier fight was famous for another reason. While that bout claimed the world's attention, a small group of anti-war activists broke into the FBI office in Media, Pennsylvania, and stole files that revealed the bureau's illicit activities. The burglars mailed the files to five news organizations, four of which immediately returned them to the FBI. After much internal debate, *The Washington Post* ran a story that turned out to be a bombshell. It revealed the existence of the FBI's Security Index, which began as a list of dissidents to be rounded up in case of a national emergency. The burglary also revealed the existence of COINTELPRO, the counterintelligence program that the FBI used to "expose, disrupt, and otherwise neutralize" the New Left, Black Panthers, and civil rights movement. FBI agents sent an anonymous letter to Dr. Martin Luther King Jr. threatening to expose his extramarital affairs and suggesting he commit suicide. Agents also burglarized a Socialist Workers Party office at least 92 times, issued bomb threats to party offices, and fired shots at one of them. As author and *Washington Post* reporter Betty Medsger noted, none of these activities served any law-enforcement purpose. "Whatever the FBI was doing as it invaded lives," she wrote, "it was not preventing violent crimes or building cases on which arrests and successful prosecutions could be based."

Four months after the FBI closed its fruitless investigation of the Media burglary, its new director came clean. Clarence Kelley admitted that the bureau's illicit activities were "clearly wrong and quite indefensible." One FBI official said the Media burglars should have been prosecuted and then pardoned for their service to the nation. The burglars were never apprehended, but some came forward later and explained their motives. The burglary was conceived by William C. Davidon, a physics professor at Haverford College. The eight burglars rarely spoke to one another during the investigation and never again met in person. "It looks like we're terribly reckless people," one of them said later. "But there was absolutely no one in Washington—senators, congressmen, even the president—who dared hold J. Edgar

Hoover to accountability. It became pretty obvious to us that if we don't do it, nobody will."

·   ·   ·   ·   ·

Despite his account's madcap escapades, Thompson considered "Fear and Loathing in Las Vegas" an epitaph for the counterculture. That was especially clear in Duke's famous speech about "riding the crest of a high and beautiful wave" in the Bay Area five years earlier. In Las Vegas, however, Duke could almost see "the high-water mark—that place where the wave finally broke and rolled back." But even if the counterculture was waning, mainstream America was by no means waxing. In Thompson's account, the mainstream culture was not only hopelessly square, but also unhinged. Lunacy became one of his major themes, and novelist Nelson Algren later remarked on that aspect of Thompson's work. "Now that the dust of the '60s has settled," Algren observed, "his hallucinated vision strikes one as having been, after all, the sanest."

Thompson suspected that *Rolling Stone* was the only American magazine that would run "Fear and Loathing in Las Vegas." His boyhood friend, Porter Bibb, who worked on the business side of *Rolling Stone*, agreed with that assessment.

> Who else would have given Hunter the encouragement? The space? The complete freedom? Who else would have let him go on and on for ten thousand, fourteen thousand words? Not Harold Hayes [at *Esquire*]. *Playboy* was rejecting his stuff. Only Jann Wenner. Without Jann, Hunter would not have become Hunter.

Thompson seemed to accept that judgment. When asked if any other outlet would publish his work, Thompson replied, "Oh yeah, but not too many places would pay for it. You know, it's hard to get people to pay you to call the president a pig-fucker." But even as Wenner made the Gonzo franchise possible, Thompson took *Rolling Stone* to another level. The magazine had never published such scorching satire, and Thompson's voice further distinguished *Rolling Stone* from its competitors. Raoul Duke's view of the San Francisco counterculture also captured the magazine's sense of itself. Every now and then, Duke says, "the energy of a whole generation comes to a head in long fine flash, for reasons that nobody really understands at the time." By the end of 1971, *Rolling Stone* was channeling that flash for a large and growing audience.

Random House planned to publish *Fear and Loathing in Las Vegas* as a nonfiction title, but the company's lawyers were concerned about Dr. Gonzo, who commits a string of felonies over the course of the story. Given that character's resemblance to Oscar Acosta, the lawyers insisted that Acosta sign a release before the book went to press. Acosta wasn't worried about felony charges, but he resented being fictionalized in the first place. Proud of his Chicano heritage, he rebuked Thompson for depicting him as a 300-pound Samoan, and he pushed to have his name and photograph appear on the cover. In his view, he and Thompson had formed a partnership on the Salazar story and, by extension, the Las Vegas adventure. "Like, did you even so much as ask me if I minded your writing & printing the Vegas piece?" Acosta asked Thompson. "Not even the fucking courtesy to show me the motherfucker." He was also dismayed by Thompson's condescension. "All I want," Acosta explained in a long letter to Thompson, "is for you to quit playing the role that I'm some fucking native, a noble savage you discovered in the woods."

Thompson wasn't having it. "You don't know how fucking lucky you are that I didn't run into you cold, as a stranger, on something like the Salazar piece—because, with an act like yours, I'd have crucified you on general principles," he told Acosta. As for the Vegas book, Thompson noted that Random House would probably use a photograph of them, taken at Caesar's Palace, on the back of the jacket without identification. When Acosta threatened a libel action, Thompson lost all patience. "Dear Oscar," he wrote in April 1972. "You stupid fuck; send me a mailing address so I can explain what's happening because of what you've done." Thompson said he assumed

Acosta had some "excellent, long-stewing reason for doing this cheap, acid-crippled, paranoid fuckaround." Nevertheless, Thompson maintained that Acosta's legal threat served neither of them.

Meanwhile, Thompson informed Rinzler that he didn't want to appear at all in Acosta's forthcoming book, *Autobiography of a Brown Buffalo*. Rinzler replied that removing that material would damage the integrity of Acosta's book, which he had no intention of doing. "What do you think?" Rinzler asked Wenner. "You're closer to Hunter, what's going on in his head? I'd hate to lose him. But I'm reconciled, if there is no other recourse, since I have no intention of fucking over Oscar or his book." Thompson's attorney fashioned a release, which both Thompson and Acosta signed, but the discord continued. Acosta told Thompson's agent he was planning to sue over the sale of the film rights to the Las Vegas book. Later, he wrote directly to Thompson. "I've been silent on the subject for almost two years because of the blackmail threats from both you and Jann that ultimately my book would be stopped," Acosta said. "Well, old pal, the book is out now, and I'm coming after you. You cocksuckers have been ripping me off for a long time."

Meanwhile, Acosta was churning out his second book, *The Revolt of the Cockroach People*. After finishing the draft, he wrote to Rinzler. "I am already thinking of the third book," he told his editor. "I don't want to make it part of the Buffalo story. I'd like to try a completely fictional thing . . . like a futuristic thing, a detective story, or a western." The *Brown Buffalo* story, he added, was also "king-sized movie material." *Rolling Stone* had the connections, and he had the talent, so why not dream big? But the same year his second book appeared, Acosta was arrested for illegal possession of Benzedrine. He told Thompson he was blackballed in San Francisco and Los Angeles and was living on food stamps and petty theft: "I am still looking to you as my only serious white connection for the big contract. . . . The way it looks from here, I'd even settle for a small one." He asked Thompson to send "seed money" to explore a political alliance between

Thompson's freaks and his cucarachas. He also asked Thompson to forward Acosta's share of the film rights for the Vegas book, to deduct his outstanding loans, and to wish him well, as he did Thompson. "Money-wise, I am desperate," he closed. "Send help to the above address, quick. . . . Thanx."

Thompson replied immediately: "What in the fuck would cause you to ask me for money—after all the insane bullshit you've put me through for the past two years?" They hadn't sold the film rights for the Vegas book, Thompson said, and Acosta's legal threats might have thwarted any such deal for good: "Anyway, good luck with your grudge. No doubt it will make you as many good friends in the future as it has in the past." He closed with another dose of sarcasm: "In the meantime, why don't you write a nice movie? Or a book? You shouldn't have any trouble selling the fucker, considering all the people you've fucked over & burned."

Acosta was also importuning Wenner. "How would you like to publish the Cockroach book in *Rolling Stone*?" he wrote in August 1973. "Can I interest you and yours in the film rights to Brown Buffalo and/or Cockroach? And how about a third contract for my next book?" In Acosta's view, Wenner was cruelly withholding the opportunities he deserved. "You could help me accomplish my goal if you wanted," he added. "I promise to make you Minister of Information after the takeover. Or whatever." Several months later, Acosta asked Wenner, "Why in the fuck won't you give me a break? I can't get either a writing gig or a lawyer gig. Even if you don't like my writing, some people do. . . . Send word." In January, Wenner finally responded.

I am dismayed that you seem to be having problems getting something together. There is just nothing I can think of that *Rolling Stone* can do for you at the current time. You have always had my fondest wishes, and I am willing to help you if there is some reasonable way to do so, but most of our professional "relationships" seem to wind up in some complicated and unsatisfying end. Meantime, we have published two of your books, and I think on balance we have done a good job with them. . . . What else can I say?

In his postscript, Wenner added that the magazine would be glad to endorse Acosta if he decided to run for sheriff again.

. . . . .

The reviews of *Fear and Loathing in Las Vegas* were overwhelmingly positive, and Wenner lashed Gonzo journalism to the magazine's masthead. Steadman and Raoul Duke were listed along with Thompson, and Wenner converted his office into the Raoul Duke Room, which he used for editorial conferences. Thompson's success was a turning point in the magazine's development as well as his own career. "The reinvention of *Rolling Stone* around Hunter Thompson," Wenner's biographer claimed, "would be nearly as important as the invention of the newspaper itself."

Largely on the strength of Thompson's example, *Rolling Stone* earned a reputation as a writer's magazine. Timothy Ferris, who had no special affection for the counterculture, joined the magazine precisely for its dedication to long-form journalism. Likewise, Joe Eszterhas, a reporter for *The Cleveland Plain Dealer*, was impressed by the freedom that *Rolling Stone* afforded its writers. When he flipped through an issue at a magazine rack, he was smitten. "It had life force," he wrote later. "It tingled in my hands. It didn't squirm around wearing a straitjacket of 'objectivity.' It told, subjectively, what it saw as the truth." Even better, the writing was powerful: "Not the homogenized, deodorized crap most magazines were dishing up but real writing. Writing that went for the funny bone, the cortex, or the jugular. Writing that—holy shit!—didn't seem to have any space limitations."

Relishing his success with the Las Vegas story, Thompson wrote to Bernard Shir-Cliff, the Bantam Books editor whom Thompson suspected of cheating him on the royalties for *Hell's Angels*. Thompson offered Shir-Cliff specific instructions on how to bid for the new book's paperback rights.

Anyway, read the fucker and then call for the corporate checkbook before you ring up [Random House editor James] Silberman. When I first called you the price was $100k—but four hours later, when you failed to call back, it was up to $110k. And by the time you get this letter, Bernard, God only knows what it might be. My guess is that we could maybe settle for $125K if you can come up with a cashier's check by this Friday.

In the meantime, read "Fear and Loathing in Las Vegas," then crank out a check for $175k. About the only guarantee I can make you right now is that you'll take any ties; that's for old times sake.

I never forget my friends, Bernard. And I know you feel exactly the same way. But keep in mind that if I don't have your check by Lincoln's birthday, you'd better put a fucking wolf-lock on the door to your office, because I'll be sending my attorney around to find out what the problem is.

Success was sweet for Thompson, but poetic justice was even sweeter.

.   .   .   .   .

In December 1971, Hunter S. Thompson was still basking in his Las Vegas glory when Wenner convened an editorial meeting at the Esalen Institute in Big Sur. For Thompson, it was a homecoming. Before Esalen became an important node in the human potential movement, Thompson was the caretaker at what was then called Slates Hot Springs. In 1961, Thompson placed his first article in a national magazine, a piece about novelist and Big Sur resident Henry Miller. After it appeared in *Rogue,* a *Playboy* knockoff also based in Chicago, Thompson found himself in hot water. His landlady, the grandmother of Esalen cofounder Michael Murphy, didn't care for the article and ran Thompson out of town. In yet another reversal of fortune, Thompson was now returning to Big Sur in triumph.

No big decisions were made in Big Sur, but the conference brought the staff together for the first time and touched off what Wenner considered the magazine's peak period. By that time, Thompson had agreed to cover the 1972 presidential campaign for *Rolling Stone*. The voting age had been lowered to 18, and Wenner hoped the magazine's coverage could push the youth vote toward Senator George McGovern, the only major candidate who promised to withdraw U.S. forces from Vietnam immediately. In Big Sur, Wenner announced that Thompson would move to Washington and begin that work. Annie Leibovitz accompanied Thompson during the primary season and later said she enjoyed her first time on the road with politicians. "I loved covering political stories then because politicians didn't have any sense of themselves," she recalled. "They were awkward. They were still putting shoe polish in their hair."

For Thompson, a longtime freelancer, the campaign assignment was a unique opportunity. The pay was steady, and his work would be disseminated quickly and broadly. After the campaign, he could assemble his dispatches into a book, perhaps even another bestseller. At the same time, the assignment was daunting. His colleagues in the campaign press corps were seasoned reporters from established outlets who didn't know *Rolling Stone* from *The Flintstones*. Thompson occupied the lowest rung of their rigid media hierarchy, and in his campaign book, he mentioned the steps he took to meet that challenge. His colorful copy contrasted sharply with the dry style that most editors preferred, and he had no interest in the care and feeding of sources. "Unlike most other correspondents, I could afford to burn all my bridges behind me—because I was only there for a year, and the last thing I cared about was establishing long-term connections on Capitol Hill," Thompson wrote. He planned to write about the campaign "the same way I'd write about anything else—as close to the bone as I could get, and to hell with the consequences."

Another asset was Thompson's work ethic. McGovern pollster Pat Caddell noted his determination to master the inner workings of the campaigns. "Hunter worked his ass off to understand what was going on," Caddell said. "He didn't know about politics, so he insisted that you explain every detail, and he would pick it up like that."

Thompson also used the force of his personality to offset his institutional disadvantages. He drank with his press colleagues, placed bets with them on election outcomes, and slowly created a niche for himself. As usual, Thompson critiqued other media accounts while covering the main story as such, but instead of singling out individual reporters or outlets for their biases or other shortcomings, he argued that traditional journalism in general was failing to meet the moment. To capture Nixon's monstrosity, journalists needed an alternative to the hard-news format that their editors demanded. If professional norms prevented reporters from capturing Nixon's depravity, he would ignore those norms and tell the unvarnished truth as he understood it.

Thompson also tapped his formidable powers of invective and satire. In the early primaries, he focused on Senator Edmund Muskie, the Democratic frontrunner and the target of Thompson's most outrageous satire. After the Wisconsin primary, Thompson wrote that Muskie was addicted to ibogaine, a psychoactive substance used for spiritual purposes in Central Africa. The Ibogaine Effect, Thompson claimed, explained why Muskie fell apart during a speech in Miami: "It is entirely conceivable—given the known effects of Ibogaine—that Muskie's brain was almost paralyzed by hallucinations at the time." The satire clicked with *Rolling Stone*'s readership. The idea that Muskie might mistake his audience for a collection of Gila monsters reinforced the hippie conviction that official America was weirder than they were.

When Timothy Crouse asked if he could cover the campaign as well, Wenner directed him to support Thompson. In the course of their daily conversations, however, Thompson suggested that Crouse observe the other reporters carefully, and Crouse soon developed a project of his own. *The Boys on the Bus* (1973), which began as a *Rolling Stone* article, offered a detailed description of the White House press corps. Crouse outlined its internal hierarchy and explained its risk-averse approach to reporting. He also quoted Brit Hume, who worked for syndicated columnist Jack Anderson. Hume had little patience with colleagues who "claim that they're trying to be objective."

> They shouldn't try to be objective. They should try to be honest. And they're not being honest. Their so-called objectivity is just a guise for superficiality. They report what one candidate said, then they go and report what the other candidate said with equal credibility. They never get around to finding out if the guy is telling the truth. They just pass the speeches along without trying to confirm the substance of what the candidates are saying. What they pass off as objectivity is just a mindless kind of neutrality.

Even if a candidate spouted demonstrable lies every day, Hume suggested, the conventions of mainstream journalism made it impossible for reporters to say so directly. After the campaign, Wenner tried to recruit Hume, who landed at ABC News and later became a fixture at Fox News.

When Muskie's campaign collapsed, Thompson trained his sights on Hubert Humphrey. Thompson's animosity for Humphrey was rooted in his pro-war stance and the chaos in Chicago, where the vice president received his party's nomination while police officers attacked protestors in the streets. Leaving the cool analysis to others, Thompson called Humphrey "a treacherous, gutless old ward-heeler who should be put in a goddamn bottle and sent out with the Japanese current." Once McGovern clinched his party's nomination, Thompson turned his guns on Nixon, but another story hijacked the campaign coverage. McGovern's running mate, Thomas Eagleton, had received electroshock treatments for depression without informing the campaign team. When the news broke, McGovern couldn't bring himself to replace Eagleton on the ticket. The story dragged on, and though McGovern finally replaced Eagleton, his campaign never recovered.

Despite committing what Thompson called "a series of almost unbelievable blunders," McGovern remained Thompson's first choice. "McGovern made some stupid mistakes," he wrote, "but in context they seem almost frivolous compared to the things Richard Nixon does every day of his life, on purpose, as a matter of policy and a perfect expression of everything he stands for." As McGovern's chances slipped away, Thompson's disappointment was compounded by his fatigue. His *Rolling Stone* dispatches merged real-time observations with flashbacks about the Hells Angels and Kentucky Derby.

Despite the campaign's unhappy ending, Thompson's reports brought *Rolling Stone* to the attention of the national establishment for the first time. Early in the campaign, Thompson noted that most of his press colleagues had never heard of *Rolling Stone*. By April, however, *Newsweek* columnist Stewart Alsop was quoting what he described as an "organ of the counterculture." As Matt Taibbi noted four decades later, Thompson's account also altered the way reporters covered subsequent presidential campaigns. Much of that influence flowed from the book's staging. Following Thompson's example, campaign books routinely included the hotshot reporter and campaign wizard, backstage gossip, and candidates who played the role of villain, sellout, and savior.

Thompson's achievement convinced Wenner that *Rolling Stone* could become a general-interest magazine and contribute to the national political dialogue. In the aftermath of the 1972 election, Wenner expanded the magazine's political coverage. In Thompson's view, that was a step in the right direction. Even after becoming the magazine's star contributor, he told Wenner that *Rolling Stone* had yet to reach a large potential readership that "doesn't give a flying fuck what the Jackson Five eats for breakfast." In the end, no one did more than Wenner to make Thompson a cultural celebrity, and no writer did more than Thompson to establish *Rolling Stone* as a political voice to reckon with.

    .   .   .   .   .

As the 1972 presidential campaign unfolded, *Rolling Stone* continued to churn out music coverage. Among the most memorable articles that summer was Robin Green's cover story on teen idol David

Cassidy. By that time, Green had become the first woman to be listed as a contributing editor at *Rolling Stone*. After moving to Berkeley with her boyfriend, Green met Alan Rinzler, who encouraged her to apply for work at *Rolling Stone*. She thought she might land a clerical position, but when Wenner learned she had worked at Marvel Comics, he asked her to write about that. That led to a cover story and more assignments, including an interview with Dennis Hopper in Taos. Never a full-time staff writer, Green avoided the office and its boys-club atmosphere. She wasn't invited to the Big Sur editorial conference in 1971, but her romance with editor David Felton allowed her to attend the second day of the meeting.

David Cassidy was famous for his role on *The Partridge Family*, a successful situation comedy that began airing in 1970. In the pilot, a widowed bank teller (played by Shirley Jones, Cassidy's real-life stepmother) helps her children record a pop song in the garage of their Northern California home. When the song becomes a hit, the family hits the road in a brightly painted school bus. It was a neater version of Further, the 1939 International Harvester that transported Ken Kesey and the Merry Pranksters only six years earlier. But whereas the message painted on Further was "Caution: Weird Load," the warning on the Partridge Family bus was "Careful: Nervous Mother Driving." The show's success revealed the remarkable dexterity of American popular culture. Network television not only absorbed the rock revolution's psychedelic style, but also converted it into wholesome family entertainment. Later, Wenner noted that *The Partridge Family* also updated *Ozzie and Harriet*, an earlier program featuring a musical family.

With the help of Los Angeles session musicians, the television show also spun off successful records. The Partridge Family's first release, "I Think I Love You," sold four million copies, making it the top-selling single of the year. The band was nominated for a Grammy Award as Best New Artist, and the television program received two consecutive Golden Globe nominations for Best TV Show. Cassidy also recorded two solo albums in 1972, both of which produced hit singles in the United States and abroad. Featured regularly in teen magazines, Cassidy received 25,000 letters each week and boasted the music business's largest fan club. The editor of *16* magazine said she had been waiting for someone like Cassidy for years.

Despite his extraordinary success, Cassidy was dissatisfied with his public image. He wanted to be seen as an adult artist, and his publicist approached *Rolling Stone* about a story along those lines. The assignment went to Green, who had little respect for Cassidy's talent or celebrity. "If the PR man or Cassidy himself had taken the time to read anything I'd written in *Rolling Stone*," she claimed later, "we could have been spared a lot of trouble." Green saw her work as "a one-woman crusade to out the pretentious, the phony, the self-deluded, the boorish, the cruel." Cassidy didn't fit that description, Green admitted, but she thought he was "lame." "He and the industries from which he sprang were such easy targets," she recalled. "I wrote the shit out of the thing, not just about him in his little androgynous white jumpsuit, but about the teen-magazine, poster, and lunch-box businesses that profited from him." Green also resented the fact that her colleagues were touring with the Rolling Stones, the Grateful Dead, and Bob Dylan while she spent five days with Cassidy and his stepmother.

"Naked Lunch Box" was another example of a *Rolling Stone* journalist taking readers behind the showbiz curtain. David Felton's title evoked William Burroughs, the subject of the Rolling Stone Interview in the same issue, even as it mocked Cassidy's profitable licensing deals for children's lunchboxes. Green's story detailed Cassidy's success, including sold-out shows at Madison Square Garden and the Houston Astrodome, and probed the nascent sexual urges those performances excited. "For many of the girls, it's the first time their little thighs get twitchy," Cassidy's road manager told Green. "This is very filthy," Cassidy added, "but when the hall empties out after one of my concerts, those girls leave behind them thousands of *sticky seats*." Cassidy also voiced his wariness about *Rolling Stone,* especially after it contrasted the Jackson 5 with white, artificially sweetened teen throbs like himself. Wounded by that comparison, Cassidy admitted to Green that his defensiveness toward the magazine was "kind of a fucked up way to be," but he said he "would really dig reading something about me that wasn't, you know, the same old bullshit."

Green's article satisfied that wish. It opened with Cassidy slumped in the back seat of a limousine, stoned and drunk, while his team encouraged him to check out a hot Manhattan nightclub. No part of that scene resembled the coverage Cassidy received in *Tiger Beat,* but Annie Leibovitz's photographs did even more to alter his public image. The cover photograph showed a Cassidy lying in repose, his torso naked, eyes shut, hands clasped behind his head in a sensual reverie. Inside, a two-page spread was more explicit. Cassidy was locked in his own embrace with the top of his pubic beard clearly visible. "It was Annie's naked photos," Green wrote later, "both on the cover and in the center spread, that finished the job." "Naked Lunch Box" parodied the sexual currents roiling beneath teen celebrity even as it exploited their power. In that sense, Green's article proved once again that selling a revolt against mass consumerism could also be a profitable enterprise.

The *Rolling Stone* profile generated considerable controversy but failed to establish Cassidy as an adult artist. Instead, he said later, it "pissed off everybody that was profiting from the business of David Cassidy." Endorsements dried up, and after the final episode of *The Partridge Family* aired in 1974, Cassidy continued to work but never achieved the same level of fame, even after he appeared on *The Celebrity Apprentice* with Donald Trump in 2011. "I was pigeon-holed as a teen idol," Cassidy said later. "I paid a tremendous personal price—it's a very empty, isolated, lonely existence." Robin Green had few misgivings about her portrait. "I can't speak for Annie, but in those days I didn't think much about the damage anything I wrote might do, how it might hurt feelings, careers," she wrote in her memoir. "It comes back to what Joan Didion wrote about our brand of journalism in the preface to *Slouching Towards*

Bethlehem: 'People tend to forget that my presence runs counter to their best interests. And it always does.'"

.   .   .   .   .

That summer, the Rolling Stones launched their first U.S. tour since Altamont. Designed to promote *Exile on Main St.*, which *Rolling Stone* panned, the tour included 51 dates crammed into eight weeks. Wenner chose Robert Greenfield, who covered the group's British tour in 1971, to report on the concerts, but he also arranged for Truman Capote to write about the shows. Capote had published *Breakfast at Tiffany's* (1958) and *In Cold Blood* (1966), which probed a 1959 murder case in Kansas. "I wanted to produce a journalistic novel, something on a large scale that would have the credibility of fact, the immediacy of film, the depth and freedom of prose, and the precision of poetry," Capote said later. Serialized in *The New Yorker*, *In Cold Blood* was a critical and commercial success, and Capote was considered a top practitioner of New Journalism.

In the end, Capote failed to submit a usable story to *Rolling Stone*. Instead, the magazine ran Capote's exchanges with Andy Warhol, who accompanied Capote on tour. Such exchanges were a staple at Warhol's *Interview* magazine, but Greil Marcus later described the arrangement with Capote as a disaster from start to finish. Jon Carroll, whom Wenner had fired two years earlier, took a different view. "Lots of times I don't think that *Rolling Stone* is the hope of the world," Carroll wrote to his former boss, "but sometimes (Capote & Warhol, of course), I do. I hate you. All love, Jon." In the same issue, Wenner ran a transcript of his own conversation with Capote. It was taped in Palm Springs, where Wenner stayed with Capote and visited a gay disco for the first time. "I wasn't bothered or worried a bit about being seen at a gay club," Wenner recalled in his memoir. "Truman was my beard."

.   .   .   .   .

One week before the 1972 election, the magazine unveiled a meaty two-part interview with Tom Hayden. Only the second Rolling Stone Interview with a nonmusician, the byline went to Tim Findley. Formerly an investigative reporter at the *San Francisco Chronicle*, Findley briefly served as an associate editor at *Rolling Stone*, where he also wrote a cover story about Huey P. Newton, cofounder of the Black Panther Party. At Hayden's request, the conversation included Richard Flacks, his mentor from the University of Michigan and a sociology professor at the University of California, Santa Barbara.

In the first part of the interview, Hayden reflected on his experience in the 1960s and grappled with that decade's political turmoil. Exposed to student activism and the farm labor movement during his first stint in Berkeley, Hayden later drafted the Port Huron Statement, pushed for civil rights during Freedom Summer in Mississippi, and served as a community organizer in Newark's poor neighborhoods. He participated in the Columbia University student strike and wrote an article for *Ramparts* called "Two, Three, Many Columbias," which celebrated the occupation and echoed Che Guevara's famous slogan about Vietnam. Casting his actions at the 1968 Democratic National Convention as a form of personal discovery, Hayden visited Czechoslovakia, the Soviet Union, and Hanoi, where U.S. adversaries hosted him and other American dissenters. Immediately before the so-called Days of Rage action in Chicago, when Weatherman led a destructive downtown rampage, Hayden gave the rioters a short pep talk using a bullhorn. By then, he considered himself a committed revolutionary.

The second part of the Hayden interview focused on the Chicago conspiracy trial, the topic of his 1970 book, as well as Weatherman, about which Hayden had mixed feelings. "I try to describe the Weather position in the best possible way, because I respect where it came from," he said. "It came from experience, from a glimpse of horror and a desire to react genuinely." Nevertheless, Hayden thought Weatherman had become too militaristic and hateful. Moreover, its members had forgotten the gradual, step-by-step process that had converted them into enemies of the government. "They could not short-circuit that process for everyone with a few bombs," Hayden said.

Asked about his own public profile, Hayden replied that the media played an outsized role in selecting movement leaders. As a result, those leaders tended to lose themselves in a media environment that claimed more and more of their attention. Worse, their comrades felt they could no longer control their own movement. For all these reasons, Hayden told Findley, "the Movement can't be built around that kind of star trip." According to Flacks, Hayden's remarks about celebrity also reflected his experience after the Chicago conspiracy trial. Returning to Berkeley, Hayden had joined a commune called the Red Family, which expelled him for manipulation and male chauvinism. Wounded by that experience, he moved to Los Angeles, took an alias, and kept a low profile. When he crossed paths with actress and activist Jane Fonda, they cofounded an anti-war organization called the Indochina Peace Campaign, which sought to defund America's involvement in Vietnam. He resurfaced in the media shortly before the Rolling Stone Interview appeared and married Fonda the following year.

The Hayden interview didn't bear directly on the imminent presidential election. He endorsed George McGovern but did so reluctantly and half-heartedly. Nixon was anathema, yet Hayden clearly found it difficult to promote a Democrat in the aftermath of the Chicago conspiracy trial. McGovern's nomination was a product of the people's resistance rather than the senator's virtue, Hayden said, and he criticized McGovern for starting his campaign at his vacation home in the Black Hills, which was sacred land for the Lakota. For Hayden, that decision was proof that McGovern didn't grasp the full horror of America's genocidal past. He also faulted McGovern for wearing a cowboy hat and jacket, thereby perpetuating an image of America that Hayden associated with the disaster in Vietnam. Finally, he cast the nation's entire political class in the harshest possible terms. "I think people ought to draw the lesson that our country is run by murderers," he said.

The interview marked a new chapter in Hayden's public life. By focusing his efforts on the Indochina Peace Campaign, Hayden pivoted from revolutionary politics to targeted lobbying. By that time, Congress wasn't rubber-stamping Nixon's requests for defense-related money. Oakland Democrat Ron Dellums introduced a bill to defund Nixon's initiatives, and later that year, Congress declined a White House request for $474 million in additional aid to South Vietnam. Opposition to the war, which had united the disparate elements of the counterculture, was finally taking hold in Congress.

.   .   .   .   .

As Hayden refashioned his public image, Hunter S. Thompson was still throwing haymakers at Richard Nixon. Only days after Nixon's landslide victory, the Gonzo journalist launched an unprecedented attack on a sitting president.

> It is Nixon himself who represents that dark, venal and incurably violent side of the American character that almost every country in the world has learned to fear and despise. Our Barbie-doll president, with his Barbie-doll wife and his boxful of Barbie-doll children is also America's answer to the monstrous Mr. Hyde. He speaks for the Werewolf in us; the bully, the predatory shyster who turns into something unspeakable, full of claws and bleeding string-warts on nights when the moon comes too close.

As Thompson waxed sinister, his hyperbole reached new heights.

> At the stroke of midnight in Washington, a drooling red-eyed beast with the legs of a man and a head of a giant hyena crawls out of its bedroom window in the South Wing of the White House and leaps fifty feet down to the lawn . . . pauses briefly to strangle a Chow watchdog, then races off into the darkness . . . towards the Watergate, snarling with lust, loping through the alleys behind Pennsylvania Avenue, and trying desperately to remember which one of those four hundred identical balconies is the one outside Martha Mitchell's apartment . . .

Thompson described his reverie as a bad dream and a joke, but Nixon's victory pushed his prose into a new and darker register.

Many writers hated Nixon, but his victory meant that Americans were willing to affirm, or at least to tolerate, everything Thompson despised.

> This may be the year when we finally come face to face with ourselves; finally just lay back and say it—that we are really just a nation of 220 million used car salesmen with all the money we need to buy guns, and no qualms at all about killing anybody else in the world who tries to make us uncomfortable.

However the blame was assigned, Thompson's contempt for Nixon and his voters fueled some of his most inspired prose. Later, when the Watergate scandal consumed the Nixon administration, Thompson's scorn seemed more justified than ever.

Stewart Brand's article for *Rolling Stone* the following month was less spectacular than Thompson's screed but even more prophetic. Brand reported from the Stanford Artificial Intelligence Lab (SAIL), which conducted research on robotics, computer vision, natural language processing, and speech recognition. He also gained access to the Palo Alto Research Center, which the Xerox Corporation had created to design the future of office work based on computers and networks. Brand was intrigued by both centers and their research, but the occasion for his visit to SAIL was a video game tournament called the Intergalactic Spacewar Olympics. Its participants included hackers who played *Spacewar!* after hours in a computer laboratory at Stanford University.

Brand featured the tournament in his article, but he also encapsulated the significant trends in computing at the time. "Ready or not," his first sentence read, "computers are coming to the people." That was good news, Brand added, maybe the best since psychedelics. The comparison wasn't gratuitous. Brand claimed that the early days of ARPANET, the prototype for the internet, were "full of freedom and weirdness," two hallmarks of the counterculture. Even the video game's symbolic violence boded well for the counterculture. "Spacewar serves Earthpeace," Brand declared. Far from being a threat to our humanity, the new technology enhanced it. Annie Leibovitz photographed the winner of the tournament, a graduate student whose research helped model eyesight for mobile robots. Her photographs indicated that many of the lab researchers were hippies.

Brand's prophecy wasn't lost on other freaks in the emergent digital culture. One of them was Steve Jobs, the cofounder of Apple Computer who would later spread the gospel of personal computing. A fan of the *Whole Earth Catalog*, Jobs brought an issue with him to college and then to the All One Farm, a hippie commune where Jobs ran the apple orchard. Decades after that, Jobs praised the *Whole Earth Catalog* in a graduation speech delivered at Stanford University that called Brand's creation "Google in paperback form, 35 years before Google came along."

Brand's techno-optimism seemed to clash with Theodore Roszak's view that the counterculture rejected technocracy, his term for the corporate regime that dominated industrial society. Shortly after hippies began leaving their mark on the computer business, Roszak predicted it was only a matter of time before the technocracy bent the new technologies to its own purposes. Yet Roszak's analysis didn't refute Brand's claim that personal computers, video games, artificial intelligence, robotics, and the internet would have far-reaching consequences for the way Americans worked, played, and lived. Brand's article pointed the way to a new digital world and the Bay Area's place in it.

PART IV Golden Age

10 Boys Club

Shortly after Richard Nixon's second inauguration in 1973, tension between Jann Wenner and Ralph Gleason flared again. In 1968, a disgusted Gleason had resigned briefly, and three years later, he demanded that Wenner stop tweaking his columns. Now he made a rare plea: Would Wenner edit an anthology of his work for Straight Arrow Books? Finding it difficult to select and arrange the pieces, Gleason concluded that Wenner was the best person for the job. "Please do this favor for me, old friend," Gleason wrote. "I need it." Wenner quickly agreed and copied Alan Rinzler on his reply.

Two days later, Wenner sent Gleason a handwritten note explaining that he didn't like Gleason's latest columns on politics or President Nixon. "At this point, they are generally getting repetitive," Wenner wrote. "Some of course have been excellent." The political columns weren't Gleason's strong suit, Wenner said, and they duplicated Thompson's work and the magazine's other features. He suggested that Gleason "stay close to areas which have proved popular and fascinating reading in the past—music, popular culture, and arts, the music business, radio, jazz artists, general musical and artistic observations, etc." Wenner said he felt strongly about this recommendation, asked Gleason to take it kindly, and added that he missed his mentor's old stuff. Gleason always claimed that politics was downstream from culture, but now Wenner was directing him to avoid political commentary in general. For the only music journalist to land on Nixon's infamous Enemies List, it was almost certainly a painful jab.

Meanwhile, Hunter S. Thompson was planning to complete his manuscript for Straight Arrow Books. By that time, presidential campaigns had produced a short shelf of acclaimed works. When it appeared in 1961, Theodore White's *The Making of the President 1960* offered a new approach to political journalism. A published novelist, White presented the entire campaign as a polished narrative whose hero was John F. Kennedy, the victorious candidate. That book won the Pulitzer Prize for general nonfiction, and White followed the same formula in 1964, 1968, and 1972. Very little in that body of work suggested that anything was amiss in American politics. Although Thompson was still an aspiring novelist, he spurned White's literary formula. Instead, he intended to produce a "jangled campaign diary" that recorded the volatile campaign in real time.

Some of the jangling arose from Thompson's use of Dexedrine. "I will definitely need speed to get the campaign book done properly and on time," Thompson wrote to Wenner. "Never mind the fucking *wisdom* of it; just gather all you can and send it ASAP—with a bill, of course." When he arrived in San Francisco, Thompson avoided the office, where space had been cleared for him. Instead, he checked into the Seal Rock Inn on Geary Boulevard, a short walk from Ocean Beach. Rinzler laid in 40 pounds of supplies, which Thompson itemized in the book: firewood, two cases of Mexican beer, four quarts of gin, a dozen grapefruits, and "enough speed to alter the outcome of six Super Bowls."

The work sessions were brutal. Thompson's book described them as "fifty-five consecutive hours of sleepless, foodless, high-speed editing." For Rinzler, the editorial process was hands-on, exhausting, and adversarial. Put off by Thompson's jabs about his Jewish ancestry, Rinzler sent Thompson a telegram when the finished books arrived.

> Working with you has been the most strenuous and stimulating experience of my twelve years in publishing. You're a bastard and sometimes a dangerous fool, with calculation, but my admiration and respect for your intelligence, courage, honesty, and style is great. In fact, I think you're a good man. Love to you on publication day of *Fear and Loathing: On the Campaign Trail 1972*. Next year in Jerusalem.

Rinzler resisted the temptation to tell Thompson that he, too, was a credit to his race.

As Thompson and Rinzler toiled over the campaign book, *Rolling Stone* ran Tom Wolfe's four-part story on the early days of NASA. By that time, Wolfe had named and popularized the New Journalism. His *New York* magazine articles on Ken Kesey and the Merry Pranksters led to *The Electric Kool-Aid Acid Test* (1969), and the following year, Wolfe skewered New York liberals in *Radical Chic & Mau-Mauing the Flak Catchers* (1970). That collection also originated with *New York* articles, one of which lampooned composer Leonard Bernstein and his friends for hosting a party for the Black Panthers. Wolfe's political views didn't square well with *Rolling Stone*'s, but Wenner was committed to running work by the leading lights of New Journalism, and none burned brighter than Tom Wolfe.

The connection between Wolfe and Thompson stretched back to the publication of Wolfe's 1965 book, *The Kandy-Kolored Tangerine-Flake Streamline Baby*. The title was drawn from a 1963 piece on Southern California's hot-rod scene, and another essay featured the frenetic action in Las Vegas. Energized by Wolfe's work, Thompson submitted a book review to his editors at *The National Observer*. When they rejected the review, Thompson sent it to Wolfe. The two began to correspond and connected despite their differences.

Thompson's juvenile delinquency prevented him from graduating with his class in Louisville, and he never finished college. Wolfe was student body president, editor of the school newspaper, and a star athlete at his all-male Episcopal school in Virginia before earning a PhD at Yale University. While Wolfe was writing for *Esquire* and *New York*, some of Thompson's early work ran in second-tier men's magazines.

For all their differences, however, the two men had much in common, including an interest in exotic West Coast subcultures. Whereas Wolfe focused on Southern California's tricked-out automobiles and those who loved them, Thompson targeted the Bay Area's most notorious motorcycle gang. For Wolfe, the extravagant tastelessness of Las Vegas was a source of amusement, whereas Thompson located the death of the American Dream there. Both writers imported the techniques of fiction into their journalism, and each forged a distinctive style. By the time Wolfe contributed his first piece to *Rolling Stone*, he and Thompson shared the same literary agent, and Wolfe's anthology of New Journalism included two pieces by Thompson.

Wolfe's series about NASA, which Wenner titled "Post-Orbital Remorse," explored the rites, rituals, and mysteries of the Brotherhood of the Right Stuff. The series had nothing to do with the counterculture or its music, but it pushed the magazine more squarely into the general-interest category. The series was also an inflection point in Wolfe's career. He dedicated several more years to the same topic before producing *The Right Stuff,* which won the National Book Award in 1979. The film version, which appeared in 1983, received eight Oscar nominations and won four awards.

·   ·   ·   ·   ·

While *Rolling Stone* featured the stars of New Journalism, it continued to nurture young writers. One was David Harris, the former student body president at Stanford University who had protested the draft and refused to report for military service. Harris was tried and convicted, but not before he married folk singer Joan Baez, whom he met while raising funds for anti-war efforts. As his case moved through the courts, the newlyweds lived on a 10-acre commune in the hills near Stanford. After his sentencing, a pregnant Baez released *David's Album* and performed at Woodstock. No less ardent in her anti-war activism than Harris, Baez offered political commentary from the stage when she went on at 3:00 a.m. Later she noted the gap between the spirit of Woodstock and her remarks. "David was in jail, I was pregnant, and it was all about changing the world and taking risks," she said. "I know people got bored with me talking about it, but my mission continued, even into this big festival."

Paroled after 20 months and divorced from Baez, Harris resumed his anti-war activism and was determined to establish himself as a journalist. He chose *Rolling Stone* as the place to start his new career. "By the time I made contact," he wrote later, "the *Stone* had solidified its reputation as the ongoing voice of the Sixties generation out among the big boys of the information world." When he met with Wenner, Harris said he wanted to write about a paralyzed Vietnam veteran he knew in Los Angeles. He and Wenner shook on a deal for ten cents a word plus expenses. A profile of Ron Kovic traced his enthusiasm as a volunteer through his second tour of duty, when Kovic was shot while leading his rifle squad. Paralyzed from the waist down, he became an anti-war activist shortly after the Kent State shootings. The *Rolling Stone* article led to the publication of Kovic's autobiography, *Born on the Fourth of July* (1976). Touted by Bruce Springsteen, the autobiography was converted into a film starring Tom Cruise that received eight Oscar nominations and won two awards, including Best Director for Oliver Stone.

Another *Rolling Stone* recruit was Tim Cahill, a graduate student in creative writing at San Francisco State College. With dreams of writing the Great American Novel, Cahill contributed stories to the *San Francisco Chronicle*'s weekend magazine. Grover Lewis noticed them, and *Rolling Stone* hired Cahill to sift through its slush pile in search of potential stories. "I didn't know what I wanted to do, what

I was good at," Cahill said later. As a result, his work ranged over various topics. He wasn't drawn to political stories, but profiling rock musicians, authors, and movie stars came easily. In 1973, Cahill joined a Christian cult to investigate charges that a foundation had hypnotized, kidnapped, and brainwashed street people in Hollywood and bussed them to a compound in Saugus. He concluded that the recruits were willing participants, but the cult leader was eventually convicted of 10 child rape offenses, received a maximum sentence of 175 years, and died in prison.

With Paul Scanlon's editorial guidance, Cahill made the work look easy, but some assignments were trickier than others. In March 1972, he picked up where Ed Ward left off and tried to interview Bill Graham. The rock impresario refused Cahill's interview request but gave the journalist a piece of his furious mind over the telephone. Cahill transcribed the exchange.

GRAHAM: But let me tell you something about the dishonest, slimy little paper you work for, mister, and that . . . evil . . . slimy little cunt, your editor. There are only a few people I'd like to take out to the street and kick the shit out of, so you tell him for me, mister, you tell that clever evil little creep who makes his living calling honest businessmen capitalist rip-off pigs . . .

CAHILL: We never called you that.

GRAHAM: Read your magazine, mister.

CAHILL: I've read the magazine, we never called you a pig of any sort.

GRAHAM: Is it morally right for that senile spot of grease, your Mister Gleason, to say when Miles Davis comes under my management that now Mr. Davis will not be playing the black clubs? Is that truth in journalism?

CAHILL: So has he played the black clubs?

GRAHAM: He always played the black clubs, he continues to play the black clubs. . . . I'm sorry to raise my voice to you. I don't know you. You're probably a decent person. But you work for . . . You just tell him this. I want him. You tell him to grow a little, put on some weight, and meet me in the street.

Cahill's profile annoyed Graham but led to a five-hour meeting between the two men and Wenner. When Graham complained about a faulty quote or factual inaccuracy, Cahill produced the notes that confirmed his reporting. The marathon meeting blunted Graham's anger and effectively concluded his feud with Wenner.

By this time, *Rolling Stone* was also featuring the work of Joe Eszterhas, the former crime reporter who specialized in tales of drugs and violence. His first piece for *Rolling Stone* described a lethal showdown in Cleveland between the Hells Angels and a motorcycle gang called the Breeds. Another Eszterhas article revisited the Kent State killings, which many Americans continued to pin on the protestors. His two-part exposé of undercover narcotics agents eventually grew into a book called *Nark!*, which Straight Arrow Books published in 1974. In it, Eszterhas maintained that local, state, and federal narcotics agents were little more than deputized gangsters.

Eszterhas also wrote about the Brotherhood of Eternal Love, which he dubbed the "Hippie Mafia." Based in Orange County, California, the brotherhood grew into a drug cartel in the late 1960s and early 1970s. Importing hashish from Afghanistan, some of it stuffed into hollowed out surfboards, the brotherhood also brewed up powerful batches of LSD called "orange sunshine" and financed Timothy Leary's escape from prison. Relying heavily on police sources, grand jury testimony, and a snitch, Eszterhas captured what author Nicholas Schou described as "the cat-and-mouse action between the cops and hippies as well as the related freakery going down in Laguna Canyon at the time." Schou, who chronicled the Brotherhood of Eternal Love in *Orange Sunshine* (2010), added that Eszterhas's story was also "a perfect example of the general shift in culture from the far-out utopianism of the 1960s to the helter-skelter paranoia of the 1970s."

Eszterhas managed to score an exclusive interview for *Rolling Stone* after oil billionaire J. Paul Getty's 16-year-old grandson was kidnapped in Rome and held for a $17 million ransom. During the negotiations, the kidnappers sliced off most of Paul Getty's right ear and sent it to his family through the mail. A postal strike delayed that package's arrival, but J. Paul Getty, who at one time was reputed to be the richest man in the world, finally agreed to pay a much smaller ransom. The story was a worldwide sensation, and a few months after his release, Paul Getty granted his first interview to Eszterhas and *Rolling Stone*. Getty recounted the entire story, including the media frenzy that surrounded his return.

> Every time I went somewhere in Rome, I had a police escort. Motorcycles, sirens. I really couldn't go anywhere. Girls were screaming whenever they saw me. I was being treated like a rock star. I got hundreds of fan letters from all over the world. Some were just addressed to "Paul Getty, the Golden Hippie," without any address and still they got to me. All the letters basically said, "Give me your cock."

Nine kidnappers were eventually arrested, including two high-ranking members of a Calabrian crime organization. Only two were convicted, and the ransom money was never recovered.

Though less sensational, another Eszterhas story hit closer to home for many Americans. "Charlie Simpson's Apocalypse" was a 17,000-word piece about a young, self-styled revolutionary in the small town of Harrison, Missouri. After contending with town elders who resented the local longhairs, Simpson killed three people (including two police officers) with an assault rifle before taking his own life. Shortly after its publication, Tom Wolfe included Eszterhas's article in the New Journalism anthology he edited. Eszterhas also parlayed the article into a book for Random House that was nominated for a National Book Award.

·   ·   ·   ·   ·

In 1973, the Wenners bought a large Victorian home in the upscale San Francisco neighborhood of Pacific Heights. With its sauna, cutting-edge sound system, and artworks by Andy Warhol, Richard Diebenkorn, and Claes Oldenburg, the house at 2018 California

Street became a bustling salon for the magazine's staff, friends, and out-of-town visitors.

Yet all was not well in the Wenner–Schindelheim clan. In June, *Rolling Stone* art director Robert Kingsbury wrote a long, unhappy letter to Wenner. Kingsbury, who was married to Jane Wenner's sister, was more than two decades older than Wenner and a veteran of the Second World War. After studying art on the GI Bill at the University of Michigan, he moved to San Francisco and met Wenner at a party on Potrero Hill. At that time, Kingsbury was fashioning roach clips with elegantly turned wooden handles. In 1968, *Rolling Stone* offered those "Handy Little Devices" as a premium for new subscribers. The ad appeared in the magazine's fifth issue and became its most famous promotion. Shortly after that, Wenner made Kingsbury *Rolling Stone*'s art director. In his letter to Wenner five years later, Kingsbury argued that his compensation should equal that of the magazine's highest-paid employee. Such a salary, he wrote, was "a minimal reward for superhuman effort over a long period of time."

After receiving Kingsbury's letter, Wenner asked Dugald Stermer, from whom Wenner borrowed the magazine's original design, to critique its latest issue. In a detailed memo, Stermer offered general recommendations and specific suggestions. Only Leibovitz and Steadman were strongly associated with the magazine's look, Stermer noted, and he urged *Rolling Stone* to develop closer relationships with its graphic contributors. He also claimed that the magazine's "major fuckups" could be traced to the editorial department, which created bottlenecks and then blamed the production department for everything from typos to factual errors. That pattern, Stermer said, had created the worst morale outside the maximum-security wing at Soledad State Prison. The cover he reviewed was satisfactory, and the masthead was "okay but cute," especially the listings for Raoul Duke (sports) and Ralph Steadman (gardening). The pull-out quotes and credit lines needed attention, and the drop cap on one article, Stermer said, "looks as if I had drawn it with a paint roller." Otherwise, Stermer concluded, the art direction was fine.

When Wenner replied to Kingsbury, he didn't offer him a raise. Instead, he announced that he was hiring a new art director, Mike Salisbury, who already had worked at *Surfer*, *Playboy*, and *West* magazine before turning 30. Wenner suggested a sabbatical for Kingsbury and offered him a job if he decided to return. Kingsbury accepted the offer and took on special projects, including books commissioned by the magazine. When Salisbury left *Rolling Stone* in 1976, his replacement sang his praises. "The fact is that Mike Salisbury turned *Rolling Stone* into a world-class design effort, with great photographs and astounding illustrations," art director Roger Black said. According to Wenner, Black also broke new ground. "He gave *Rolling Stone* a look that reflected our early attempts at classic design, but which was far more sophisticated and felt new," Wenner said. "There was no room left for the hippie potpourri that had been so much a part of our early years."

.   .   .   .   .

As the magazine changed around him, Ben Fong-Torres continued to coordinate *Rolling Stone*'s music coverage. His dealings with Wenner were generally cordial, but he was no pushover. When Wenner asked to review the questions Fong-Torres had prepared for Art Garfunkel, who was also Wenner's tennis partner, Fong-Torres replied that he had spoken with Landau and Gleason, made notes on the Paul Simon interview, and scoured the Simon & Garfunkel file. "So I'm ready for the interview," he told Wenner, "but I don't need to go over the questions with you. That's fifth-grade untrusting bullshit I can do much better *without*. Love, Ben."

Shortly after conducting that interview, Fong-Torres returned to the office to find Wenner and Garfunkel tweaking the article. He also learned that Garfunkel had written a letter to Wenner setting out the terms of use for the interview and Leibovitz's photographs. When

Fong-Torres saw the letter, he wrote to Wenner. "I am of course offended by the whole tone of Garfunkel's letter," Fong-Torres said. He believed that Garfunkel was using his star power and friendship with Wenner to control the rights and permissions for the work. Fong-Torres also expressed regret about his own role. "I am really sorry that I didn't disassociate myself from that interview by removing my byline," he wrote, "and sorrier than ever about the direction Garfunkel was able to take with the 'agreement' with you."

For Fong-Torres, complaints from record companies also came with the territory. In 1974, he received a letter from David Geffen, cofounder of Asylum Records, who objected to Fong-Torres's article about Bob Dylan. "Dear Ben," Geffen wrote. "I have just read your latest bit of bullshit." Geffen claimed that Fong-Torres had joined the ranks of Hollywood gossip columnists Rona Barrett and Joyce Haber as well as paparazzo Ron Galella. "Congratulations," Geffen concluded, "you finally made the small time."

During those years, Fong-Torres became a mentor to Cameron Crowe, the magazine's youngest contributor. At age 13, Crowe began writing reviews for an underground newspaper called the *San Diego Door*, where his sister worked part-time. The owner of a local head shop slipped him an issue of *Rolling Stone*, and Crowe later recalled his reaction.

> I was hooked. I ordered back issues and read interviews with all the important musicians, like David Crosby, who gave their writer Ben Fong-Torres a spectacular unguarded interview. Their regular feature Rolling Stone Interview was my favorite. Even John Lennon sat down for a no-holds-barred conversation. Everybody said "fuck" a lot. Janis Joplin posed nude. *Holy shit.* Reading *Rolling Stone*, I felt older, cooler, and in the know.

By the time he was 14, Crowe was corresponding with Lester Bangs, who also wrote for reviews for the *Door* but was by then editing *Creem* in Detroit. "How could it be that my rock-writing hero was also published in our tiny local give-away paper?" Crowe wondered.

"His rants about the latest records by Iggy Pop or Van Morrison spun dizzily through my head like crazy jazz." Bangs asked him for 1,000 words on Humble Pie and ran it in *Creem.*

Soon after that, Crowe contributed a blurb to *Rolling Stone* based on interviews he had conducted with Kris Kristofferson and followed up with a long feature article about Yes. When Fong-Torres called the house in San Diego, Crowe's sister answered and told Fong-Torres how old her brother was. Fong-Torres added an author's note that said Crowe was "going on 16." When the two next spoke, Fong-Torres laughed and said, "Half the staffers hate you."

While interviewing Dickey Betts for *Rock* magazine that year, Crowe learned how difficult it was for Betts and his colleagues to carry on after Duane Allman's death. Neither Betts nor Gregg Allman had publicly discussed that topic in detail, and Crowe pitched the story to Fong-Torres. The main obstacle was the band's residual hostility over Grover Lewis's profile two years earlier, but Crowe's youth and sincerity worked to his advantage. When Betts and the label's publicist reassured the other musicians, Crowe joined the tour. The cover story ran in December, when Crowe was 16 years old.

Rolling Stone quickly saw the value of making peace not only with the Allman Brothers Band, but also with Led Zeppelin and other groups the magazine had alienated or neglected. "I was aware of that situation, and I wore it like a badge of honor," Crowe later told author Alan Paul. "To me, those bands were as deserving and passionate as the acts that had gotten such great play in *Rolling Stone.* I wanted to put my guys on the team." That remark accurately reflected Crowe's contribution to *Rolling Stone,* but it also indicated a shift in emphasis at the magazine. Its earliest coverage presumed that rock music was animating a social revolution. Later, it featured its own brand of New Journalism, which showcased writers and their sensibilities. Now the emphasis fell heavily on which bands deserved a place in the rock pantheon.

.   .   .   .   .

In the same issue that featured Crowe's first cover story, Wenner interviewed Daniel Ellsberg, who was tried under the Espionage Act for leaking the Pentagon Papers. The charges against Ellsberg and his colleague, Anthony Russo, were dismissed due to what the defense called "the totality of government misconduct, including the suppression of evidence, the invasion of the physician-patient relationship, the illegal wiretapping, the destruction of relevant documents, and the disobedience to judicial orders." The judge decided that declaring a mistrial was inadequate, especially given the series of "bizarre events" that had "incurably infected the prosecution of this case." The same day the judge dismissed the case, U.S. Attorney General John Mitchell was indicted for the crimes he committed during the Watergate scandal. He was convicted and served 19 months in prison.

Like the Hayden interview, the Ellsberg interview was remarkable for its length and substance. As Wenner noted, Ellsberg's remarks were "intricately detailed, with many ideas interwoven and cross-referenced into a dissertation of extraordinary complexity, some 500 typewritten-pages long." As the Watergate scandal continued to unfold, Ellsberg justified his decision to release top-secret files to the public. "We were facing a massive and urgent threat to our remaining democratic institutions, a coup on the eve of its completion," he said. "People who carried out this coup are still in power, starting with the President."

Ellsberg also described his relationship with Henry Kissinger, who served as President Nixon's national security advisor and secretary of state. Ellsberg said he thought Kissinger had "no originality whatsoever as an intellect" and shared Nixon's belief in the use of violence to maintain world order. According to Ellsberg, Kissinger knew as early as 1967 that the only objective in Vietnam should be to create a decent interval before the Communists took over. Nevertheless, Kissinger presided over the massive bombing of Vietnam as well as the destruction of Cambodia and Laos. Ellsberg also thought that Kissinger was the driving force behind many domestic decisions, including the formation of the White House Plumbers. When asked why Kissinger had escaped what Wenner called "the curse of Watergate," Ellsberg credited Kissinger's public relations operation. "So he's pretty immune," Ellsberg said. "And the man who, with his boss, has dropped more bombs than any human being in history, bugging and lying as necessary, is perceived as a peacemaker, as a lovable wit, a charming fellow, as anything but the murderous creep that he obviously is."

Ellsberg's impression of Nixon was similarly negative, but he viewed the Nixon administration as the culmination of a long-term trend that served the nation poorly, especially on matters of war and peace. The greatest evil, Ellsberg thought, was an unnecessary war, and the recipe for it was concentrating power in an unchallenged executive body cloaked in secrecy and mystery. Asked what would happen if President Nixon weren't impeached, Ellsberg claimed that the evidence against him was sufficient for a conviction and that more was coming in every day. For that reason, it was "getting harder and harder to say that we could live with letting the President off and still think of ourselves as a country of laws."

The Ellsberg interview showed once again that *Rolling Stone* was far more than a rock magazine. Indeed, by that time it was a logical outlet for the story Ellsberg wanted to tell.

·   ·   ·   ·   ·

When Thompson's campaign book appeared in 1973, the Watergate scandal was dominating the news. The story began the year before, when five men were arrested for breaking into the offices of the Democratic National Committee in the Watergate complex in Washington. Reporting for *The Washington Post*, Bob Woodward and Carl Bernstein discovered an extensive campaign of political spying and sabotage on behalf of President Nixon's reelection campaign. A Senate investigation, which aired on television that summer, drew a large audience. During his testimony, White House counsel John

Dean revealed that the president's public statements about the scandal were lies. After Nixon lost a legal battle over his tape-recorded White House conversations, the transcripts revealed his direct role in the crimes. They also dramatized the gap between his stiff public persona and brutal political style.

The scandal retroactively justified Thompson's attacks on Nixon and affirmed *Rolling Stone*'s place in the national media ecology. Like all good hyperbole, Thompson's polemic exaggerated his subject's defects not to deceive readers, but rather to make those defects visible to all. With Nixon's resignation, however, Thompson lost the public figure that his biographer described as his muse. Although Thompson's political commentary continued to figure in the national conversation, his subsequent work for *Rolling Stone* rarely matched the intensity of his Nixon screeds.

As the Watergate scandal widened, the magazine's political coverage bulked larger. In 1973, *Rolling Stone* began running articles by Richard Goodwin, a former speechwriter and aide to John F. Kennedy, Lyndon Johnson, and Robert Kennedy. Impressed by Goodwin's insider status and access to the Kennedy family, Wenner asked him to open a Washington bureau. He also offered Goodwin a six-month contract, an expense account, a housing allowance, and a personal loan of $20,000. Goodwin's charge was to edit a new section of the magazine called "Politics," which had its own gossip column, "Capitol Chatter." Wenner considered creating a new spinoff magazine called *Politics*, which would resemble a juiced-up version of *The New Republic*. Goodwin moved from Boston to Washington, but his first stop was Hickory Hill, the Virginia estate where Ethel Kennedy lived with her 11 children. He issued a weekend invitation to Wenner, who was delighted to meet John F. Kennedy Jr. and Caroline Kennedy, the former president's teenage children.

In his memoir, Wenner acknowledged that many *Rolling Stone* editors had grave misgivings about Goodwin, whom they referred to as "Wenner's Folly." Wenner also admitted that he was starstruck by the "President Kennedy magic dust," which Goodwin sprinkled generously on him. Larry Durocher, who replaced Porter Bibb on the magazine's business side, later described that relationship and its effect on the magazine.

> *Rolling Stone* readers would never read Goodwin's political pages. What they wanted to read was cultural politics, the kind of stuff Hunter Thompson and Timmy Crouse wrote. But along came Dick Goodwin, and Jann once again got starfucked. He walked into the room and said in a sense, "What does it cost me to kiss your ass?"

If Wenner was starstruck by Goodwin's connections, he also wanted "every office on the Hill, and every wing in the White House" to read *Rolling Stone.* Toward that end, Goodwin brought in articles by *Washington Post* national reporter William Greider, Robert Shrum, Pat Caddell, and Daniel Yergin. Greider would join *Rolling Stone* in 1982 and contribute more than 200 additional articles.

With Landau's recommendation, Goodwin also hired Joe Klein, the news editor at *The Real Paper* in Boston. Klein turned down other offers, including one from *The Boston Globe,* to write for what he called "*The New Yorker* of my generation." Klein first met Goodwin at Hickory Hill, where he discovered his new boss smoking a cigar in the swimming pool. When Goodwin noticed him, he barked, "Tax reform!" Klein considered that issue negligible compared to the Watergate scandal, but he later expressed his gratitude to Goodwin, both for the sources he acquired during that period and for what he learned about the legislative process.

Goodwin leased expensive office space at 1700 Pennsylvania Avenue, next door to the Executive Office Building. He also sprang for a series of lavish lunches and dinner parties, some of which Wenner attended. According to Klein, Goodwin "was skinning Jann for all he could get." Others were more concerned about Goodwin's prose style, which was out of place at *Rolling Stone.* Wenner later conceded the point even as he plumped Goodwin's output. "Dick had written three brilliant essays for us already; his style was elegant, and it was academic, and it suited the lessons of American political history he was trying to explain," Wenner wrote. "It didn't resonate with our readers." That was giving Goodwin the best of it. When the magazine polled its readers, it found that Thompson and Fong-Torres were the most popular contributors, whereas Goodwin finished dead last.

Goodwin arranged an informal colloquium at his Georgetown home, invited foreign policy experts, and fielded their story ideas. Wenner, who also attended, met with Klein the next day and asked for his impressions of the previous evening. Klein replied that he didn't think the story ideas would work for *Rolling Stone*. Wenner agreed and then fired Klein, explaining that he needed to send a message to Goodwin. It was another example, Klein said, of what he called Wenner's "painful honesty." A crestfallen Klein returned to Boston, and Wenner later opted not to renew Goodwin's contract. "He had done an impressive job editing the Politics section," Wenner recalled, "but I decided not to evolve that section into a national magazine for Dick to edit." As a parting gift, Goodwin left a slew of unpaid bills and kill fees. He also purloined both a *Rolling Stone* tape recorder and bedsheets from Hickory Hill. A furious Wenner considered suing Goodwin before opting for what he called the "good karma" of letting it slide.

After Goodwin's departure in 1974, Klein returned to *Rolling Stone* as the DC bureau chief and stayed on as a contributing editor until 1980. His only music story featured Arlo Guthrie, but that article led to his first book project, a well-received biography of Woody Guthrie. When it came to political coverage, Klein noted the gap between Wenner's outlook and his own. Whereas he understood politics as a process, Wenner was drawn to its star power. "When Jann said politics was the rock and roll of the 70s," Klein said, "it was clear he thought of politicians as rock stars." Later, Klein said Wenner "was disappointed that I wasn't a starfucker." Nevertheless, Klein was grateful for his time at *Rolling Stone*, which he described as a reportorial magazine. "It wasn't an opinion magazine, though you could express your opinion," he said. More important, he could report without fear or favor and tell the truth as he understood it. Klein went on to write for *Newsweek*, *New York*, *The New Yorker*, and *Time*, but only his Substack column, he later noted, afforded him the same sense of freedom that he enjoyed at *Rolling Stone*.

.   .   .   .   .

In the years after Ellen Willis's 1970 letter to Ralph Gleason, the magazine took modest but measurable steps to hire more women. Robin Green appeared on the masthead as a contributing editor, and Ben Fong-Torres recommended Judith Sims to serve as *Rolling Stone*'s Los Angeles bureau chief. From 1966 to 1969, Sims edited *TeenSet* magazine, where she covered rock groups from a fan's perspective and ran articles by Fong-Torres and music critic John Mendelsohn. The magazine also featured 250 photographs by Jim Marshall, including many from the Monterey Pop Festival, where Marshall was on assignment with *TeenSet*. Founded before *Crawdaddy* and *Rolling Stone*, the magazine played a largely unrecognized role in the history of rock journalism and photography. After struggling to attract advertisers, however, *TeenSet* shut down in 1969. Three years later, Sims joined *Rolling Stone*, where she contributed almost 80 articles over the next four years.

While female journalists remained heavily outnumbered at *Rolling Stone*, female staffers were busily contending with the office's male culture. "There was a sign over Jann's secretary's desk in huge letters: 'Boys' Club,'" said Barbara Downey, a proofreader who later married Jon Landau. "I'll never forget that." Christine Doudna, who started as an editorial assistant, acknowledged that *Rolling Stone* was "a guy's magazine," adding that it had "a very male sensibility, always." Sarah Lazin, who also started as an editorial assistant, added that the office remained "a rollicking male culture, spearheaded by Hunter and Hunter wannabes." Given the magazine's readership, Robin Green said later, a preponderance of male writers was predictable. Even so, women were making major editorial contributions at *Creem, The Village Voice,* and other outlets.

In October 1973, Wenner hired John Walsh as managing editor and asked him to professionalize the magazine. Walsh, the former sports editor at *Newsday,* quickly determined that the magazine needed a copy and research department. One candidate for copy chief, Marianne Partridge, had worked for *Time, Forbes, The New York Times,* and the McGovern campaign. Having cold-called the magazine, she assured Walsh she could form the copy department. Later, she admitted she knew nothing about copyediting apart from what she observed at other outlets. Nevertheless, Partridge thought Walsh was amiable and welcoming, and she was impressed by the magazine's female staffers. Walsh offered her the position in January 1974, urged her to hire from inside, and added that female staffers might qualify for the newly created jobs.

Doudna recalled the changes following Partridge's arrival: "Marianne just talked to each of us and asked, 'Do you want to train to be an editor or fact-checker or proofreader?' We all just leapt at the chance. . . . She trained us all." Harriet Fier, a Smith College graduate whose first job at the magazine was answering telephones at night, rose quickly through the ranks. "She helped lead a remarkable women's editorial takeover at the magazine," recalled Felton. "Fier was key in convincing [Wenner] to trust and empower his young female staff."

Doudna identified Partridge as the key to their advancement but also credited Wenner. "It's sort of amazing that we were able to do what we did, and that Jann supported us," she said. "Marianne was one of the first women who really gained his trust. He was so dependent on her." Some writers resisted the new department's copyediting and fact-checking, but the work went more smoothly after Wenner read an unedited submission. "What is this shit?" he asked Partridge. "This is the shit we get all the time," she replied. "What do you think we're doing over there? Getting manicures?"

Less than a year later, Partridge was promoted to senior editor, the first woman to hold that position at *Rolling Stone*. Wenner later said she wasn't as attuned to the magazine's culture and mission as some editors were, but she was supple enough to adapt. After accepting the job, Partridge contacted Ellen Willis, whom she knew socially. There had been little explicit coverage of rape, Partridge reminded Willis. The word *rape* was never used in print, and prosecutors found it difficult to secure convictions in those cases. Willis took Partridge's point and found a case in Boston to write about. Partridge knew the topic was groundbreaking, and she later said she wanted to break that ground. *Rolling Stone* was a trailblazer in many ways, but not when it came to women's issues. She wanted to change that and also make a statement to her male colleagues.

Partridge decided to present Willis's project at her first story-idea meeting, where she was the only woman in the room.

> I was sitting next to Jann, and I started to talk and I realized my hands were shaking so bad, I put them in my lap. At the far end of the table, Eszterhas says, "Why don't you just lie back and enjoy it?!" and everybody laughed. I was looking at Jann, and he was the only person at the table that didn't laugh. He was nodding his head, like please continue. I got through, and he said, "That sounds great. How long do you think that's going to take? O.K., four months. It's going to run then." Who knows why Jann did that, but he didn't laugh, and I don't care why.

Rolling Stone ran Willis's "Rape on Trial" in August 1975. After it appeared, Willis encountered William Shawn, editor at *The New Yorker*, who said he admired the piece but "could never run something like that." Willis left *The New Yorker* shortly after that exchange, and over the next three years, she published 22 more articles at *Rolling Stone*.

When Partridge was offered an editorial position at *The Village Voice*, Willis implored her to stay. There were plenty of people like Partridge at the *Voice*, Willis maintained, but not nearly enough women like her at *Rolling Stone*. Partridge wasn't unhappy at *Rolling*

Stone—indeed, she admired Wenner and worked well with him—but the magazine and counterculture had entered a new phase. "The times had changed," Partridge said later. "The drugs had changed. I wasn't into drugs. I mean, let's not lose our minds, I smoked a little pot, but I never did coke." Rock music had also changed, Partridge said. As the 1970s wore on, its stars had less in common with their audiences, and their output was rarely mistaken for important social commentary.

By the time Partridge decamped for *The Village Voice* in the summer of 1976, more women were working in *Rolling Stone*'s editorial department, but female journalists were still rare. "The single highest priority must be to find competent women critics, which is my and the rock press in general's biggest failing," Jon Landau told Wenner privately. "Ellen Willis remains the only one with a significant reputation, although she writes so much better about other subjects."

The media ecology was also shifting. The extraordinary success of *People* magazine, which appeared in 1974, tapped a strong demand for celebrity journalism. "Our focus is on people, not issues," publisher Richard Stolley stated in the first issue. Inheriting most of its staff from *Life* magazine, which folded the previous year, *People* quickly reached millions of readers and attracted substantial advertising. Many *Rolling Stone* staffers scorned celebrity journalism, but Wenner understood its appeal. Ironically, the magazine's top writer was now a celebrity himself. Hunter S. Thompson was the subject of a high-profile *Playboy* interview in 1974, the same year cartoonist Garry Trudeau introduced a character based on Thompson (and Raoul Duke) in his award-winning *Doonesbury* strip. Thompson hated the cartoon character, but *Doonesbury* kept Thompson in the public eye long after his output began to decline.

Oscar Acosta never experienced that level of celebrity. He was last heard from in May 1974, when he called his son from Mazatlán and said he was "about to board a boat of white snow." A private investigator concluded that Acosta's disappearance was probably a political assassination or murder at the hands of drug dealers. In 1977, *Rolling Stone* ran Thompson's elegy for Acosta. "The Banshee Screams for Buffalo Meat" was a long piece, even by Thompson's standards. "Oscar was one of God's own prototypes—a high-powered mutant of some kind who was never even considered for mass production," Thompson wrote. "He was too weird to live, and too rare to die." The article reflected an important fact: Acosta contributed directly to "Strange Rumblings in Aztlan," one of Thompson's most significant works of journalism, as well as *Fear and Loathing in Las Vegas*, his famous comic novel. By doing so, Acosta also helped reinvent *Rolling Stone*.

11   After the Revolution

Shortly after President Nixon's resignation, Jann Wenner directed managing editor John Walsh to devote an entire issue to that historic event. Hunter S. Thompson, Wenner added, should write the cover story. Thompson failed to produce, but the staff pulled together copy and photos from back issues, and David Felton coined the title. "The Quitter" was well received, but Wenner later concluded that Walsh didn't have the editorial or cultural touch that his job required. When he fired Walsh after eight months on the job, he credited Walsh for his contributions. "On the professional side," Wenner wrote, "I want to commend you for setting up our first copy desk and research operation, for bringing in two first-rate editors, polishing up the weak spots that existed when you came, and managing *Rolling Stone*'s wild-eyed bunch."

Walsh's departure prompted an article by Alexander Cockburn, the press critic at *The Village Voice*. The son of a leftist journalist, Cockburn graduated from Oxford University and worked for several British publications before moving to the United States in 1972.

Along the way, he developed a knack for pointed correspondence. Wenner wrote to Cockburn, questioning the accuracy of his story and noting that Cockburn had failed to contact him prior to running it. Cockburn fired off a saucy rejoinder.

> Re your pompous letter: if you have a real complaint, why don't you send it for publication in the normal way? You say, "It is possible and indeed probable that the conclusions you have drawn are unwarranted and unsupportable . . ." Well, are they or aren't they?

Cockburn then addressed Wenner's claim that he hadn't been contacted.

> So far as calling you is concerned: between the time I started on that story and deadline—a matter of some five hours—I made every effort to call you, both at *Rolling Stone* and the number I have for your home. I left messages—none of which you seem to have bothered to return, even the next day. So stop telling me what "it behooves me" to do.

Cockburn closed his letter with advice for Wenner. "By and large you have had a pretty good deal from the press," he wrote, "so I think it behooves you, Wenner old chap, to get off your high horse when the salt gets into those sweet winds you're accustomed to sniffing." Cockburn's tart letter didn't prevent him from writing seven articles for *Rolling Stone* in the 1980s, all of them coauthored by investigative reporter James Ridgeway.

Wenner replaced Walsh with Paul Scanlon, who had embraced the magazine's growing reputation for long-form journalism. In a 1973 television documentary, he outlined the magazine's appeal to working journalists.

> I can speak for editorial, the people that are here have come here because they wanted to be here, because they were sick of the newspaper game, myself included. They were looking for an area of creativity in the print media, which is very hard, if not impossible, to find anymore. And *Rolling Stone* is one of the frankly few places where you

can find where you have the unlimited ability to write what you want to write professionally, with high professional standards, keeping with the libel laws. You're not going to be shackled by some idiot publisher, who says you can't write this because you're going to upset X advertiser, or you can't say this because you're going to upset the sensibilities of someone in Oshkosh, Wisconsin, or something like that.

Later, Wenner credited Scanlon's stint as managing editor. "I had found someone with the same sensibilities and standards I had, with a greater knowledge of reporting and writing, great taste, and, as far as I could tell, someone who wasn't particularly bothered by my ego," Wenner wrote. "Paul became my right-hand man through the next five years, what came to be called 'The Golden Age of Rolling Stone.'"

Wenner hired Chet Flippo as the New York bureau chief in 1974. Before that, Flippo covered Timothy Leary's trial in Texas and wrote about country music, blues, bluegrass, and Austin's lively music scene. Flippo's articles about Willie Nelson, Waylon Jennings, Kris Kristofferson, Roy Orbison, Freddie King, Kinky Friedman, Doug Sahm, Doc Watson, Leon Russell, and Dolly Parton helped those artists reach new audiences and added another dimension to the magazine. In 1974, Flippo also completed an astute master's thesis at the University of Texas on the origins of *Rolling Stone*, where he would eventually place over 200 articles.

Change was underway on the business side as well. In 1973, the same year Mike Salisbury redesigned the magazine, Wenner hired Joe Armstrong as its advertising director. His predecessor, Laurel Gonsalves, collected ads from the music labels, landed several stereo and apparel accounts, and persuaded Wenner not to accept ads from cigarette companies or the U.S. Army. A native Texan based in New York, Armstrong had a different ambition. He wanted the car, liquor, and cigarette ads that padded the upscale magazines and their profits. Moreover, he wanted to address the mismatch between mainstream advertising firms and the magazine's countercultural reputation. Armstrong hired a new sales staff and chipped away at Madison Avenue's indifference to *Rolling Stone*. On his watch, ad sales jumped 50 percent in 1974, then another 50 percent in 1975. Wenner rewarded Armstrong by naming him publisher, the position previously held by Porter Bibb and Larry Durocher. Armstrong's success in those roles moved the magazine's center of gravity toward New York.

·   ·   ·   ·   ·

In December 1974, *Rolling Stone* ran Tom Hayden's profile of Jerry Brown, who was elected governor of California the month before. The fourth and lengthiest contribution from Hayden that year, "The Mystic and the Machine" figured Brown as an important part of a national political realignment. Flying around California with Brown in the final days of the campaign, Hayden felt the campaign's surging energy. Delivered in Fresno, Brown's stump speech received cheers from Chicanos waving *Huelga* flags, which the United Farm Workers carried during their labor strikes. Unlike his father, former governor Pat Brown, Jerry Brown had marched with Cesar Chavez in support of farmworkers. Hayden's report documented Brown's victory over GOP candidate Houston Flournoy, but it also imagined a reformed Democratic Party, one that might have room for someone like Hayden.

The next month, Wenner received a note from Ralph Gleason: "Janno—Just finished reading the manuscript of Greil's book, and it's a gas. It's going to be an important book. I think it's the most important book on rock yet written, and RS ought to grab some of it a.s.a.p. Have you read it?" Wenner scribbled his reply on Gleason's letter: "No. But I saw Greil, who continues his active distaste for RS, which inspires a similar feeling in me toward him." Gleason typed his rejoinder on the same letter: "Ah, you don't have to dig *him*. It would be good for RS to print some of it. Be BIG."

Wenner never ran an excerpt of *Mystery Train* in *Rolling Stone*, but Gleason reviewed it glowingly in the *San Francisco Chronicle*. *Mystery Train* was about rock and roll, but it also sought to portray "the American character and the American soul in this time," Gleason wrote. "As such, it is the best thing I have read in ages." Jon Landau also touted *Mystery Train* to Wenner, and in his review for the magazine, he described the book as dazzling and original. Although he faulted Marcus for his promiscuous theorizing and arbitrary musical judgments, he credited his intellectual imagination and knack for connecting disparate phenomena. Soon after that, Wenner invited Marcus to rejoin the magazine. Marcus asked for a full-page book column in every other issue, but when Wenner countered with two-thirds of a page in every issue, Marcus happily accepted.

. . . . .

During this time, Wenner was also focusing on *Rolling Stone*'s youngest contributor. "I just finished reading the galleys of the Joe Walsh piece," Wenner wrote to Cameron Crowe in 1975, "and I thought you turned out a most professional and well written profile." Wenner told Crowe he was generally pleased with his progress and the maturity of his writing. When Crowe submitted a Led Zeppelin piece, Wenner wrote to him again: "I'd like you to come up for a visit. Who knows, you may turn out to be the youngest *Rolling Stone* man ever." Despite the compliments, Crowe suspected he was in trouble. "What wafted back to me was that Jann thought it was a puff piece," Crowe said. In fact, Tim Cahill expressed that exact opinion. Acknowledging that the reader feedback was highly favorable, Cahill described the interview as "soft, slushy, and sycophantic."

The day Crowe flew to San Francisco, Gleason suffered a massive heart attack. The news shattered Wenner, but he kept his appointment with Crowe. As he offered his advice to the teenage journalist, Wenner felt as if he were channeling the hospitalized Gleason. "If you want to be a *real* writer, you've got to read real writing," he told Crowe. He disappeared into a back room and returned with a well-thumbed copy of Joan Didion's *Slouching Towards Bethlehem*. "Read this book. The whole book. It's going to inspire you. Take my copy.

Return it when you're done," he told Crowe. "Read the [Jim] Morrison piece. It's the best profile of the band ever written, and she's already nailed it before Morrison even enters the room." In his 2025 memoir, Crowe admitted that he still hadn't returned the book.

Years later, the magazine's chroniclers hailed Crowe's contributions. "Had it not been for the discovery of a teenaged southern Californian named Cameron Crowe," Robert Draper wrote, "*Rolling Stone* might have trundled through the seventies like a blind man in a wheelchair." Abe Peck, the former *Chicago Seed* editor who was then working at *Rolling Stone*, said that many senior writers were unmoved by the rock music of those years, but that Crowe embraced it.

> And then here's Cameron, reacting the same way that everyone from Jann on did in 1967. This is his first flush of rock and roll. He's the guy that's getting a kick out of the dressing room experience, a kick out of dangling groupies out the window, and a kick out of the music in a way that thirty-year-olds weren't.

Crowe's affability was another asset. "Cameron possessed the ability to make people root for him," Peck said.

Shortly after Crowe's visit to San Francisco, Ralph Gleason died in a Berkeley hospital at age 58. He hadn't been a major presence at the magazine for years, but Wenner and the staff assembled a tribute issue that included praise from Duke Ellington, Dizzy Gillespie, Frank Sinatra, Miles Davis, Jerry Garcia, Marty Balin, and John Lennon. Tributes also came in from Nelson Algren, Studs Terkel, Lawrence Ferlinghetti, Luria Castell, and Ken Kesey. Mary Ann Pollar, who founded the Rainbow Sign, an African American cultural center in Berkeley, wrote that Gleason "spoke for black people for so many years in places we were not allowed to speak for ourselves, and he told the truth." The issue reflected Gleason's immense contribution, both in the magazine's pages and behind the scenes. The role of mentor now fell to the 29-year-old Wenner.

·   ·   ·   ·   ·

Two months after Gleason's death, *Ramparts* magazine published its final issue. Much had changed since Warren Hinckle ran the hippie story that enraged Gleason. Circulation had plunged, sympathetic millionaires were no longer willing to cover the magazine's losses, and David Horowitz and Peter Collier were writing a book about the Rockefeller dynasty.

In contrast, *Rolling Stone* was thriving. The total readership averaged two million, and net paid circulation stood at 417,000, higher than that of *New York* magazine and similar to the numbers at *Harper's*, *The Atlantic Monthly*, and *The New Yorker*. An internal memo that year explained the magazine's success to itself. It described *Rolling Stone* as a "biweekly, general-interest magazine covering contemporary American culture, politics, and arts with a special interest in music." Rock music, the memo maintained, expressed a less repressed attitude toward sex and pleasure, and as American society opened up, the magazine expanded its coverage to include film, books, and television. In 1971, when the voting age dropped to 18, it also began covering politics and national affairs full-time. The memo credited the magazine for stimulating an interest in politics among its readership.

The memo also claimed that *Rolling Stone* covered stories the straight press missed, including the Altamont debacle, the Manson Family saga, the drug culture, and West Coast stories more generally. Moreover, *Rolling Stone* capitalized on youthful distrust of the "Eastern Establishment Press" and its so-called objective perspective. "This distrust," the memo stated, "comes mainly from the way young people have seen themselves portrayed by the media as a group." *Rolling Stone* differed from the eastern establishment press in several ways. It favored New Journalism, gave writers freedom and space, and dismissed claims about objectivity as "semantic bullshit." At the same time, the memo insisted, *Rolling Stone* writers were fanatics about factual accuracy, and editors held them to the highest standards. "A lot of our success has to do with the honesty our readers perceive in *Rolling Stone*," the memo concluded. "We tell the truth." It was a savvy if self-serving assessment of the magazine's strengths, but one idea was conspicuous by its absence. At no point did the memo mention the political consequences of the rock revolution, which the magazine's founders once claimed were inevitable.

For all its success, *Rolling Stone* still faced significant challenges, some of which were related to a downturn in the record business. Album sales had softened, and the major labels were signing fewer groups and offering lower advances. To maintain his magazine's edge, Wenner commissioned a study to determine which covers boosted or depressed newsstand sales. The study concluded that covers should feature major stars, not necessarily musicians, preferably those with sexual charisma. The study also indicated that the quality of a star's work was secondary. Wenner took those findings to heart. As Tim Crouse said later, "The fatal discovery on Jann's part was that movie stars sold more of the magazines when they were on the cover than anybody else."

Even when it focused on musicians, *Rolling Stone* wasn't discovering talent so much as ratifying it. The record industry read that pattern as a sign of the magazine's declining taste. "They have moved, shall we say, from being the boutique of the music industry to being the supermarket," one record executive said. That change wasn't lost on Greil Marcus. "That's the period where *Rolling Stone* really does turn into a promotional vehicle," Marcus said later. "Whether it's promoting a rock-and-roll performer, or a TV performer, or a movie star." Negative album reviews, which Marcus once regarded as a sign of the magazine's integrity, were more likely to be seen as problematic. Indeed, Wenner temporarily banished Lester Bangs—who called 1972 "one of the stalest years in the history of popular music"—precisely for his negative reviews.

Although Bangs panned *Greetings from Asbury Park* (1973), Bruce Springsteen's arrival gave Jon Landau hope. Landau later admitted that he turned to film criticism in part because he found so many rock acts tiresome. In 1974, however, a Springsteen show he attended changed his outlook. "Last Thursday, at the Harvard

Square Theatre, I saw my rock-and-roll past flash before my eyes," he wrote in *The Real Paper*. "And I saw something else: I saw rock-and-roll future, and its name is Bruce Springsteen. And on a night when I needed to feel young, he made me feel like I was hearing music for the very first time." Landau marveled at Springsteen's skill: "He leads a band like he has been doing it forever. I racked my brains but simply can't think of a white artist who does so many things so superbly." The following year, Landau coproduced *Born to Run* (1975) and became Springsteen's manager.

Landau's editor at *The Real Paper*, Dave Marsh, also saw Springsteen's show. Marsh had written for *Creem* and *Newsday* before joining the Boston alternative weekly. Like Landau, Marsh hitched his wagon to Springsteen's star. He eventually wrote four books about Springsteen, and his wife became Landau's partner in the talent management business. In 1975, Marsh accepted a position at *Rolling Stone*, where he eventually wrote hundreds of reviews, columns, and feature stories. He also coedited two important reference works for the magazine's imprint: *The Rolling Stone Record Guide* (1979) and *The Book of Rock Lists* (1981).

· · · · ·

Even as *Rolling Stone* evolved, it maintained its niche in the media ecology. As Abe Peck observed, the magazine was hipper than anything better and better than anything hipper. The book division, however, was on the chopping block. Between 1970 and 1975, Straight Arrow Books had published the Lennon and Garcia interviews, Thompson's campaign volume, Acosta's two books, and a volume of rock photography edited by Annie Leibovitz. Other titles included Ann Charters's biography of Jack Kerouac, Kenneth Anger's *Hollywood Babylon*, Joe Eszterhas's *Nark!*, anthologies by Jon Landau and Jonathan Cott, *The Smokestack El Ropo Bedside Reader*, and a global energy manifesto by Stewart Brand. *The Connoisseur's Handbook of Marijuana* and *The Art of Sensual Massage* were especially popular, but Wenner saw little reason to continue the book operation. It wasn't losing money, he told Rinzler, but its profit margin depended on free office space and other services provided by the magazine.

Although Rinzler worked well with Wenner, he occasionally took issue with decisions that affected the book division. In 1972, Wenner asserted that he alone had final approval on all covers and interior designs. He needed that creative control, Wenner explained, because the books also represented the magazine to the public. Rinzler challenged that prerogative.

> On Straight Arrow Books, I cannot accept your unilateral decrees on jacket or interior design. Your opinion is respected and welcome, as I hope mine is on all matters of *Rolling Stone* content and design. But, as with all Straight Arrow Books ... these matters must be determined by mutual agreement. Book publishing is not like magazine publishing. It involves not only the publisher and the designer but the author himself and cannot be subject to this kind of unilateral approval.

Rinzler also chided Wenner for the way he handled Hunter S. Thompson during the 1972 presidential campaign. "Your note to Hunter re: his personal expenses is ill-advised and contrary to our agreement," he told Wenner. "To wit, we agreed to leave him alone until he's done. For obvious reasons. Now you've hit on him for a crummy $363.39. If this freaks him, you're responsible. And listen: your end runs around our careful plans are tiresome as usual . . ."

The decision to shut down Straight Arrow Books surprised Thompson, who was counting on a healthy advance for the 1976 sequel to his campaign book. "I am immensely fucking pissed off about that vicious sandbag job you laid on me vis-a-vis the C-76 book contract," he wrote to Wenner in March 1975. The news about the book division, which Wenner mentioned only after a pleasant and productive visit to Woody Creek, "drove a stake through the heart of the whole relationship," Thompson added. He charged

Wenner with laying "a near-perfect con job" on him while "wallowing in an atmosphere of friendliness and hospitality that might be hard to revive on your next visit." Like many of Thompson's communications with Wenner, the letter was meant to secure an even better deal with *Rolling Stone*, but Thompson seemed genuinely put out that Straight Arrow Books was shuttered and that Wenner didn't inform him earlier.

Meanwhile, Rinzler was assembling an anthology of Thompson's work for publication. Wenner told Rinzler he would receive his final check when the anthology was complete, prompting an angry response. "There has never been any 'verbal understanding' that my final check was to be contingent on the completion of Hunter's anthology," Rinzler said, "nor has there been any conversation whatsoever between us connecting those two disparate events. This is a preposterous, complete, and utter lie, as you know, and I will be happy to so testify under sworn oath in a court of law." Rinzler added, "It's sad to see how little you have learned about dealing with people on a human level." Rinzler and Wenner parted on bad terms, and Simon & Schuster eventually published the Thompson anthology as *The Great Shark Hunt* in 1979.

Despite closing Straight Arrow Books, Wenner continued to sponsor a steady stream of book titles. In 1975, he signed several book deals with Random House, one of which led to *The Rolling Stone Illustrated History of Rock & Roll* (1976). The oversized volume was edited by Jim Miller, who had contributed scores of record reviews to the magazine. Raised in an academic family in Chicago, Miller grew up listening to the blues and reading *DownBeat, Sing Out!, The Little Sandy Review*, and *The Realist*. As an undergraduate at Pomona College, he scoured the magazine racks and noticed *Rolling Stone* when it first appeared. Responding to a house ad soliciting reviews, he contributed his first article in February 1968. That summer, he returned to Chicago and demonstrated outside the Democratic National Convention. The following year, he attended SDS's final conferences in Flint, Michigan. There was talk about a staff position for Miller at *Rolling Stone* if his graduate school plans went awry, but he earned a PhD in the history of ideas at Brandeis. He also wrote for *The Real Paper* in Boston, where he met Jon Landau and succeeded Dave Marsh as music editor.

The book project Miller inherited had a backstory. Wenner and Jerry Wexler assembled the pitch and were originally slated to coauthor the book. Wexler would write about the 1950s, and Wenner would focus on the 1960s. When their other responsibilities made that plan impractical, Wenner approached Jon Landau and Greil Marcus, both of whom declined to edit the volume and recommended Miller without his knowledge. Miller accepted the invitation to develop the project, but he rewrote the outline extensively. His plan was to ask top critics to deliver chapters on specific artists, groups, genres, and regions. When Miller received all the draft chapters, he flew to San Francisco, settled in at Marcus's house, and worked closely with Sarah Lazin at the office. As the magazine's fact-checker, Lazin was familiar with the dearth of reliable sources on rock history. "If we're going to do this, it should be fact-checked," she told Wenner. "If we're going to be the source, then it has to be accurate." Shortly after that, Lazin found herself managing not only the illustrated history, but also *Rolling Stone*'s other book projects.

The final manuscript for Miller's volume included essays by Ellen Willis, Peter Guralnick, Langdon Winner, Robert Christgau, Jonathan Cott, John Morthland, Ed Ward, Greil Marcus, Jon Landau, Paul Nelson, and Charles Perry. Their chapters situated rock and roll in a tangle of vernacular musical traditions, most of them rooted in the South and dominated by black performers. The photographs, which Robert Kingsbury arranged for maximum effect, highlighted the importance of those artists. Many were publicity shots that photographer and Columbia Records publicist Michael Ochs acquired from the labels at little or no cost. According to Miller, Wenner seemed to have little confidence in his judgment. Wenner wondered, for example, why Miller included essays on Jackie Wilson and Sam Cooke but neglected Simon & Garfunkel.

Marcus, who served as a consultant on the project, later told Miller that Wenner almost fired him midway through the project.

The Rolling Stone Illustrated History of Rock & Roll was a critical and commercial success, selling more than 100,000 copies and producing two more editions. Later, Lazin reflected on its significance.

> Growing up in the 50s and 60s and having no one take music seriously at all—it's just something for the kids, right?—there was no history. You can't imagine how revolutionary *The Rolling Stone Illustrated History of Rock & Roll* was. The idea of having a chapter on New Orleans music, a chapter on Stax Records, and then a chapter on Chuck Berry, just starting to pinpoint who was important by creating a history.

In his introduction, Miller considered rock's early appeal and present status. "At the outset," Miller wrote, "rock and roll was a *succès de scandale*, an outrage to an older generation's aesthetic and sexual tastes." By 1976, however, rock music was "first and foremost a member in good standing of the American entertainment industry, welcome in Las Vegas and Hollywood, on the screen and over the air, in homes and theaters." Rock gossip sold newspapers, rock concerts packed stadiums, and rock records dominated the radio. Meanwhile, predictions about the music's social and political consequences had "died a quiet death."

. . . . .

Rolling Stone's original thesis, it seemed, was a dead letter. No single idea would replace the notion that rock music was animating a social revolution. Instead, several long-standing concerns came to the fore. One was a growing interest in rock history, especially questions of influence and who belonged in the rock pantheon. That concern drove the success of *The Rolling Stone Illustrated History of Rock & Roll* and prefigured the Rock & Roll Hall of Fame, which the magazine was already constructing in the public imagination. In 1983,

Ahmet Ertegun established the hall of fame's foundation, whose board of directors included Wenner, and the museum opened in 1995.

A related editorial theme was the ratification of talent, which became especially prominent after the magazine's move to New York. Edited by Dave Marsh and John Swenson, *The Rolling Stone Record Guide* (1979) used a five-star system to rate almost 10,000 albums. It became an indispensable source for aficionados, and the magazine switched to that rating system two years later. *The Book of Rock Lists,* edited by Marsh and Kevin Stein, appeared in 1981. The magazine noticed that such lists were a good way to generate reader engagement with little effort or expense.

A growing emphasis on celebrity was also plain even before the move to New York. The Haight-Ashbury days—when rock musicians lived, shopped, and ate with their fans—were over. Now the magazine invited fans to glorify superstars whose lives bore little resemblance to their own. Advertisers had long known that selling aspiration was a winning strategy, but as art critic John Berger later maintained, that technique robbed viewers of their self-respect and sold it back to them for the price of the product. To the extent that *Rolling Stone* invited readers to participate vicariously in a rock-star lifestyle that lay beyond their grasp, it downplayed the counterculture's emphasis on authenticity and community. Many longtime contributors lamented the turn toward celebrity coverage, but the appetite for it was undeniable.

The magazine's editorial mix was changing in other ways as well. With the emergence of New Hollywood, Wenner began beefing up the magazine's film coverage. That movement's point of origin is often traced to *Easy Rider* (1969), which flaunted its countercultural credentials and became one of the highest-grossing films of the year. By that time, weekly movie attendance had dropped to a postwar low, but the major studios were still churning out expensive musicals, big-budget epics, and formulaic genre pictures. Awakened from their slumber by *Easy Rider*'s success, veteran studio heads wondered how to reach younger audiences with little interest in *Hello*

Dolly! or *Doctor Dolittle.* The expensive and time-consuming nature of filmmaking made it harder for the industry to adapt quickly. "Hollywood is always the last to know, the slowest to respond," film historian Peter Biskind claimed, "and in those years it was at least half a decade behind the other popular arts."

Out of desperation, studio executives empowered a new generation of directors, many of whom were recent film-school graduates. Over the next several years, Steven Spielberg, Francis Coppola, George Lucas, Martin Scorsese, Roman Polanski, Peter Bogdanovich, Hal Ashby, Brian De Palma, and Robert Altman fashioned some of their signature works. Not everyone celebrated the industry's youth movement. Director Billy Wilder, for example, dismissed the new directors as "the bearded horde." But their films revived the industry and enhanced its artistic and intellectual cachet. Writer and critic Susan Sontag noted that "going to movies, thinking about movies, talking about movies became a passion among university students and other young people. You fell in love not just with actors but with cinema itself."

Rolling Stone had published film reviews from its inception, but now it started running cover stories, profiles, and interviews with actors and directors. Robin Green's 1971 piece about Dennis Hopper, who directed *Easy Rider*, was one of her most significant contributions to the magazine. When *Paper Moon* was released in 1973, nine-year-old Tatum O'Neal appeared on the magazine's cover and later earned an Oscar for her performance. Not all the magazine's film coverage focused on New Hollywood. Grover Lewis profiled veteran actors and directors, including Paul Newman, Lee Marvin, Robert Mitchum, John Huston, and Sam Peckinpah. Foreign films were also grist for the magazine's mill. Jonathan Cott interviewed Bernardo Bertolucci, director of *Last Tango in Paris* (1972), and the magazine reviewed films by Luis Buñuel, Federico Fellini, and François Truffaut.

Some of *Rolling Stone*'s own reporting spawned critically acclaimed films that extended and deepened its cultural influence. Those films included *Silkwood* (1983), *The Right Stuff* (1983), *Born on the Fourth of July* (1989), and *Fear and Loathing in Las Vegas* (1998). Other efforts were less successful. *Where the Buffalo Roam* (1980) was a loose adaptation of Hunter S. Thompson's Gonzo journalism and persona, and though Thompson credited Bill Murray's performance, he dismissed the film as a "horrible pile of crap."

Alert to the connection between magazine stories and Hollywood film properties, Wenner later arranged a deal with Paramount Pictures to deliver original screenplays. One was *Key West*, a drug-smuggling caper written by Thompson. Another was Ben Fong-Torres's *Somebody to Love*, which featured a rock star who resembled Janis Joplin. None of the screenplays made it out of development. Wenner also hoped to land a script by Cameron Crowe, who adapted his 1981 book, *Fast Times at Ridgemont High*, for the screen. That project went to Universal, however, and launched Crowe's Hollywood career. *Almost Famous* (2000) was the only film written and directed by Crowe that drew directly on his experience at *Rolling Stone*. Set in the early 1970s, the coming-of-age comedy featured a teenage journalist who covers a rock tour for the magazine. With Terry Chen as Ben Fong-Torres and Philip Seymour Hoffman as Lester Bangs, the winsome period film received four Oscar nominations and won the award for Best Original Screenplay.

.   .   .   .   .

Crime stories also became a more important part of *Rolling Stone*'s editorial formula. From the outset, the magazine covered drug busts and the dope trade, but the Altamont and Manson pieces were major triumphs, and much of Joe Eszterhas's output hinged on crime. If such reports were the archetypal news story, as media scholar Todd Gitlin once asserted, two blockbuster stories during this period showed that the magazine was carving out a place in that tradition. Both stories involved Howard Kohn, who had written about the heroin racket and official corruption for the *Detroit Free Press*. After leaving the newspaper amid controversy, Kohn drove from Michigan to San Francisco to join forces with David Weir, whom he met at the University of Michigan campus newspaper. Weir, who was also Kohn's brother-in-law, was an editor at *SunDance* magazine, which also listed Kohn on its masthead. When that magazine folded after three issues, Weir and Kohn formed *Sun* magazine, a countercultural version of *Parade,* the newspaper insert that reached 50 million readers every Sunday. They hoped it would appear in college newspapers across the country, but it folded after a single issue.

While Kohn and his wife were honeymooning in Marin County, he saw a bulletin about the death of Karen Silkwood, a lab technician at the Kerr–McGee plutonium plant in Oklahoma. Silkwood had agreed to collect evidence of unsafe and illegal practices at the plant, but the week before she was scheduled to deliver that evidence to her union, she and her apartment were contaminated with plutonium that was traced to her workplace. Soon after her release from the hospital, Silkwood was delivering the evidence to a union official and a *New York Times* reporter when she died in a single-vehicle car accident.

Kohn wanted to follow up on the Silkwood story immediately. He cut short his honeymoon, drove to the *Rolling Stone* office, and began pitching the story to David Felton. Felton cut him off, saying he had an even better idea for Kohn. As it turned out, Felton also had the Silkwood story in mind. Kohn began his research but encountered stiff resistance from Kerr–McGee. The company was "its own kind of god in Oklahoma," Kohn wrote later, "and it did not suffer gladly reporters from outside the state, let alone someone from *Rolling Stone.*" When company officials told Kohn that their libel lawyers would scrutinize every word he wrote, he was unsure how Wenner would respond to that warning. "Start writing," Wenner told Kohn. "Sounds like you're onto a hell of a story. I love it!"

Karen Silkwood's story coincided with rising concerns about the environment in general and nuclear power in particular. Kohn's first installment generated more mail than any previous *Rolling Stone* story, and Jane Fonda expressed interest in the film rights. When the

Silkwood family was slow to file a lawsuit against Kerr–McGee, in part for lack of funds, Wenner donated $10,000 to that effort and promised to match contributions from readers. Kohn felt the story crossing into advocacy, but he stuck with the civil case as it worked its way through the courts. Company officials, he wrote, described Silkwood as "a union zealot, a kook, a patron of liberal parties, a dope smoker, and a nymphomaniac." They blamed Silkwood for her own contamination, arguing that she had smuggled the plutonium out of the plant in her vagina. To explain a package of contaminated bologna in her refrigerator, an FBI agent maintained that Silkwood used the package as a dildo. Meanwhile, the plaintiffs argued that the plant's operation was grossly negligent, that the company defrauded the government by producing defective fuel rods, and that its security system was so poor that 40 pounds of plutonium, enough for four bombs, had gone missing.

In the end, the jury awarded $500,000 to the Silkwood estate for her injuries and $10.5 million in punitive damages. It was the largest penalty a trial court had ever assessed against a U.S. corporation. (After Kerr–McGee appealed the ruling, it settled with the Silkwood estate for $1.38 million and admitted no liability.) The judge declined to hear testimony about the company's role in Silkwood's death, and no criminal charges were ever brought. Between 1975 and 1979, Kohn wrote nine articles on the Silkwood story for *Rolling Stone*, and his book on the same topic appeared in 1981. The film adaptation, which starred Meryl Streep, Kurt Russell, and Cher, received five Oscar nominations.

Not long after the Silkwood jury returned its verdict, a partial meltdown at the Three Mile Island nuclear plant in Pennsylvania stoked concerns about nuclear power. The meltdown was the worst accident in the industry's history and occurred less than two weeks after the premiere of *The China Syndrome* (1979), which was based on that exact scenario. The film starred Jack Lemmon, Jane Fonda, and Michael Douglas, who also produced it, and *The China Syndrome* received four Oscar nominations. By that time, Wenner had developed a friendship with Michael Douglas and featured him on the cover of *Rolling Stone*. The accident at Three Mile Island also led to a series of high-profile protests, including a five-night "No Nukes" concert series at Madison Square Garden with Bruce Springsteen, Bonnie Raitt, Jackson Browne, Graham Nash, and the Doobie Brothers. Organized in part by Kohn and *Rolling Stone* employee Susan Kellam, the concerts led to a triple-album release and live concert film.

. . . . .

Rolling Stone's second big crime story began when Patricia Hearst, a Cal student and the granddaughter of media titan William Randolph Hearst, was kidnapped from her Berkeley apartment in 1974. Little was known about her abductors, a radical group called the Symbionese Liberation Army (SLA), even after it assassinated Marcus Foster, the first black superintendent of the Oakland Unified School District. Tim Findley, who covered the Foster assassination for the *San Francisco Chronicle*, eventually learned that the SLA was led by Donald DeFreeze, an escaped convict who was serving time for armed robbery. Days after the abduction, the SLA began releasing communiqués to KPFA and KSAN. The recordings included demands as well as messages from Hearst, who assured her parents she was fine. Within weeks, however, she embraced the SLA's revolutionary agenda and took a nom de guerre, Tania.

Competing only with the Watergate scandal for public attention, the Hearst story touched off a media frenzy. It played out over years, had widespread appeal, and radiated danger. Another reason for the frenzy was the media's own role in the story. The SLA kidnapped a media heiress and then used the mass media to propagate its message. As *San Francisco Examiner* reporter Carol Pogash noted, the SLA's entire membership could fit in a single elevator, but the extensive media coverage effectively converted the ragtag group into a certified revolutionary organization. The SLA's motto—"Death to the fascist insect that preys upon the life of the people!"—reverberated through the media's echo chamber. According to one *San Francisco Chronicle* reporter, that motto was also popular at his workplace. "Around the newsroom," the reporter said, "this became an all-purpose slogan for telling off editors."

The media frenzy reached new heights when Patricia Hearst, wielding an M1 rifle, helped the SLA rob a bank in the Sunset District of San Francisco. The following month, she also sprayed bullets at security guards who scuffled with her SLA comrades outside a sporting goods store in Los Angeles. Shortly after that, police identified the SLA's hideout in South Central Los Angeles. A shootout ensued, and when police officers shot tear gas into the house, it caught fire. When the smoke cleared, six SLA members were found burned or shot to death in a crawl space. A new gadget, the minicam, allowed a local CBS affiliate to broadcast the entire event live from the SLA's hideout, thereby producing an unprecedented media spectacle.

Hearst and two SLA comrades, Bill and Emily Harris, watched the conflagration on television in their Orange County motel room. Hearst reportedly wanted revenge, but the trio returned to the Bay Area in a dilapidated car and virtually broke. Two gestures encouraged them. First, the Weather Underground bombed the Los Angeles office of the state attorney general and dedicated the attack to its sisters and brothers in the SLA. Second, a woman named Kathy Soliah, whose friend perished in the Los Angeles shootout, pledged her support at a rally held in Berkeley. Soliah met with the fugitives, gave them $1,500 in cash, and introduced them to activist Jack Scott, the sports editor at *Ramparts* magazine. Scott said he was collecting information for a proposed book about the SLA, and though the SLA members had little interest in his project, they accepted his offer to drive them to a farm in Pennsylvania, which Scott's wife had rented for the summer.

Upon Hearst's return to the West Coast, she and the Harrises combined forces with Soliah and her comrades to rob a bank in Sacramento. When they pulled off another bank job in nearby Carmichael, Emily Harris blasted a 42-year-old nurse who was depositing her church's weekend collection. She bled to death on the floor, implicating Hearst in a capital offense. Meanwhile, Jack Scott's brother contacted the police about Hearst's disappearance. Scott turned to Michael Kennedy, a radical defense lawyer in San Francisco who advised the Scotts to call a press conference and announce that they wouldn't cooperate with law enforcement.

After the press conference, Randolph Hearst called David Weir, who had recently finished a *Rolling Stone* article about Timothy Leary's legal problems. Weir put Hearst in touch with Kennedy, from whom Hearst hoped to learn more about his daughter's condition and whereabouts. Weir began investigating Patricia Hearst's time as a fugitive, and Kohn, who was by then an associate editor at *Rolling Stone,* also began working on the story. Their unnamed sources included Jack Scott, Michael Kennedy, and Patricia Hearst's cousin, Will Hearst, whom Wenner met and befriended as the story took shape.

In September 1975, the FBI arrested Patricia Hearst and her comrades in San Francisco. Meanwhile, *Rolling Stone* was preparing layouts for "The Inside Story: Tania's World." Its timing, Wenner said later, was dumb luck. Published after the arrest but before the trial, the two-part article detailed Hearst's underground movements, which the FBI had yet to pin down. Wenner later described the story as "the scoop of the seventies." It marked the first time an issue of *Rolling Stone* sold more than one million copies, and though the trial was another media spectacle, no other outlet matched *Rolling Stone*'s investigative work on Hearst's disappearance.

.   .   .   .   .

The Hearst story, and the circulation bump that accompanied it, prompted Wenner to expand the magazine's investigative staff. On Weir's advice, Wenner hired Lowell Bergman, a New York native who had studied with philosopher Herbert Marcuse and cofounded an alternative newspaper in San Diego. Bergman's investigative work led to a 1975 *Penthouse* article coauthored by Jeff Gerth, who contributed to *SunDance* magazine and later became an investigative reporter for *The New York Times*. The *Penthouse* article linked the La Costa Resort and Spa in Carlsbad to organized crime. The developers, who included former bootlegger and casino owner Moe Dalitz, sued *Penthouse* for libel. In an article for *Rolling Stone*, Weir summarized the *Penthouse* article and the ensuing legal actions. Years later, the parties agreed to drop the case.

Bergman's first article for *Rolling Stone* appeared in 1976. Coauthored by Kohn, "Reagan's Millions: Inside the Candidate's Closet Cabinet" described the former governor's land deals as well as the support he received from rich Southern California businessmen. One of those supporters was Jules Stein, who in 1924 cofounded the Music Corporation of America (MCA), a talent agency in Chicago. In 1939, Stein moved MCA to Beverly Hills and quickly became a powerful force in the film industry. With the help of MCA executive Lew Wasserman, Ronald Reagan became president of the Screen Actors Guild, which issued MCA a special waiver allowing it to produce television shows in addition to representing talent. When MCA's waiver came through, the company hired Reagan to host *General Electric Theater* for $125,000 per year. After MCA merged with Universal Studios, Wasserman became the most powerful man in Hollywood. A staunch Reagan supporter, he was also a key fundraiser for the Democratic Party. So was his best friend of fifty years, attorney Sidney Korshak, whom *The New York Times* described as "the fabled fixer for the Chicago mob."

Bergman's next article, "Revolution on Ice," was coauthored by Weir. It recounted the FBI's determination to undermine the Black Panthers through its counterintelligence program. According to a 1967 FBI memo, the purpose of the bureau's Racial Intelligence Section was to "expose, disrupt, misdirect, discredit, or otherwise neutralize the activities of black nationalists." The following year, another FBI memo warned agents to prevent the rise of a "messiah" who could "unify and electrify" the militant black nationalist movement. One month after Martin Luther King and Stokely Carmichael were identified as potential messiahs, King was assassinated, and Carmichael left for Africa five months after that. In the aftermath of King's assassination, a shootout between Black Panthers and Oakland police officers led to the death of Black Panther treasurer Bobby Hutton. Fred Hampton died in a hail of bullets the following year. In all, the Panther organization listed 31 "fallen comrades" who were killed by police, suspected agents, or "renegade" elements of the party. "The FBI played a documentable role in provoking, if not actually causing, a number of these deaths," a sidebar in *Rolling Stone* noted. The Racial Intelligence Section, for example, worked feverishly to incite a conflict between the Black Panthers and United Slaves of Southern California. That conflict left at least four dead.

Another Bergman collaboration with Weir explored the death of American Indian Movement (AIM) activist Anna Mae Aquash. After two FBI agents were killed serving a subpoena at the Pine Ridge Indian Reservation in 1973, the bureau located and questioned Aquash, who believed the interrogation put her in danger. Two AIM activists were charged with the murders, and the FBI issued an all-points bulletin for a third suspect, Leonard Peltier. Aquash went underground with Peltier and AIM leader Dennis Banks, but she was apprehended and sent to South Dakota to stand trial on an explosives charge. Released on personal recognizance the day before her trial, she again became a fugitive. When her body was found on the Pine Ridge reservation, the initial coroner's report failed to identify her and attributed her death to exposure. A second report, however, revealed that Aquash had been shot in the back of the head. AIM leaders accused the FBI of killing her, while the FBI speculated that AIM executed her for being an informant. The piece by Weir and Bergman ended inconclusively, but decades later, two AIM members were convicted of Aquash's murder.

.　.　.　.　.

Even as *Rolling Stone* became an outlet for investigative reporting, Hunter S. Thompson's appetites were hampering his productivity. Blending booze and Dexedrine no longer helped him complete his work, and David Felton noted that cocaine sometimes turned Thompson's brain to cement. To keep the Gonzo franchise alive, Wenner gave Thompson unprecedented editorial support. His Las Vegas piece, Thompson said later, marked the last time he produced a second draft of anything. According to Wenner, every subsequent assignment became a full-out siege. Instead of submitting complete drafts, Thompson transmitted short fragments over the so-called Mojo Wire, an early fax machine, and editors fashioned those into cohesive pieces. It was a protracted and frequently contentious process that extended far beyond the usual queries and revisions. "When Hunter had problems, they became your problems," David Felton said. "And they could be quite excruciating." In the end, Thompson's editors paid a physical and emotional price. "I don't think there's an editor that's worked with Hunter that hasn't, at some point in the process of a story, broken down in tears," Felton said.

Even with extensive editorial support, Thompson sometimes failed to produce the necessary copy, and two botched assignments during this period were especially significant. Shortly after President Nixon resigned, Thompson traveled to Zaire to cover the heavyweight championship fight between Muhammad Ali and George Foreman. By that time, Ali was a global media superstar as well as Thompson's personal hero. The match with Foreman appeared to be Ali's final chance to regain the title he lost in 1967 for resisting the draft, but when the bell rang, Thompson wasn't ringside. Instead, he was floating in the hotel swimming pool and ignoring Ralph Steadman's pleas to leave for the event. Nearly one billion viewers, the largest television audience ever at that time, watched what was later described as the greatest sporting event of the twentieth century. Ali scored a knockout in the eighth round, and Thompson returned home without the story. According to Thompson's wife, he slept for a day and a half and had trouble writing afterward.

Thompson's excursion to Vietnam the following year was another setback. As the American phase of the conflict came to a close, Thompson flew to Saigon, whose fall was imminent. Few veteran journalists took him seriously, and after a month, Thompson returned to the United States with little to show for his efforts. Upon his arrival, he quickly changed the subject to Wenner's treachery. Before departing for Saigon, Thompson wrote a scathing letter to Wenner about his decision to close Straight Arrow Books. He claimed that Wenner fired him and canceled his health insurance, and though Wenner contested that account, Thompson could focus on little else. He criticized Wenner publicly and insisted that his own name (and Raoul Duke's) be removed from *Rolling Stone*'s masthead.

The flap marked a low point in Wenner's complex dealings with Thompson. "I would like to rescue our relationship," Wenner wrote to Thompson in July 1975. "But I'm coming to believe that we may not be able to do it." Exasperated by Thompson's haggling and personal attacks, Wenner confessed that he no longer wished to speak with Thompson on the telephone. "Zaire is blown and Indochina is promised but not in; you indicate no faith in me; and I am sick and tired of the abuse, private even more than public, drained of any desire to work with you in the near future," Wenner wrote to Thompson. In the end, Wenner offered Thompson a new contract and didn't remove any names from the masthead. Nevertheless, Thompson claimed that the relationship ended with what he called his firing. "The attempt was enough," he told his biographer.

12 The Establishment

As Jann Wenner steered *Rolling Stone* through the mid-1970s, a new political coalition was gaining traction in San Francisco. Led by Democratic legislators Phillip and John Burton, the so-called Burton machine included labor movement activists, environmental advocates, and leaders from the city's racial and ethnic communities. The machine went into high gear when George Moscone won a narrow victory in San Francisco's 1975 mayoral election. The next year, San Francisco voters passed a proposition that substituted district elections for citywide races. Among the newly elected county supervisors was Harvey Milk, who represented the Castro District. A New York transplant, Milk was a pot-smoking hippie in the Haight before he moved to the Castro, cut off his ponytail, and became the first openly gay man to be elected to public office in California.

Milk was a natural ally of the Burton machine, but it was slow to recognize the growing power of the gay community. Scores of gay bars, restaurants, bathhouses, health clubs, newspapers, bookstores, and shops had opened in the Castro. An estimated 100,000 of the city's 700,000 residents were gay, and half had arrived during the previous decade. When Phil Burton faced a serious opponent, he moved to shore up his support in the gay community. Learning that two parades—one made up of gay activists, the other of labor supporters—would converge on City Hall for a massive rally, Burton took one labor representative aside. "Just one thing," he said. "Don't let your Teamsters go near my cocksuckers."

By that time, *Rolling Stone* had run several stories about the gay community, including a report on the Stonewall uprising of 1969, when patrons of that New York bar turned on the police who raided it. The following year, John Lombardi wrote about the Cockettes, a drag troupe that regarded its Palace Theatre shows as a form of gay liberation. The year after that, *Rolling Stone* featured a cover story on the same troupe, which a *San Francisco Chronicle* columnist described as "an outrageous tribe of cockflapping transvestites" and "the satiric cutting edge of Gay Liberation." "We're freaky and funky, not female impersonators," said one Cockette, who called himself Harold Thunderpussy and described the troupe's appetite for psychedelics. "We're closer to [French dramatist Antonin] Artaud than anything else around," said another member of the troupe. In 1972, Annie Leibovitz photographed the spectacular gender-bending on display at another Palace Theatre event. The accompanying text maintained that most participants were "humble folks with a closet of silly rags and occasional bent for sexual improvising. And, well, isn't that what America's all about—the land where any citizen has the opportunity to become . . . something else?"

The Cockettes were the latest wrinkle in a San Francisco tradition. Queerness, one historian claimed, was "sewn into the city's social fabric." The Gold Rush brought an overwhelmingly male population to the city in the nineteenth century, and female impersonation in the minstrel, burlesque, and vaudeville traditions was especially popular. Prohibition drove gay bars and nightclubs underground, but they remained vital social hubs. When they resurfaced after the repeal of Prohibition, female impersonation experienced a revival, and queer culture became more visible along the waterfront, on Market Street, in the Theatre District, and in North Beach. The Second World War also brought thousands of soldiers and sailors through San Francisco and expanded its queer entertainments.

By the 1950s, the gay bar had become what one historian described as "a public institution—a legitimized public space—without forfeiting its history of difference and defiance." In 1964, *Life* magazine ran a two-part article on homosexuality in American cities that bolstered San Francisco's reputation as a gay mecca. Decades later, a character in a memoir-novel compared that article to "an engraved invitation to every faggot in America." The "gay stampede" that ensued, one historian noted, "utterly transformed the culture, politics, and social geography of San Francisco."

Although *Rolling Stone* had not ignored the gay community, Wenner later acknowledged the magazine's shortcomings in that department. In his memoir, which recounted his own homosexual encounters, Wenner wrote, "As busy as we had been fighting the war in Vietnam, the War on Drugs, and on behalf of racial justice, we hadn't covered gay rights or touched gay culture." He also recalled a 1971 letter to the magazine asking *Rolling Stone* to acknowledge "gay people who are struggling for some peace, along with everyone else."

The magazine's coverage began to shift with Tom Burke's 1973 story "Violet Millennium or The Invert Comes of Age." A tour de force of New Journalism, the article claimed that public references to the gay community had become commonplace, at least in the nation's major cities. Even so, gay men continued to face stubborn challenges. "Fags still drink more than turned-on straights," Burke wrote, "because, frankly forgetting all this gay-is-proud bullshit, it's a rough life—rougher than straight, even less permanent, if that's still possible." Burke recounted the Stonewall uprising as well as a meeting where the president of the Mattachine Society, an early gay rights organization, called for a letter-writing campaign and candle-light march on New York's City Hall. A street boy, Burke reported, was "already on his feet, and then up in front facing the crowd, shouting fuck that, bullshit, gays are never going to beg for rights again. They're gonna fuck in the streets if they want; let the straights watch." The rest of Burke's article considered various fissures and fractures within the gay and lesbian communities. Some gay men, Burke noted, were much more interested in Bette Midler's bathhouse rendition of "Friends" than in political drama.

Responses to Burke's article were mostly negative. "I'm 17 and I've read your magazine for some four months now," one letter read. "I think it's a bunch of shit to publish a seven-page article about a bunch of faggots." Another reader took a different tack.

> I hope in the future you decide not to write any more articles on gays. . . . The good gays are still in their closets. I know 'cause I've gone to bed with them. . . . They won't come out because who wants to march down the street with a bunch of people who are really an insult not only to straights but gays as well?

Yet another letter from a New York resident complained about "Fun City's dykes and fags" as well as the old codger in lipstick at the local Blarney Stone bar. The letter concluded, "So I am moving into the basement and not coming out again until this fucking world gets itself straight again, and you can believe that if Bette Midler comes on my radio, I am turning it off." A letter from the Mattachine Society president complimented the article's accuracy but claimed that Burke "needs to open his closet door a little wider to find out how great gay lib is." The dissension that Burke found worrisome, the letter claimed, demonstrated the movement's strength and breadth.

The same year, *Rolling Stone* ran Perry Deane Young's "So You're Planning a Night at the Tubs? Here's Some Advice Your Mother Never Gave You." It quoted a customer who found the earlier New York bathhouse scene depressing. "You went into the old gay baths feeling guilty," he said, "and you came out feeling dirty." That changed when Steve Ostrow, the president and cantor of a Reform temple in New Jersey, opened the Continental Baths in the basement of the Ansonia Hotel on the Upper West Side. At the time, it was illegal for two people of the same sex to dance together, much less to have sex in a bathhouse. Nevertheless, business was brisk. Later, Ostrow hired decorator Richard Orbach, who was also a customer, to redesign the space. It eventually included a disco, black marble steam room, restaurant, chapel, gym, boutique, and a clinic for sexually transmitted diseases.

In 1975, *Rolling Stone* profiled *The Advocate*, calling it "the best gay news medium in the country," and Burke followed up on Young's article by featuring Steve Ostrow in a 1976 piece called "King Queen." Police officers raided his "gay fantasia" 200 times in its first year, Ostrow said, but the raids stopped when he began to donate 10 percent of his profits to a fictitious policeman's ball. Ostrow also began to feature live musical acts that were open to the public. Performers included Bette Midler, Barry Manilow, Melissa Manchester, Labelle, and the Manhattan Transfer. Activist and playwright Larry Kramer later credited Ostrow's operation. "I think the Continental Baths changed things more than Stonewall," he wrote in *New York* magazine. "They were clean, and you could talk to people, and Bette Midler sang to you." Ostrow offered Burke a different view of his achievement.

> We're close now to total sexual liberation here, but I wish everybody in the world could have witnessed the first awakening down there, the dawn of the revolution, the first girl turning on to beautiful boys in towels, the first straight guy who did, the first gay guy turning on to naked women. . . . The world comes here now to feel the release of decades of pent-up sexuality, all those years of inhibition are *splattered*, if you will, against my walls! Enough semen has been excreted here to populate the world to infinity!

Much of Burke's article described Ostrow's political ambitions, but the baths closed shortly after the story appeared. Plato's Retreat, a swingers club for heterosexuals, opened in the same location the following year. Ostrow began to perform with various opera companies and eventually settled in Australia. He later received the Medal of the Order of Australia for his service to the LGBTQ community and the performing arts.

Gay and bisexual identity also figured in *Rolling Stone*'s music coverage. An early example was John Mendelsohn's 1971 article about David Bowie and *The Man Who Sold the World*. Mendelsohn considered that album one of the most interesting of the year, but Bowie remained unfamiliar to many American rock fans. Appearing for an interview at the KSAN studios, Bowie wore a floral-patterned velvet midi-gown and a hat purchased in the ladies section at the City of Paris department store in San Francisco. Mendelsohn described Bowie as "ravishing" and "almost disconcertingly reminiscent of Lauren Bacall, although he would prefer to be regarded as the latter-day Garbo." His new album, Bowie told his KSAN host, was "a collection of reminiscences about his experiences as a shaven-headed transvestite." He planned to appear onstage, he told Mendelsohn, "decked out rather like Cleopatra, in the appropriate heavy make-up and in costumes that will hopefully recall those designed in the Thirties by Erte." Claiming that fans and critics took rock and pop music too seriously, Bowie offered Mendelsohn some advice. "Tell your readers that they can make up their minds about me when I begin getting adverse publicity; when I'm found in bed with Raquel Welch's husband."

The same year, David Felton's cover story on Elton John reported that he had no time for love affairs. He was still single, Felton wrote, though an earlier pregnancy scare almost led to marriage. In a *Rolling Stone* cover story five years later, Elton John was more forthcoming. "I haven't met anybody that I would like to settle down with—of either sex," he told Cliff Jahr. When Jahr asked whether he was bisexual, he claimed everyone was to a certain degree. "There's nothing wrong with going to bed with somebody of your own sex," John said. He then predicted that his answer would rile up the soccer club he played for: "It's so hetero, *it's unbelievable*. But I mean, who cares!" Wenner called Elton John to make sure he wanted those remarks to appear in the magazine. John said he wasn't worried, and the comments made national news, including a mention by Walter Cronkite on the *CBS Evening News.*

The letters to *Rolling Stone* were less vitriolic than the responses to Burke's piece three years earlier. It was about time, one reader wrote, that someone had the balls to ask Elton John about his sex life. Another reader said he had avoided David Bowie's albums on the grounds that gay and bisexual people were "gross" or mentally ill. The reader credited the Elton John interview, however, for prompting more reflection: "He's opened my mind completely, and I'm never going to judge anyone by what they are physically, but instead by what an individual is inside." Not everyone came to that conclusion. One Elton John fan said she didn't need to know that her hero was bisexual. "My disgust is matched only by my disappointment, while both are overshadowed by my pity," she concluded. "I pity him for his sexual illusions and perversions."

·   ·   ·   ·   ·

As the 1976 campaign season shaped up, Wenner focused on two elections that involved *Rolling Stone* contributors. He supported Tom Hayden's run for a U.S. Senate seat in California, offered advice to his communications director, and produced a list of potential donors plucked from his own Rolodex. On the day Hayden announced his candidacy, Wenner made stops with him in San Francisco, Los Angeles, and San Diego. Hayden's stump speech claimed that 1960s radicalism was fast becoming the common sense of the 1970s, but he lost his primary race to incumbent John Tunney. Wenner also supported David Harris for the House seat on the San Francisco Peninsula, but Harris had his hands full with Pete McCloskey, the anti-war Republican who cowrote the Endangered Species Act and cofounded Earth Day. After losing to McCloskey, Harris continued to write for *Rolling Stone.*

As important as those races were to Wenner, the presidential campaign was his chief concern. He urged Joe Klein to cover Jerry

Brown's primary bid in Maryland, which came less than two years after Brown's first gubernatorial victory. His campaign enlisted Linda Ronstadt, the Eagles, and Chicago to perform in Baltimore. Klein's piece, which was accompanied by Leibovitz's photographs, pondered Brown's enigmatic campaign.

> He was surrounded by few of the trappings of the usual presidential campaign—no press releases, no position papers, no pollsters, no media advisor, and only a benighted stab at scheduling. Even the words "Brown for President" were expunged from some of the buttons, and they simply became brown buttons. Later, he would dub himself "The Uncandidate."

Despite his unconventional style, Brown clobbered Governor Jimmy Carter of Georgia in the Maryland primary. "At age 38," Klein noted, "he was a national figure, a potent political force to be reckoned with, whoever he was." Although Klein wanted to call his piece "The Mad Prince of the West," the final title omitted the adjective. Brown also prevailed in the Nevada and California primaries, but he lacked the time, organization, and resources to wage a national campaign.

Unwilling to reprise his 1972 campaign coverage, Hunter S. Thompson eventually agreed to write something about the race. "Hunter couldn't stay away from Washington," his biographer noted, "and he couldn't stay away from *Rolling Stone*." Thompson's most important article recalled an experience two years earlier. While following Senator Ted Kennedy through the South, Thompson attended Law Day at the University of Georgia. As he refilled his glass of iced tea with Wild Turkey, he heard Carter quote Bob Dylan, whom the governor considered a personal friend, and criticize Georgia's dirty politics and rotten judicial system. Thompson described Carter's remarks "a king hell bastard of a speech" and the most impressive piece of sustained political oratory he ever heard.

In a long, rambling story for *Rolling Stone*, Thompson recalled that speech and his reaction to it. The cover blared "Jimmy Carter and the Great Leap of Faith: An Endorsement, with Fear and Loathing, by

Hunter S. Thompson," but the piece was called "Third-Rate Romance, Low-Rent Rendezvous," a nod to the 1975 hit single by the Amazing Rhythm Aces. Thompson began by dismissing generations of Dixie politicians as "thieves, bigots, warmongers, and buffoons." That group included Lester Maddox, Carter's predecessor, whom Thompson called "a white trash dingbat." Along the way, Thompson also claimed that the recent failures of radicals and reformers had turned the middle of the road into the high ground in American politics. Evangelical Christians made him uncomfortable, Thompson admitted toward the end of the piece, but he liked Carter, whom he described as one of the most intelligent politicians he ever met. "At the moment," he wrote, "failing any new evidence that would cause me to change my mind, I would rather see Jimmy Carter in the White House than anyone else we are likely to be given a chance to vote for. And that narrows the field right down, for now, to Ford, Reagan, and Humphrey."

Thompson maintained that his story wasn't an endorsement, but David Felton, who wrote the cover headline, disagreed. After the story appeared, Wenner recalled, the magazine was "virtually an official part of the Carter campaign, and they treated us as such." Carter also benefited from the active support of musicians Gregg Allman, Willie Nelson, Bob Dylan, and Jimmy Buffett. The counterculture's music had been reaching large audiences for years, but the establishment was finally recognizing its political utility. That wasn't the case ten years earlier, when *Rolling Stone* didn't exist, or even four years earlier, when Thompson and Crouse covered the 1972 campaign. Back at *Rolling Stone*, however, Marianne Partridge and Joe Klein had misgivings about the Carter endorsement. Partridge knew it was Wenner's privilege to endorse a candidate, but she felt that it would do no harm, and perhaps much good, to discuss the matter internally before issuing an endorsement. Much to Klein's dismay, associate publisher Anne Wexler stuck a "Carter for President" sticker on the front door of the DC bureau. A political consultant, Wexler was also doing advance work for the Carter campaign on the side.

Rolling Stone didn't cover the Democratic National Convention in New York, but Wexler and Wenner arranged a party for Carter's staff during the event. Renting a converted townhouse on East Sixty-Eighth Street, they invited 400 guests to the star-studded evening. An estimated 800 guests showed up, and the overflow crowd clogged the sidewalk and street. The fire department told Wenner that no one else was allowed in the building. "I waved at [*Washington Post* publisher] Kay Graham, sitting on the hood of a car with Warren Beatty," Wenner recalled, "but there was nothing I could do." Wenner was a long way from the Acid Tests, but not so far from the 1964 GOP convention at the Cow Palace or the high society he read about in the *San Francisco Chronicle*.

After Carter's victory in the general election, Jimmy Buffett remarked on the changes it ushered in.

> This is the first time young people were kind of in charge. This was really groundbreaking when you'd come out of the Nixon era, you know? And so actually they liked and listened to rock and roll, and weren't just window dressing. And then when you went to the White House, we were welcomed in.

A peanut farmer and devout Baptist, Carter was no hipster, but his authenticity, which the counterculture prized, distinguished him from many politicians. Both his candidacy and his connections in the music community seemed to fulfill Gleason's prophecy about the downstream effects of rock music on American politics.

.   .   .   .   .

The *Rolling Stone* bash in New York highlighted two major developments in the magazine's history. First, it pointed to its expanding niche in the national media ecology. Whereas Hunter S. Thompson and Tim Crouse began as lowly figures in the 1972 campaign press corps, *Rolling Stone* figured prominently in presidential politics, at least on the Democratic side, only four years later. The New York event was the culmination not only of Thompson and Crouse's work, but also of the magazine's deeper commitment to politics, current affairs, and investigative reporting. Wenner's fascination with political celebrity strengthened that commitment, but *Rolling Stone* published many hard-news stories that would have been welcome in other major outlets.

Second, the blowout in New York reflected Wenner's growing attraction to that city. In his memoir, Wenner noted that the appeal was both professional and personal.

> I was spending more time in New York; the magazine business was there, as were many of the writers I wanted to work with. New York was more fun than San Francisco. There were places to go; there were parties, small ones, medium ones, and big ones.

New York was indeed the nation's publishing capital, but as Wenner's remark suggests, its vibrant social scene also figured heavily in Wenner's thinking.

A close friend and frequent host in New York was Earl McGrath, whom Wenner met in Los Angeles. McGrath was the son of a short-order cook in Wisconsin, but his wife Camilla's wealth and aristocratic background helped him assemble an impressive social network in Los Angeles and New York. Eve Babitz based one of her protagonists on McGrath, Joan Didion dedicated *The White Album* to him, and Ahmet Ertegun eventually hired McGrath to run a record label. McGrath knew little about the music business, but the other executives valued his taste, company, and social connections.

McGrath invited the Wenners to Tuscany, where Camilla's family owned a large estate. The villa was previously owned by Napoleon's sister, and Camilla's family at one time employed 25 gardeners to maintain the grounds. During the Wenners' first visit, McGrath also took them furniture shopping in Milan. Later, he persuaded the couple to sublet an apartment in New York and hosted a party for them. "If you went to Earl's," Michelle Phillips said later, "you were going to a party that you knew would be staffed and stuffed with the most beautiful, interesting people you could find. Always, always the most fuckable people." The McGraths, Wenner recalled in his memoir, became central to his and Jane's lives on both coasts. When asked about his friendship with the Wenners, McGrath said he taught them how to be rich.

In 1973, McGrath introduced Wenner to Lorne Michaels. By that time, Michaels had written for *Rowan & Martin's Laugh-In*, another television show inspired in part by the counterculture, but he wanted to produce a show that combined music, sketch comedy, and political satire in the British tradition of *That Was the Week That Was*. Michaels's program, *Saturday Night Live*, first aired in 1975. Soon after that, Wenner invited Michaels and cast member Chevy Chase to lunch on the Upper East Side. "We all just hit it off great, and we were all the same age and rebellious and breaking through the establishment," Wenner said later. When Wenner asked Tom Burke to write about *Saturday Night Live*, Burke delivered a rave review.

Michaels, his program, and its success furnished more reasons for Wenner to be in New York. Attending the show became a weekly ritual.

> Every weekend we went to the NBC studios in Rockefeller Center and watched *Saturday Night Live*. Lorne let us stand with him on the studio floor while the show was being broadcast, and we could wander freely around to wherever a sketch was being done or in front of the stage with the band. Following every show, an after party would begin at some secret location where cast and friends would stay until dawn.

Hoping to tap that energy, Wenner commissioned a story by SNL cast members Dan Aykroyd and John Belushi called "Jimmy Carter: New South Burn." The piece, which ran one week before Carter's inauguration, described a road trip across the South and leaned heavily on Gonzo tropes. Indeed, Aykroyd and Belushi visited Hunter S. Thompson at his home before driving to Atlanta to celebrate Carter's victory. "It was totally inspired by Hunter," said Aykroyd.

"We were gonzo apprentices." Paul Scanlon was unimpressed, privately describing the piece as "a towering monument to banality." Wenner ran it anyway and added the reading line, "Two Famous Television Personalities, Both Personal Friends of the Editor, Risk Their Jobs, Their Reputations, Their Lives, and Your Patience."

As Wenner expanded his new social network, he distanced himself from the San Francisco counterculture that had powered his magazine's growth. Meanwhile, his interest in the establishment, whose media arm his magazine frequently critiqued, remained robust. That fascination was on display in 1976, when Annie Leibovitz was touring with the Rolling Stones and Thompson was sitting out the presidential campaign. Looking to replace some of the magazine's missing firepower, Wenner approached photographer Richard Avedon and asked him to produce portraits of the presidential candidates. After hearing Wenner's pitch, Avedon suggested a different approach. He wanted to photograph the American establishment, broadly defined to include politicians and bureaucrats, captains of industry, media moguls, and the military's top brass. He also laid out his non-negotiable terms. "He wanted to have an entire issue and total control," Wenner recalled, "not just choice of photos but of subjects, copy, and the cover." Wenner agreed to those terms and later described "The Family" as another landmark for *Rolling Stone*.

Appearing less than one month before the election, Avedon's black-and-white portraits put memorable faces on American power. The subjects included AT&T Chairman John deButts, Secretary of State Henry Kissinger, President Gerald Ford, Jimmy Carter, Ronald Reagan, CIA Director George H. W. Bush, and Defense Secretary Donald Rumsfeld. Avedon also photographed House Speaker Carl Albert, Hubert Humphrey, George McGovern, Edmund Muskie, Nelson Rockefeller, Ted Kennedy, Eugene McCarthy, Jerry Brown, Andrew Young, Barbara Jordan, and Bella Abzug. George Meany of the AFL-CIO was included, as was Frank Fitzsimmons, Jimmy Hoffa's successor at the Teamsters union. The Joint Chiefs of Staff appeared in a single portrait, and F. Mark Felt represented the FBI.

Decades later, Felt was identified as "Deep Throat," the key source for the Watergate stories by Bob Woodward and Carl Bernstein. Avedon also photographed staunch critics of the establishment, most notably consumer advocate Ralph Nader and labor leader Cesar Chavez.

Few of the mainstream media figures resembled old-school patricians. The son of an immigrant farmer, A. M. Rosenthal attended City College of New York before joining *The New York Times* and rising through the ranks. Katharine Graham was born into a wealthy New York family that purchased *The Washington Post*, but she took the reins only after her husband committed suicide in 1963. The son of a dry goods merchant, Jules Stein grew up in Indiana and trained as a physician before cofounding MCA in Chicago. William Paley's father started a successful cigar business in Chicago and invested in radio stations. Paley was expected to take over the cigar business but instead parlayed the radio properties into the CBS radio and television networks. In addition to building a strong news division, CBS owned Columbia Records, a major force in the music business. Walter Annenberg's immigrant father sold newspapers as a boy, became circulation manager for the Hearst Corporation in Chicago, and deployed mob muscle in that city's violent circulation wars. Moses Annenberg then purchased the *Daily Racing Form* and used its profits to buy *The Philadelphia Inquirer*. When Moe Annenberg was prosecuted for tax evasion, he struck a deal to spare his only son and died shortly after his own release from prison. Walter Annenberg acquired *TV Guide* and *Seventeen*, became a vocal supporter of the Vietnam War, served as U.S. ambassador to Great Britain in the Nixon and Ford administrations, and entertained presidents and royalty at his Palm Springs estate. He later sold most of his holdings to Rupert Murdoch for $3.2 billion and established the Annenberg Foundation, which has supported educational and arts institutions since 1988.

Wenner was proud of Avedon's work. "*Rolling Stone* would decide who was the Establishment in our country," he later wrote. If he meant that the magazine conferred that status on its subjects by photographing them, his claim was grandiose. Later, however, Wenner said he was more struck by the irony of a hippie magazine running such a feature. "The Family" didn't define the nation's ruling class, much less critique it, but the portraits came together as a politically suggestive and aesthetically powerful representation of American elites. The piece also expanded *Rolling Stone*'s reputation for working with top artists. After "The Family" appeared, the magazine ran letters from five figures who were profiled. Their tone suggested that they felt honored to be included not only in the piece, but also in the establishment. Indeed, George H. W. Bush's letter was something of a thank-you note. "It was a pleasure having Mr. Avedon out here at CIA," Bush wrote. "I don't know if he was as scared to come as I was in posing for the great Avedon, but he sure has a neat way of putting his victims at ease, and I enjoyed our time together."

"The Family" broadened the typical conception of the establishment to include its critics and nonpatricians of various stripes, but its own politics were otherwise subtle. The interpretive challenges began with the title. What kind of family was this? A ruling or aristocratic family? Or something more akin to a mob family as depicted in *The Godfather*, the popular novel and landmark film of the same period? The article also raised questions about the magazine's political posture. *Ramparts* and *The Village Voice* wouldn't have run such portraits without a pointed critique of the establishment. *Rolling Stone* was never a radical magazine, but its roots in the San Francisco counterculture made it an anti-establishment symbol. As the 1970s wore on, those roots became less visible, and if there was a rock-and-roll establishment, *Rolling Stone* was already part of it.

·   ·   ·   ·   ·

Even before *Rolling Stone* turned its gaze to the 1976 presidential election, it pondered the history of the San Francisco counterculture. In a cover story called "From Eternity to Here: What a Long Strange Trip It's Been," Charles Perry moved swiftly through Ken Kesey and the

Merry Pranksters, Chet Helms and the Family Dog, the Mime Troupe and the Diggers, the Acid Tests and the Trips Festival, the Human Be-In and the Summer of Love, and the back-to-the-land movement. "Even for the people who were there," Perry noted, "it was going too fast to follow." Perry referred to that period's lunacy, much of which he located in the mainstream culture. "It seemed like a nation gone mad," Perry wrote, "at war with Asian peasants, with its own black citizens in urban ghettos, and with its own white children."

Perry also charted Haight-Ashbury's rapid decline after the Summer of Love, but he maintained that the neighborhood's survival was miraculous, especially given the depth of the heroin epidemic that followed. "That is the new mystique of the Haight," Perry concluded, "that it's gone through hell and pulled itself out. A chastened mystique, but still, like the old one, one of hope." That sense of hope, however, was masked by the elegiacal tone of the cover copy, which referred to "the Late, Great Haight."

Shortly after that issue appeared, Wenner convened a meeting in Hilton Head, South Carolina, where he told *Rolling Stone*'s key managers that he was moving the magazine to New York. He cited several advantages, including a larger talent pool, a higher profile for the magazine, and huge savings on travel and long-distance telephone calls. Back in the San Francisco office, Wenner gathered the staff and announced, "We're all going to New York! . . . Or at least some of us are." Most of the staff saw little to celebrate. "I spoke to sad and long faces," Wenner recalled, "hiding my own excitement, trying to do what I could to be comforting." When *The New York Times* reported Wenner's decision, publisher Joe Armstrong rattled off the advantages. "We're active in book publishing—that's in New York," Armstrong said. "Advertising—that's in New York. Circulation—that's in New York. Syndication—that's in New York. And about fifty percent of our editorial right now is coming from staff or freelancers in New York." The stated reasons were long on corporate logic and short on countercultural values, but an unstated reason was more personal: The Wenners wanted to be in New York.

Charles Perry was briefed in advance and shattered by the news. He later said he never heard a single good reason for moving the magazine.

> I had given them my goddamn life's blood, and now it seemed to me a betrayal of everything I did. I'd been suckered into seeing *Rolling Stone* as this new voice, and now it was obvious that [Wenner] just wanted to publish the same people that were being published everywhere else.

Perry stayed in the Bay Area and parlayed his Haight-Ashbury article into a book for *Rolling Stone*'s imprint. Ben Fong-Torres also remained in the Bay Area, as did Tim Cahill, who joined the newly formed *Outside* magazine. Of the staff members who moved to New York, many left the magazine within a few years.

Rolling Stone had shown it could survive a major editorial shake-up, but in his memoir, Wenner admitted that he didn't appreciate how profoundly the move would affect his staff. He also acknowledged that the relocation changed the magazine more drastically than even he suspected. Nevertheless, he stood by his decision and offered additional reasons for it.

> It was becoming clear that the cultural center of the country had moved away from San Francisco, and the greater part of it was back in New York again. San Francisco, as a new and dynamic city of the arts, politics, and rock and roll, had gone quiet. Rock and roll now included television, movies, and literature; we broadened our coverage accordingly. We even had a rock and roll president, of sorts, in Jimmy Carter. The saga of the hippies was losing its story line, though the relevance of its many concerns—drug use and enforcement, healthy living, care for the environment, sexual freedom, and human rights—were more urgent than ever. Flower power was dead, and it was time to move on.

Wenner was correct that rock music's place in American culture was firmly established, and many would agree that the counterculture's concerns remained relevant or even urgent. It was less clear that San Francisco itself had gone quiet. The media coverage of hippies, campus activists, and Black Panthers had crested, but the Bay Area was still experiencing what author David Talbot later called its season of the witch. The Haight's decline, the Altamont debacle, and the SLA saga were traumatic, but the horrors to come—the slaughter in Guyana at the behest of the Reverend Jim Jones, the City Hall assassinations of George Moscone and Harvey Milk, and the ravages of the AIDS epidemic—made those events seem tame by comparison. Flower power was dead, but the next chapter of San Francisco history was truly lethal.

Wenner's claim that San Francisco had lost its cultural centrality was also misleading, for the region's marginality was always the source of its cultural vitality. Ever since the Gold Rush, San Francisco had been commercially connected but culturally isolated, and in the absence of any firmly rooted cultural orthodoxy, the region was fertile ground for wave after wave of bohemianism. From its perch on the West Coast, the city served as a Beat outpost, a global rock capital, and a gay mecca. Occasionally it attracted the national media spotlight, but it was never the nation's cultural center. It wasn't even California's cultural center, especially as the film, television, and music industries turned Los Angeles into a major media hub.

The Bay Area's media environment, always small compared to New York's, was no worse than it was a decade earlier, when *Ramparts* was peaking and Wenner launched *Rolling Stone* with $7,500 in seed money. Indeed, the same year Wenner moved *Rolling Stone* to New York, he launched *Outside* magazine in San Francisco. The year before that, a trio of *Ramparts* veterans founded *Mother Jones* in the city and later moved into *Rolling Stone*'s old office at 625 Third Street. Those magazines faced the same costs and constraints that Wenner cited to justify the relocation. The Center for Investigative Reporting (CIR)—which David Weir, Lowell Bergman, and journalist Dan Noyes cofounded in the Bay Area the same year *Rolling Stone* decamped—faced those same challenges. Much like *Mother Jones*, with which it eventually merged, CIR nevertheless managed to sponsor an impressive body of award-winning journalism.

In 1977, *Rolling Stone* moved to its new office. In Sarah Lazin's view, the layout did not encourage editorial creativity.

> The editors had these big corporate offices, and their assistants had cubicles outside their offices, which was a big change. It really imposed a hierarchy that had not existed. When we got there, Harriet [Fier] and Christine [Doudna] and I just looked around, and there were all these assistants, who were not really editorial assistants at all, but secretaries, with their Bloomingdale outfits and their high heels and their makeup, sitting outside the offices of the editors, who were inside being important.

Hunter S. Thompson also had misgivings about the move and what led up to it. "*Rolling Stone* began to be run by the advertising and business departments and not the editorial department," he told biographer William McKeen. "It was a financial leap forward for Wenner and *Rolling Stone*, but the editorial department lost any real importance." The relocation also underscored Thompson's estrangement from the magazine. "Essentially, the fun factor had gone out of *Rolling Stone*," he said. "It was an outlaw magazine in California. In New York, it became an establishment magazine, and I never worked well with people like that." For him, the New York office resembled "an insurance office with people communicating cubicle to cubicle."

If *Rolling Stone* was becoming an establishment magazine, it had not lost its bite. That fall, *The New York Times* picked up two major *Rolling Stone* stories. In the first, former *Washington Post* reporter Carl Bernstein claimed that 400 American journalists secretly shared information with—and in some cases, provided operational assistance to—the CIA during the previous 25 years. According to CIA officials, the agency's most valuable associations were with *The New York Times*, CBS News, and *Time* magazine, but the agency established similar arrangements with *The Washington Post*, ABC, NBC, the Associated Press, United Press International, Reuters, Hearst Newspapers, and *Newsweek*.

In the second article, Howard Kohn and NPR correspondent Barbara Newman revealed how Israel assembled its nuclear arsenal. The piece claimed that Israel not only purchased enriched uranium from West Germany and France under the cover of staged hijackings, but also that it smuggled several hundred pounds of weapons-grade uranium from a nuclear plant in Pennsylvania. Their reporting also revealed that two presidents, Lyndon B. Johnson and Gerald R. Ford, knew about the smuggling but declined to investigate it. Appearing on *The Today Show*, Kohn and Newman fielded questions about the story and referred to Israel's nuclear arsenal as an "open secret."

The two stories were yet another indication that the magazine had arrived—not only to New York, the center of U.S. publishing, but also to the top ranks of American journalism. Its place in the emergent rock establishment was also secure. What seemed solid and permanent, however, proved to be fluid and contingent. *Rolling Stone*, the magazine business, and the record industry would soon face challenges that few of its leaders saw coming.

Epilogue

Rolling Stone's move to New York was an important turning point in the magazine's history, but other factors shaped its fortunes even more profoundly than the relocation. The rise of cable television altered the way music was marketed and consumed. For promotional purposes, a catchy music video and heavy rotation on MTV, which launched in 1981, trumped a rave review in *Rolling Stone*. New digital technologies, which Stewart Brand presaged in 1972, were even more transformative. File-sharing and then streaming services decimated record sales and became a primary way for audiences to discover new music. The magazine business was also taking its lumps. Search engines and social media sapped the advertising revenue that magazines needed to survive, and a tweet from a pop star could send a new single up the charts faster than a full-page ad in a rock magazine. By that time, *Rolling Stone* had altered popular culture so profoundly that many Americans no longer remembered what it replaced. The magazine continued to publish top writers and award-winning journalism, but as the record business, *Rolling*

Stone's place in that business, and advertising revenue continued to shrink, the magazine lost much of its clout and relevance.

Along the way, Wenner declined personal invitations to invest in MTV, Netscape, and *Wired* magazine, which described itself as "the *Rolling Stone* of tech." Wenner and Steve Jobs also crossed paths and shared many musical interests, but the two never hit it off. "We had a conventional occupational disagreement about the future of print," Wenner said later. "He turned out to be right." Instead of investing in new technologies, Wenner Media bought *US Weekly* in 1985 and founded *Men's Journal* in 1992. In 1995, Wenner also invested in *Salon*, an early online magazine founded in San Francisco. *Salon*'s first editor was David Talbot, who had contributed to *Rolling Stone* and described it as formative. But when the two outlets copublished "Deadly Immunity," a 2005 article by Robert F. Kennedy linking vaccines to autism, a wave of objections from experts led both outlets to retract the piece.

As the magazine business cratered, *US Weekly* remained Wenner Media's cash cow. In 2017, Wenner sold it to American Media, which also owned the *National Enquirer*. At that time, *US Weekly*'s average paid circulation was close to 1.95 million, its total readership exceeded 50 million, and the magazine accounted for almost two-thirds of Wenner Media's profits. The same year, *Rolling Stone*'s 50th anniversary, Wenner sold a controlling interest in that magazine to the Penske Media Corporation (PMC), which owned *Variety* and later bought *Billboard* and *The Hollywood Reporter*.

In 2017, HBO also released a two-part documentary film, *Rolling Stone: Stories from the Edge*. In its review, *Variety* summarized the first part of the film, which focused on the San Francisco years.

> At the center of it all is the fresh-faced young man with the bushy hair, giant bell-bottoms and a series of ever-wider ties, whose undeniable brilliance as an editor and self-promoter led him and the magazine from "counter-culture" to the center of the culture to the establishment, all of which happened by the time the magazine relocated from San Francisco to New York in 1977.

The same year that film appeared, Knopf published Joe Hagan's biography of Wenner. *Sticky Fingers* wasn't the first book to chronicle *Rolling Stone* or its chief figure, but it was the only one to scrutinize five decades of Wenner's personal and professional relationships. The book critics at *The New York Times* named it a top-ten title of the year, but Wenner, who recruited Hagan for the project, denounced the book as "deeply flawed and tawdry."

Shortly after that, Wenner began working on his memoir. When it appeared in 2022, *The New York Times* ran a mixed review, but the *Vogue* review by Corey Seymour, who had worked for *Rolling Stone*, credited the book's detail, range, and emotional depth. Seymour claimed that the memoir invited readers to come for the celebrity gossip and stay for what he called "the moving account of how a college dropout with a big idea turned his vision into an empire—and changed the country and the world in the process." He also compared the memoir to "an eerie trumpet call over a lost battlefield." It was a reference to Wenner's long march from cofounding what Joe Klein called *The New Yorker* of his generation to presiding over an award-winning but troubled magazine in a declining industry. "Jann came, he kicked ass, had his own ass kicked, and walked away with his head held high," Seymour concluded.

By that time, Wenner had attracted accolades and stinging criticism for more than five decades. The same was true of *Rolling Stone*, but only a fraction of that coverage could be described as searching or substantive. Much of the criticism fell back on countercultural stereotypes and the magazine's reputation for excess, which it shared with the rock stars it covered. A two-dimensional version of *Rolling Stone* made it easier for commentators to overlook, minimize, or distort the magazine's early achievements, especially after Wenner's disastrous *New York Times* interview while promoting his latest book, *The Masters*, in 2023.

How then should we understand *Rolling Stone*'s achievement during its first and most important decade? I've offered four related answers to that question. The first is that *Rolling Stone*, for all its setbacks and shortcomings, was one of the most important American magazines of the 1970s. It earned that accolade not only with its unmatched music journalism, but also with its political reporting, commentary, satire, interviews, investigative reporting, media criticism, photography, illustrations, and design. It broke major stories, challenged the establishment's hypocrisy and mendacity, and set new journalistic standards for its competitors and successors. Contemporary observers also applauded the magazine's effective targeting. J. Anthony Lukas, a Pulitzer Prize–winning journalist who contributed to *Rolling Stone*, described its appeal in those terms. "I feel that, of all the magazines in this country, only two have any real idea of who their audience is and how to reach that audience," Lukas told Chet Flippo in 1974. "Those two are *The New Yorker* and *Rolling Stone*."

Despite these accomplishments, I don't share Joel Selvin's view that *Rolling Stone* was "the journalistic voice of its generation." The magazine spoke to and for a large audience, but its core demographic—young white men with relatively high levels of education—was too narrow to earn that honor. Indeed, Evelyn McDonnell, a journalism professor who contributed dozens of articles to *Rolling Stone* in the 1990s, maintained that the magazine's conception of rock music marginalized the voices of female and nonwhite journalists, distorted our understanding of popular music, and skewed inductions into the Rock & Roll Hall of Fame. That Lukas and McDonnell are both right attests to the magazine's complex history. Indeed, the marginalization that McDonnell cited was the flip side of the successful targeting that Lukas applauded. Moreover, the forms of exclusion that McDonnell identified were all the more important precisely because *Rolling Stone* was the most influential rock magazine of its era.

My second claim is that a cohort of talented writers, photographers, illustrators, and designers were crucial to the magazine's success. That group included Ralph Gleason, Baron Wolman, Jon Landau, Jonathan Cott, Charles Perry, Dugald Stermer, Robert

Kingsbury, John Burks, Ben Fong-Torres, Annie Leibovitz, Hunter S. Thompson, Ralph Steadman, David Felton, Greil Marcus, Lester Bangs, Paul Scanlon, Mike Salisbury, Roger Black, Joe Eszterhas, Marianne Partridge, Howard Kohn, and Cameron Crowe. My third claim follows closely on the second: Jann Wenner deserves much of the credit not only for conceiving and growing the magazine, but also for recruiting and deploying that talent. As Abe Peck observed, Wenner knew how to pick a horse. Here again, however, it would be a mistake to overlook the other *Rolling Stone* staff members who recruited and mentored the magazine's key personnel. That group included Ralph Gleason, John Burks, Jon Landau, Ben Fong-Torres, David Felton, Paul Scanlon, John Walsh, and Marianne Partridge.

Fourth, *Rolling Stone* was an important magazine for the reason its cofounders identified at its creation. Gleason and Wenner grasped the significance of the counterculture when most media outlets were denigrating or dismissing it. Wenner also had a strong sense of what his audience wanted to read and needed to know. The magazine's internal disputes led to rifts, departures, and occasional reunions, but the staff never doubted its mission, and the editorial changes during its first decade grew its audience and expanded its influence. The proof that *Rolling Stone* was a good idea, Gleason claimed, was that it survived Wenner's management of it. If Wenner was the sine qua non of the magazine's success, Gleason's quip correctly emphasized the sturdiness of the founding concept.

In my introduction, I claimed that *Rolling Stone* effectively created the rock music beat and insisted on its importance. Above all, however, I have argued that *Rolling Stone* was always more than a rock magazine. Neglecting that fact is the most common way to misunderstand the magazine's achievement. Another trap is to fall back on stereotypes that trivialize the counterculture. As we've seen, contemporary media outlets invited their audiences to do exactly that. To repeat that mistake now, however, is to underestimate both the counterculture and the magazine that covered it. Yet another error is to assume that *Rolling Stone* was a hippie publication. By focusing on the counterculture and its music, the magazine became a symbol of that movement, but its key contributors weren't hippies, it wasn't a hippie operation, and its relationship with the counterculture was complex. Ignoring or discounting that complexity also leads to a distorted understanding of the magazine and its chief topic.

.   .   .   .   .

What then of the counterculture, which *Rolling Stone* wrote off even before its move to New York? Historians often cast it as part of the Long '60s, an idea that emphasizes how the decade's major figures, events, institutions, and movements continued to shape American culture for years after that. As late as 2023, for example, prominent historian Eric Foner asked, "When did the decade of the Sixties end? Did it end at all?" In the aftermath of the Vietnam War, the hippie ethic didn't suddenly vanish. Rather, the loosely affiliated groups that made up the counterculture recombined with other cultural formations to shape American public life. In this sense, the counterculture was a quiet river that flowed through the second half of the twentieth century.

Well after its first epitaphs were written, the counterculture continued to influence popular music. In a 1987 *Rolling Stone* interview, Mikal Gilmore began by asking Bruce Springsteen about that influence. In his reply, Springsteen mentioned the youthful response to "the dehumanization of society" as well as the tendency to draw moral lines that "busted up nearly every house in the nation." It was a childlike fantasy, Springsteen said, to believe that "radical, joyous energy" was going to sweep away "all the bullshit and all the Nixons." Nevertheless, Springsteen claimed, "a lot of those ideas were good ideas."

> It's funny, but because of the naiveness of that era, it's easily trivialized and laughed at. But underneath it, people were trying in some sense to redefine their own lives and the country they lived in, in some more open and just fashion. And *that* was real—the desire was real.

Springsteen's reply channeled Theodore Roszak, who also critiqued the counterculture but never trivialized it, and echoed Greil Marcus, who argued in *Mystery Train* that musicians were continuously reworking or reinventing American culture. Springsteen also claimed a lasting personal connection to countercultural values. "The values from that time are things that I still believe in," he said. "I think that all my music—certainly the music I've done in the past five or six years—is a result of that time and those values."

If not typical of the 1980s, Springsteen's personal statement was far from unique. Moreover, his endorsement of countercultural values was especially significant given its timing. When the interview appeared, the Age of Reagan was in full swing. The scourge of the hippies no longer linked rock music, dancing, and marijuana to the international communist conspiracy, but his administration's War on Drugs and retrogressive vision of America drove a new cohort of young people toward cultural and political alternatives. It was no accident that the Grateful Dead, a symbol of the 1960s countercul-ture, scored its first top-ten single during Reagan's second term. Indeed, the Dead tended to thrive when Reagan was in power, first as California governor and then as U.S. president.

Countercultural values also found expression in the environmen-tal movement, which Roszak cast as "the most durable offshoot of countercultural protest." One environmental historian, Andrew Kirk, noted that the counterculture consistently promoted the theme of "reconciling nature and culture toward a sustainable future." Wenner founded the short-lived *Earth Times* and featured environ-mental issues in *Rolling Stone,* but Kirk maintained that Stewart Brand's *Whole Earth Catalog* made an especially important contri-bution to pragmatic environmentalism, which touted practical alternatives and meaningful optimism when other parts of the envi-ronmental movement favored jeremiads and protests. Kirk also emphasized Brand's role in the greening of American business, an effort that resonated with the founders of Apple, Smith & Hawken, Williams-Sonoma, Patagonia, and other major companies. What

Kirk called "counterculture green" also figured heavily in the creation of Earth Day in 1970 and the rise of organic farming, organic grocery stores, farmers markets, renewable energy, and recycling.

Another important manifestation of the counterculture was its influence in Silicon Valley. In his 2005 commencement speech at Stanford University, Steve Jobs highlighted that influence.

> When I was young, there was an amazing publication called the *Whole Earth Catalog*, which was one of the bibles of my generation. It was created by a fellow named Stewart Brand not far from here in Menlo Park, and he brought it to life with his poetic touch. This was in the late 1960s, before personal computers and desktop publishing, so it was all made with typewriters, scissors, and Polaroid cameras. It was sort of like Google in paperback form, 35 years before Google came along. It was idealistic and overflowing with neat tools and great notions.

Jobs called attention to his hippie roots in other ways as well. In one interview, he said that taking LSD was one of the two or three most important things he had done in his life. He also claimed that Microsoft founder Bill Gates would be "a broader guy if he had dropped acid once or gone off to an ashram when he was younger."

The counterculture's influence on Apple was evident well after Wenner wrote off the hippies. In 1984, for example, Apple reinforced its countercultural identity with a Super Bowl advertisement for its new personal computer. In the ad, a young woman sprints toward a large screen on which a stern speaker exhorts his audience of gray drones to celebrate "a garden of pure ideology" and "the unification of thought." The woman stops, pivots, and hurls a sledgehammer at the screen, which explodes. The ad then informs viewers, "On January 24th, Apple Computer will introduce Macintosh. And you'll see why 1984 won't be like *1984*." The iconoclasm was on brand for Apple, whose "Think Different" ad campaign later celebrated "rebels and troublemakers" such as Bob Dylan, Martin Luther King Jr., John Lennon, and Muhammad Ali. Apple also ran ads that presented a Mac, played by Justin Long, as casual, relaxed, and authentic, while the Microsoft PC, played by John Hodgman, comes off as bumbling, nerdy, and hopelessly square. The power of Apple's brand, which some observers credit with keeping the company afloat while Jobs was out of power, was deeply rooted in the Silicon Valley branch of the counterculture.

The countercultural strain in Silicon Valley has been well documented by John Markoff, Fred Turner, and others, but decades before their books appeared, Theodore Roszak was writing about the links between hippie culture and the computer industry. In *From Satori to Silicon Valley: San Francisco and the American Counterculture* (1986), Roszak connected the counterculture's utopianism to Silicon Valley's technophilia. For him, the "mystic tendencies and principled funkiness" of the counterculture maintained "a certain irrepressible Yankee ingenuity, a certain world-beating American fascination with making and doing." Roszak honored that ingenuity, but he didn't believe that the industrial process, when pushed to its limits and divorced from its social and political context, would save us with its gadgets. Indeed, he dismissed that belief as little more than "an attractive hope." He also challenged Big Tech's conflation of data with knowledge, the erosion of human values in public education, and a digital oligarchy whose interests were strongly linked to the national security state. None of those concerns turned out to be idle. At Donald Trump's 2025 inauguration, for example, the tech barons literally lined up behind the nation's most divisive political figure. In short, Roszak admired the counterculture when it was resisting the technocracy, but not when it was enabling Big Tech.

A more spectacular example of the counterculture's legacy is the Burning Man Project, which is based in San Francisco and describes itself as "a global ecosystem of artists, makers, and community organizers who co-create art, events, and local initiatives around the world." The project hosts "a participative temporary metropolis" that has drawn 70,000 participants to its weeklong celebration of art, music, psychoactivity, and clothing-optional fashion in the Nevada desert. One can draw a straight line from the Trips Festival to the annual event, which San Francisco artists began on Baker Beach in 1986. Noting that Burning Man became especially popular in the digital subculture, *The New York Times* quoted its principal cofounder on the connection. "Both Burning Man and the Internet make it possible to regather the tribe of mankind," said Larry Harvey, who saw a "deep parallel between desert and cyberspace." Harvey was also responsible for codifying the event's principles: radical inclusion, gifting, decommodification, radical self-reliance, radical self-expression, communal effort, civic responsibility, environmental stewardship, participation, and immediacy. Those principles, which grew out of the mid-century San Francisco art scene, continue to reflect the counterculture's core values.

Given Burning Man's appeal to the tech community, it was no surprise that it became a place for Silicon Valley executives to meet and play. The cofounders of Google began attending regularly and once brought a CEO candidate to see how he would respond to its unique atmosphere. Mark Zuckerberg and Jeff Bezos have attended, Elon Musk has described himself as a fan, and Airbnb's CEO referred to Burning Man as "what life would be like if artists ruled the world." Wenner attended Burning Man with a former MTV executive, found the experience enthralling, and returned the following year with his partner Matt Nye and son Theo.

The counterculture's influence also can be detected in the so-called sharing economy, at least in the public statements of its flagship companies. When ride-sharing and home-sharing apps began to appear, there was much happy talk about community, sustainability, and other countercultural virtues. As these companies scaled up, however, they began to change the cities in which they operated. Landlords evicted tenants to convert whole buildings into unregulated hotels. At least one ride-sharing app set fares, skimmed tips, and imposed strictures on its drivers, even as it maintained that they were independent contractors, not employees. Heavily regulated hotel chains and taxi companies complained that sharing-economy companies were systematically skirting—or encouraging their users to skirt—labor, zoning, tax, insurance, access, and public safety laws. Over time, those companies began to resemble Gold Rush miners, not hippie collectives, especially in their anarchic urge to move fast and break things.

In his book about the sharing economy, Tom Slee maintains that it is indeed a movement, but not a countercultural one. "It's not about building an alternative to a corporate-driven market economy, it's about extending the deregulated free market into new areas of our lives," Slee concludes. Writing for *The Nation,* Doug Henwood seconded that criticism and linked the sharing economy to the so-called Californian Ideology, a term coined by two British media theorists in the mid-1990s to describe the Silicon Valley mashup of countercultural, libertarian, and neoliberal values. In addition to critiquing the sharing economy, Slee admits to a sense of betrayal. What seemed to be "an appeal to community, person-to-person connections, sustainability, and sharing" became "the playground of billionaires, Wall Street, and venture capitalists extending their free-market values ever further into our personal lives." Slee's admission suggests that appeals to countercultural values, whether or not those appeals were authentic, continued to resonate long after the 1970s.

As these examples illustrate, Bay Area firms, industries, and institutions continued to tap the counterculture's spirit—or at least its rhetoric—long after *Rolling Stone* moved to New York. That track record, however, has done little to enhance the region's image in the national political conversation. Consider the long-standing complaints about "San Francisco values," whose point of origin was the Democratic National Convention in 1984. In his speech to the delegates in San Francisco, Jesse Jackson described the United States as an interracial, interdenominational, and intergenerational quilt that included places for gays and lesbians. In doing so, Jackson became the first speaker to mention those groups at a national convention. In her speech at the GOP convention later that summer, U.N. Ambassador Jeanne Kirkpatrick contrasted President Reagan with "San Francisco

Democrats." Unobjectionable on its surface, her phrase was construed as an appeal to the electorate's homophobia and racism.

Cruising to victory in 1984, Reagan was well on his way to becoming the most important American politician in the second half of the twentieth century, but the attacks on San Francisco extended well beyond Reagan's second term. In 1996, a North Bay congressman became the first politician to criticize his opponent's "San Francisco values." GOP leader Newt Gingrich and Fox News host Bill O'Reilly added that phrase to their arsenals, and it enjoyed a resurgence when San Francisco Democrat Nancy Pelosi became the first female House Speaker. By that time, Gingrich had relinquished his seat after one of his extramarital affairs became public. Later, O'Reilly was fired after he and his employer settled lawsuits with five women who accused him of sexual misconduct. Another GOP leader, former House Speaker Dennis Hastert, was later convicted of financial offenses linked to his sexual abuse of four teenage boys while he was a high school wrestling coach. Despite those falls from grace, San Francisco values were still considered uniquely problematic. For a conservative movement preoccupied with God, guns, and gays, the city remained a perfect target.

As I was finishing this book, the GOP candidate for president cast his Democratic opponent as a "San Francisco radical." A former prosecutor who grew up in the Bay Area, she called herself a daughter of Oakland, where she lived in her twenties, but she was born and raised in Berkeley and attended law school in San Francisco. That she erased Berkeley from her campaign biography was widely seen as a response to the city's reputation as a countercultural hotbed. Meanwhile, her opponent was rarely described as a radical, even though he instigated a violent assault on the Capitol while Congress was ratifying the 2020 election results. On the campaign trail in 2024, he promised to root out radical leftists, whom he described as vermin, by deploying the National Guard or U.S. military. His values weren't a deal-breaker for a plurality of U.S. voters, even though he was convicted of falsifying business records to cover up a tryst with a porn star, indicted for election interference, and found liable for fraud, sexual assault, and defaming the victim of his sexual assault. Fifty years after Hunter S. Thompson suggested that a werewolf was living in the White House, the state of American politics reflected Peter Coyote's trenchant observation: The counterculture won all the cultural battles and lost all the political ones.

Perhaps a more direct way to observe the counterculture's enduring influence is to walk through a typical American city. If you spot a Whole Foods supermarket, Apple Store, yoga studio, cannabis dispensary, farmers market, or recycling center, you're looking at the counterculture's long tail. If you snap a picture with your smartphone and post it on social media, you're living in its shadow. *Rolling Stone* didn't build those enterprises or institutions, but it credited their source when other media outlets were disparaging, trivializing, or stereotyping it. Indeed, those modes of dismissal are still very much with us.

In 2023, Wenner opened *The Masters* with his mentor's favorite passage from Plato.

> Forms and rhythms in music are never changed without producing changes in the most important political forms and ways. . . . The new style quietly insinuates itself into manners and customs and from there it issues a greater force. It goes on to attack laws and constitutions, displaying the utmost impudence, and it ends by overthrowing everything, both in public and private.

That passage underwrote Gleason's conviction that the counterculture would "change heads" and usher in a new age of progressive politics. If the strong version of that prophecy was obviously false, a more modest version was just as obviously true. The counterculture and its impertinent style did transform many important aspects of American culture. By documenting that transformation and playing a significant role in it, *Rolling Stone* fostered a new generation of writers, influenced countless others, and left an indelible mark on American journalism, media, and culture.

Random Notes

VINCE ALETTI was the art editor and photography critic at *The Village Voice*. He also curated photography exhibitions and reviewed others for *The New Yorker*.

JOE ARMSTRONG left *Rolling Stone* in 1977 and became publisher and editor in chief of *New York* and *New West*. In the 1990s, he also served as publishing director of *Garden Design* and *Saveur*.

LESTER BANGS left *Creem* in 1976 and moved to New York, where he wrote for *The Village Voice* and other publications. At age 33, he overdosed on a mixture of opioid analgesic, Valium, and cough syrup.

LOWELL BERGMAN cofounded the Center for Investigative Reporting and produced news stories for ABC's *20/20*, CBS's *60 Minutes*, and PBS's *Frontline*. His work at *60 Minutes* was the basis for *The Insider* (1999), which received an Oscar nomination for Best Picture. From 2006 to 2019, he held an endowed chair in journalism at the University of California, Berkeley.

JOHN BURKS was a reporter for the *San Francisco Examiner* before accepting a position at San Francisco State University, where he taught from 1979 to 2011. He died in 2021.

TIM CAHILL was a founding editor of *Outside* magazine, where he wrote a long-running column. The author of ten books, many on travel and adventure, he lives in Livingston, Montana.

JON CARROLL won a National Magazine Award during his three years as editor of *New West* magazine. From 1982 to 2015, he was an award-winning daily columnist for the *San Francisco Chronicle*.

JONATHAN COTT is the author of 19 books, including *Dylan on Dylan: The Essential Interviews*, *Days That I'll Remember: Spending Time with John and Yoko*, and *Let Me Take You Down: Penny Lane and Strawberry Fields*.

TIMOTHY CROUSE was the Washington columnist for *Esquire* and wrote for *The New Yorker* and *The Village Voice*.

CAMERON CROWE is a screenwriter and director whose credits include *Fast Times at Ridgemont High*, *Say Anything*, *Jerry Maguire*, and *Almost Famous*. *The Uncool: A Memoir* was published in 2025.

JOE ESZTERHAS wrote the screenplays for *Jagged Edge*, *Basic Instinct*, *Showgirls*, *Jade*, and other films. His autobiography, *Hollywood Animal*, appeared in 2004.

DAVID FELTON left journalism in the early 1980s and worked for MTV, where he helped develop *Beavis and Butt-Head* and became a senior vice president.

HARRIET FIER helped launch *Outside* magazine and was *Rolling Stone*'s managing editor from 1978 to 1980. She was an assignment editor at *The Washington Post* and a senior editor at Time Inc., Simon & Schuster, and Bantam Books. She died in 2018.

TIMOTHY FERRIS became an award-winning science writer and professor at the University of California, Berkeley. The author of twelve books, he also produced three PBS documentaries on astronomy and space exploration.

CHET FLIPPO left *Rolling Stone* in 1980. He wrote a biography of Hank Williams, taught journalism at the University of Tennessee, became the Nashville bureau chief for *Billboard* magazine, and served as the editorial director at cable channel CMT. He died in 2013.

BEN FONG-TORRES wrote a history of Top 40 radio, a memoir, and books about Gram Parsons, the Doors, the Grateful Dead, the Eagles, and Little Feat. His column "Radio Waves" ran in the *San Francisco Chronicle* from

2005 to 2019. *Like a Rolling Stone: The Life and Times of Ben Fong-Torres* began streaming on Netflix in 2022.

JERRY HOPKINS wrote *Elvis: A Biography* in 1971. Later, he served as *Rolling Stone*'s London correspondent and wrote biographies of Jim Morrison, David Bowie, Jimi Hendrix, and many other figures. He died in Bangkok in 2018.

HOWARD KOHN left *Rolling Stone* as a senior editor in 1981. He served as an investigative and wire service reporter, a columnist at the *Takoma Voice*, and a writer for Fenton Communications. His books include *The Last Farmer: An American Memoir* and *We Had a Dream: A Tale of the Struggle for Integration in America.*

JON LANDAU manages Bruce Springsteen and other artists. He also heads the nominating committee for the Rock & Roll Hall of Fame and received that institution's Ahmet Ertegun Award for Lifetime Achievement in 2020.

SARAH LAZIN established Rolling Stone Press in 1976 and represented it for three decades. In addition to creating book packaging divisions for *Ms. Magazine*, *The Village Voice*, *Playboy*, and *Vibe*, she served as a literary agent.

ANNIE LEIBOVITZ joined *Vanity Fair* in 1983 and began contributing to *Vogue* four years later. The author or editor of several books, she has received awards from the International Photography Hall of Fame and Museum, the Royal Photographic Society, and the Rhode Island School of Design.

GROVER LEWIS freelanced for *Playboy* and *Oui* before moving to Los Angeles in 1976 and writing for *New West*. He later wrote for *The Washington Post, Los Angeles Times, St. Petersburg Times,* and *Texas Monthly*. He died of lung cancer in 1995.

MICHAEL LYDON began performing music in the 1970s. He also published a biography of Ray Charles, an anthology of his music writing, and a memoir. He died in 2025.

SUSAN LYDON wrote "The Politics of Orgasm," a widely anthologized feminist essay, for *Ramparts* magazine in 1970. Her 1993 memoir recounted her life, work, and struggles with drug addiction. She wrote two books about knitting and conducted related seminars at Esalen. She died of liver cancer in 2005.

GREIL MARCUS wrote for *Creem, The Village Voice, Interview,* and *The Believer*. He now publishes his column on Substack. His many books include

Lipstick Traces: A Secret History of the Twentieth Century; *The Old, Weird America: The World of Bob Dylan's Basement Tapes*; and *The History of Rock 'n' Roll in Ten Songs*. He has taught at the University of California, Berkeley, the New School, and the University of Minnesota.

JAMES MILLER is a professor of politics and liberal studies at the New School. His six books include *Flowers in the Dustbin: The Rise of Rock & Roll, 1947–1977*, *The Passion of Michel Foucault*, and *Democracy Is in the Streets: From Port Huron to the Siege of Chicago*.

JOHN MORTHLAND wrote for *Creem* and published *The Best of Country Music* in 1984. After relocating to Austin, he contributed to *Texas Monthly* and wrote *Texas Music: Legends from the Lone Star State*. He was Lester Bangs's literary executor and edited *Main Lines, Blood Feasts, and Bad Taste: A Lester Bangs Reader*. He died in 2016.

PAUL NELSON was the record review editor at *Rolling Stone* from 1978 to 1983. After resigning from that position, he turned his attention to film, worked at Evergreen Video in Greenwich Village, and wrote an unfinished screenplay. He died in 2006.

MARIANNE PARTRIDGE is editor in chief of the *Santa Barbara Independent*, the alternative weekly she cofounded in 1986.

CHARLES PERRY wrote *The Haight-Ashbury: A History* (1984) and was a food writer at the *Los Angeles Times* from 1990 to 2008. He also has written, edited, or translated several cookbooks.

PAUL SCANLON is the author of *Reporting: The Rolling Stone Style* (1977). From 1984 to 1996, he was an assistant managing editor at Condé Nast.

JUDITH SIMS left *Rolling Stone* in 1976, wrote about gardening and cooking for various outlets, and became an assistant editor at the *Los Angeles Times Magazine*. She died of cancer at age 56.

HUNTER S. THOMPSON wrote *The Great Shark Hunt*, *The Curse of Lono*, *Generation of Swine*, two volumes of edited correspondence, and several other books. The film adaptation of *Fear and Loathing in Las Vegas*, which starred Johnny Depp and Benicio del Toro, appeared in 1998. He committed suicide in 2005.

JOHN WALSH joined ESPN as a managing editor in 1988. During his 27-year-stint, he also served as an executive vice president and chairman of its editorial board.

ED WARD was the West Coast correspondent for *Creem*, the music critic at the *Austin American-Statesman*, and the rock-and-roll historian at NPR's *Fresh Air* from 1987 to 2017. He wrote books about the history of rock and roll and a biography of guitarist Michael Bloomfield. A cofounder of South by Southwest, he died in Austin in 2021.

DAVID WEIR cofounded the Center for Investigative Reporting in 1977 and worked at *Salon, Wired Digital, Mother Jones,* and KQED, where he was senior editor of digital news. The author or coauthor of four books, he taught journalism at the University of California, Berkeley, Stanford University, and San Francisco State University.

JANN WENNER cofounded the Rock & Roll Hall of Fame and Museum, which opened in 1995. Two years later, he became the youngest editor ever inducted into the American Society of Magazine Editors. After separating from Jane Wenner in 1995, he started a new family with fashion designer Matt Nye, with whom he has three children. His memoir, *Like a Rolling Stone*, appeared in 2022.

ELLEN WILLIS taught journalism at New York University, where she also headed the Center for Cultural Reporting and Criticism. She died of lung cancer in 2006. A collection of her essays, *The Essential Ellen Willis* (2014), received the National Book Critics Circle Award for Criticism.

LANGDON WINNER is the Thomas Phelan Chair of Humanities and Social Sciences in the Department of Science and Technology Studies at Rensselaer Polytechnic Institute. His books include *The Whale and The Reactor: A Search for Limits in an Age of High Technology* (1986).

BARON WOLMAN founded Squarebooks, which published books on photography, in 1974. He later moved to Santa Fe and released an autobiographical book of photographs, *The Rolling Stone Years*. He died in 2020.

Acknowledgments

Friends, family, colleagues, and many experts have helped me conceive and execute this project.

I wish to thank Jann Wenner for his cooperation. In addition to arranging access to the Straight Arrow Papers, he spent many hours answering my questions, correcting my account, and challenging my claims and interpretations. His feedback made for a stronger manuscript, and though I'm solely responsible for its shortcomings, I'm grateful for Jann's interest and input. Many thanks also to his assistant, Susan Kerner, who helped me locate the relevant material in the Straight Arrow Papers.

I'm grateful to the *Rolling Stone* veterans who fielded my questions. Over the course of this project, I interviewed or corresponded with Vince Aletti, Lowell Bergman, Roger Black, Renshin Bunce, Tim Cahill, the late Alec Dubro, David Felton, Tim Ferris, Ben Fong-Torres, Laura Fraser, Michael Goldberg, Robin Green, Susan Kellem, Joe Klein, Howard Kohn, Jon Landau, Sarah Lazin, Suzanne Locke, Greil Marcus, Evelyn McDonnell, James Miller, Marianne Partridge, Abe Peck, Charles Perry, Alan Rinzler, Corey Seymour, David Talbot, David Weir, Sheila Weller, and Langdon Winner.

For teaching me about the magazine's key figures and historical context, I wish to thank Judy Gumbo Albert, Lili Anolik, Don Armstrong, Allison Bumsted, Stef Burns, Mat Callahan, Judy Clancy, Raechel Donahue,

Arthur Eckstein, David Farber, Richard Flacks, Elizabeth Fracchia, Ben Grant, Marianne Hinckle, Pia Hinckle, Adam Hochschild, Sean Howe, Ron Jacobs, Denise Kaufman, Michael Koncewicz, Ellen Mandel, Regan McMahon, Greg Mitchell, Alan Paul, Carol Pogash, Craig Pyes, Tim Riley, David Rubinson, Nicholas Schou, Gene Sculatti, Joel Selvin, Derek Shearer, Chris Sterba, David Talbot, Jeff Tamelier, Pat Thomas, Jay Williams, Yumi Wilson, and Justin Wyatt.

This project's peer reviewers—Michael J. Kramer, Evelyn McDonnell, and John McMillian—offered probing questions, helpful corrections, practical suggestions, and tactful objections. I'm grateful for their expertise and willingness to share it.

Many thanks to Susan Hoffman and her staff for allowing me to teach a course on this topic at the Osher Lifelong Learning Institute at the University of California, Berkeley. I also thank Ben Fong-Torres, Greil Marcus, and David Weir for visiting that class and sharing their reflections. I'm grateful to Ben Stone and Kathryn Roszak, who invited me to appear at the opening of the Theodore Roszak Papers at Stanford University.

Sincere thanks to Nicholas Meriwether, Sue Balter-Reitz, and Granville Ganter, all of whom encouraged me to present my work-in-progress at the Popular Culture Association meetings in San Antonio, Chicago, and New Orleans. My exchanges with other colleagues there also helped me conceptualize this work. I discussed material related to this book at GonzoFests in Louisville and New Orleans, at the Canessa Gallery in San Francisco, and at the Wellstone Center in the Redwoods in Soquel. For those opportunities, I thank Kent Fielding, Margaret Harrell, Steve Kettmann, Christopher Tidmore, and Ron Whitehead. At those events, I also benefited from the expertise and intellectual generosity of John Brick, Tim Denevi, Rory Feehan, Kurt Hemmer, Bill McKeen, Curtis Robinson, and David Streitfeld. I thank Dan Lewis, Abe Peck, Michael Kramer, Steve Savage, and Nicholas Meriwether for the chance to co-organize a 2017 conference in San Francisco called "Revisiting the Summer of Love, Rethinking the Counterculture." The presentations there and at a follow-up conference informed my thinking about the counterculture and its significance.

I wish to thank Jon Lebkowsky, David Gans, and other members of the WELL, the online community that Stewart Brand cofounded in 1986. Since joining the WELL in 2009, I've learned a great deal about topics that figure in this project. The WELL hosted conversations about three of my earlier books and put me in touch with Ed Ward's sister Louise, who kindly granted me permission to quote his WELL posts. Thanks also to David

Gans and Amelia Davis, who asked me to contribute an essay to a volume about Jim Marshall's photographs of the Grateful Dead. Some of Marshall's images appear in this book with Amelia's permission. I also thank the other photographers whose work I've included here, especially Annie Leibovitz and Allan Tannenbaum. For help with permissions, I'm grateful to Marco Acosta, Nona Willis Aronowitz, Ruby Booth, Stewart Brand, Tim Cahill, Jon Carroll, Weyaka Cassero, Robert Christgau, Daisy Cockburn, Ben Fong-Torres, Toby Gleason, Evelyn Haralampu, Jon Landau, Tracy Johnston, Denise Kaufman, Megan Stermer, Anita Thompson, and Jann Wenner. Their permission to quote unpublished correspondence and internal memos made this a better book.

Over the course of my research, I was hosted by Greg and Rhonda Aplet in Colorado, Brian May and Betsy Talbott in Virginia, and Nicholas Maybank in North Carolina. I thank them once again for their warm hospitality.

I offer my heartfelt thanks to Kim Robinson, Aline Dolinh, Julie Van Pelt, and the staff at the University of California Press. I'm especially grateful to Kim for her interest, support, and editorial guidance. I also thank copyeditor Nicholas Taylor for his meticulous work on the manuscript and assume all responsibility for remaining errors.

Beth Tudor encouraged me to undertake this project and several others before it. For that encouragement and everything else, I dedicate this book to her.

Notes

Introduction

2   **Only four years earlier:** Browne 2017.

2   **sex, drugs, and rock and roll:** Throughout this book, the spellings *rock and roll* (noun) and *rock-and-roll* (adjective) are standardized, even in quotations, for consistency.

2   **He compared it to a medieval crusade:** Roszak 1969, p. 48.

6   **Wenner's introduction acknowledged:** Wenner 2023, p. x.

6   **That he had neglected important black artists:** Wenner 2023, p. x.

6   **Yet when journalist David Marchese asked:** Marchese 2023.

7   **If the interview exposed Wenner's prejudices:** Farhi and Sommer 2023.

Chapter 1. Hippies

13   **Even its chief nemesis:** *Time* 1967a.

14   **"The danger in the hippie movement":** Hinckle 1967.

14   **That neighborhood was steeped in:** Cohen 1993, p. 23.

15   **Alert to connections:** Armstrong 2024, p. 87.

15 **At the same time, Gleason privately:** Gleason 1963.

16 **It was a profound shock:** Gleason 1975, pp. xvi–xvii.

16 **"I read him," Miles Davis once said:** Armstrong 2024, p. 231.

16 **"I don't care if I make it":** *New York Times* 1975.

16 **"He is saying something":** Gleason 1965b.

18 **"So there was a bit of mystery":** Hagan 2017, p. 60.

18 **The following year, Gleason wrote:** Gleason 1966.

18 **"There has been no point":** Gleason 2013–14, p. 120.

18 **Eric Hobsbawm later claimed:** Hobsbawm 2005, p. 399.

19 **"The batting average is sensational":** Gleason 1969a, p. 68.

19 **"Everybody felt it":** Gleason 1969a, p. 38.

20 **Gleason knew about the incident:** Armstrong 2024, pp. 167–68.

20 **"The media delighted in":** Gitlin 1987, p. 211.

21 **"For the reality of what's happening today":** Gleason 1967.

21 **According to one observer:** Anson 1981, p. 43.

21 **In a letter to a friend:** Gleason 1963.

21 **In his *American Scholar* article:** Gleason 1967.

22 **"To their deeply worried parents":** *Time* 1967b.

22 **Appearing in *The Saturday Evening Post*:** Didion 1967.

23 **Yet as the Summer of Love approached:** Harris 1967.

23 **"The 'Hashbury' Is the Capital of the Hippies" traced:** Thompson 1967a.

24 **Alan Watts, the popular philosopher:** Conners 2010, pp. 272–73.

25 **"Wherever I went in the state":** Schrecker 2022.

26 **In fact, the FBI was already investigating:** Rosenfeld 2012, p. 311.

26 **As Todd Gitlin observed:** Gitlin 1980, p. 28.

27 **"Today there is no place without its hippies":** M. Lydon 1970.

28 **"I think that the revolution":** *Hard Road* 1970.

Chapter 2. Counter Culture

29 **"Basically we want to meet people":** Gleason 1965a.

30 **"About 400 or 500 people":** Weller 2012.

30 **"They entered into the occasion":** Gleason 1969a, p. 8.

30 **"After the dance, on the long bridge":** Gleason 1969a, p. 8.

30 **Gleason endorsed it:** Armstrong 2024, p. 134.

31 **But when push came to shove:** Thompson 1967b, p. 236.

31 **According to one music scholar:** Bernstein 2008, p. 5.

31 **"We're not in the business of doing benefits":** Graham and Greenfield 1992, p. 131.

32 **"We thought it was *hilarious":** Graham and Greenfield 1992, p. 219.

32 **"What the *fuck* do you know":** Fong-Torres 1976.

32 **"I have heard him scream":** Graham and Greenfield 1992, p. 278.

32 **"All that bullshit about vibes":** Anson 1981, p. 90.

33 **Specifically, he "put a toughness":** Graham and Greenfield 1992, p. 279.

34 **"These were tribal rites":** Selvin 1994, p. 2.

34 **"He always had this rap":** Graham and Greenfield 1992, p. 202.

34 **"In the first days," one musician said:** Greenfield 1996, p. 125.

35 **After visiting San Francisco in the spring of 1967:** Williams 1967.

35 **In his history of Haight-Ashbury:** Perry 1984, p. 271.

36 **The Haight, he wrote:** Thompson 1970.

36 **The statement concluded that:** Hartlaub 2018.

37 **One of their prophets:** Frank 1997, p. 76.

37 **With his deep voice and massive body:** Selvin 1998, p. 9.

38 **"In radio, I found out about":** Fong-Torres 1998, p. 143.

38 **"Do you realize that we sit here":** Fong-Torres 1998, p. 207.

40 **"If you examine San Francisco closely":** Williams 1967.

40 **That effort included serving free food:** Callahan 2017, pp. 85–91.

40 **"There never was a free concert":** Goodwin 1971.

41 **In another interview, Garcia dismissed:** *Creem* 1970.

41 **At first, Roszak agreed:** Roszak 1969, p. xiii.

42 **"The young, miserably educated as they are":** Roszak 1969, p. 41.

42 **"If there is one aspect of the period":** Roszak 1969, p. xxxiv.

Chapter 3. Plan B

45 **One observer described the GOP convention:** Skipper 2016, p. 2.

45 **The Goldwater delegates had put out their cigarettes:** Clark 1993.

45 **That sort of mistreatment:** Robinson 1972, p. 340.

46 **Belva Davis, who later became:** Davis 2010, pp. 1–5.

46 **"The Goldwater delegates went completely amok":** Thompson 1973, p. 336.

46 **"I was in the heart of the machine":** Wenner 2022, p. 25.

46 **"We didn't realize it then":** Wenner 2022, p. 26.

47 **During the 1930s, its president:** Blauner 2009, p. 27.

48 **"It was a torch":** Wenner 2022, p. 27.

48 **Although Wenner welcomed the opportunity:** Wenner 2022, p. 26.

48 **"The wealth was on display, the booze":** Hagan 2017, p. 42.

48 **When he returned from a ski trip:** Wenner 2022, p. 27.

48 **The Free Speech Movement, he recalled:** Wenner 2022, p. 28.

49 **"In Ralph, we found someone who spoke our language":** Wenner 1975.

49 **"Denise and LSD changed my life":** Wenner 2022, p. 232.

49 **"She combined those two worlds":** Hagan 2017, p. 52.

50 **Wenner revered Gleason's *Chronicle* column:** Gleason 2016b, p. xi.

50 **"Their sound is very tight and very beautiful":** Wenner 1966b.

50 **"The group which, if it ever makes it":** Wenner 1966a.

50 **"Ralph liked that I was an enthusiastic student":** Wenner 2022, p. 39.

51 **"I thought that sounded funny":** Reynolds 2012.

51 **"Everything we were doing in that seminar":** Richardson 2017.

52 **"The Free Speech Movement had an enormous effect":** Richardson 2017.

52 **In his view, Gleason "wrote the same three columns":** Hagan 2017, p. 61.

52 **"My view was, let the young guys take the floor":** Richardson 2017.

52 **"I left walking on air":** Richardson 2017.

52 **"Everything that I had learned":** Richardson 2017.

53 **"We will cover the local stories the metros don't cover":** Wenner 2022, p. 46.

54 **"She wasn't a hippie":** Hagan 2017, p. 69.

54 **Recalling her signature trench coat:** Hagan 2017, p. 70.

55 **"They were oblivious to the cultural changes in San Francisco":** Richardson 2009, p. 108.

55 **"I don't think there is any possibility whatsoever":** Gleason 2013–14, p. 117.

55 **Adam Hochschild, a *Ramparts* staff writer:** Richardson 2009, p. 97.

56 **"It was a breakthrough magazine of its time":** Hagan 2017, p. 74.

56 **"And finally, Jann came over one day":** Shamberg and Rucker 1973.

56 **"I felt that rock and roll was also about imagery":** Wenner 2022, p. 59.

56 **The only problem with Marshall:** Wenner 2022, p. 59.

57 **"There was nothing that gave Bob Dylan his due gravitas":** Wenner 2022, p. 57.

57 **"I was a hippy, I was taking LSD":** Thomas with Gurk 2001.

57 **"I recognized from the beginning":** DeRogatis 2000, p. 50.

58 **"We created *Rolling Stone* in Ralph's living room":** Wenner 2022, p. 58.

58 **"I was headed to a shirt, tie, and jacket professional career":** M. Lydon 2018, pp. 78–79.

58 **"Much of this was tongue in cheek":** M. Lydon 2018, p. 109.

59 **"He was from Boston and a family of staunch Kennedy Democrats":** S. Lydon 1993, p. 52.

59 **Although she later described him as:** S. Lydon 1993, p. 75.

59 **"At the time," she recalled:** S. Lydon 1993, p. 76.

59 **According to Susan Lydon, Wenner said his ambition:** S. Lydon 1993, p. 77.

60 **"Go fuck yourself, Jann":** S. Lydon 1993, p. 77.

60 **Michael Lydon later described:** M. Lydon 2003, p. 22.

61 **"He'd sit there at that corner desk":** Anson 1981, p. 25.

61 **"Ralph and I have done it":** Straight Arrow Papers (hereafter cited as SAP).

62 **"At the age of 19, my objectives were messianic":** Landau 1972, p. 13.

62 **During his sophomore year:** Author interview with Jon Landau.

62 **"Looking forward to a long and mutually profitable relationship":** SAP.

62 **"I too look forward to a long and mutually profitable relationship":** SAP.

62 **He assured Landau:** SAP.

63 **"I wrote for *Rolling Stone* for ten years":** Hanley 2020.

66 **"I hadn't read a paragraph of it before I realized":** Author interview with Greil Marcus.

Chapter 4. Early Days

69 **"This was vital information":** Author interview with Joel Selvin.

70 **"I walked into a Frisco record store":** Gene Sculatti Facebook post.

70 **"It was the issue with Eric Clapton on the cover":** Green 2018, p. 19.

70 **"I bought the very first issue":** Flippo 1974, p. 72.

70 **"These were your lifelines":** Hagan 2017, p. 96.

71 **"It treated rock and roll *seriously*":** Author interview with Michael Goldberg.

71 **Jon Carroll, who would later appear on the masthead:** Richardson 2017.

71 **"The *Barb* was exciting, the *Oracle* was peculiar":** Peck 1985, p. 107.

71 **"He didn't like the prose":** Peck 1985, p. 107.

71 **Although Wenner and Marcus strongly distinguished:** McMillian 2011, p. 122.

72 **"If you touched the stuff about the Byrds":** SAP.

72 **Although his views focused on the musical deficiencies:** Author interview with Jon Landau.

72 "I just finished looking at the latest *Eye* magazine": SAP.

72 "Jann wanted a big, popular, successful magazine": Anson 1981, p. 69.

73 "I wanted to take the opportunity": SAP.

73 "Briefly: First issue was strong": SAP.

74 "We are operating on at least four premises": SAP.

75 "The back page of our next issue": SAP.

75 "I was anxious to help *Rolling Stone*": Anson 1981, p. 224.

75 "I always took it personally": Davis with Willwerth 1975, p. 271.

76 "I am feeling very frustrated in this regard": SAP.

76 Writing to Wenner, he said Landau: SAP.

76 "As I explained to you on the phone": SAP.

77 "I was shocked to see a Carole King ad": SAP.

77 "The decision was made to promote and advertise in print media": SAP.

77 "Three grand for an ad?": SAP.

77 "It's nice to see your concern": SAP.

77 After noticing that Wenner's letter: SAP.

78 "Dear Jann: Go fuck yourself":

78 Returning the memo to *Rolling Stone*: SAP.

78 "Let me tell you, Jann": SAP.

78 "I just saw the latest issue of *Eye*": SAP.

80 In 1970, *Rolling Stone* reported that Marin County: Kamin 1970.

80 He later admitted that the Trips Festival: Bernstein 2008, p. 244.

81 He asked Wenner to write: SAP.

81 "From one point of view": Albright 1969.

82 "If rock can change the business world": Gleason 1968a.

82 "Music, if Plato was right, may save us yet": Gleason 1968b.

82 Although the Youth International Party: Farber 1988, p. xvii.

83 "I remember once being at a be-in": Carroll 1982.

83 "A movement that isn't willing to risk injuries": Rubin 1970, p. 43.

83 "I learned the hard way that you can't build a new society": Rubin 1970, p. 51.

83 "I had disliked Jerry Rubin": Wenner 2022, p. 70.

84 "A self-appointed coterie of political 'radicals'": Wenner 1968b.

86 Wenner's article was predictably controversial: Hagan 2017, p. 150.

86 According to historian John McMillian: McMillian 2011, p. 122.

87 Thompson called him "a plastic man in a plastic bag": Thompson 1968.

87 **"I witnessed at least ten beatings":** Thompson 2000, p. 119.

88 **It was, Wenner later said:** Hagan 2017, p. 111.

88 **"This was our first experience with controversy":** Hagan 2017, p. 168.

88 **"The point is this, print a famous foreskin":** Wenner 1968b.

Chapter 5. Staffing Up

90 **In November 1968, he also wrote:** Perry 1968.

90 **"When I started working at *Rolling Stone*":** Email message to author.

90 **"Jann was kind of into Leary":** Email message to author.

91 **"Your provincialism still shows":** SAP.

91 **"It was about issue No. 18, I guess":** Flippo 1974, pp. 76–77.

92 **"When John was at *Rolling Stone*":** Whiting 2021.

92 **"Those articles were about rock and roll":** Fong-Torres 2006, p. xiv.

92 **Fong-Torres also cast the magazine:** Fong-Torres 2006, p. xvii.

93 **"The whole point about *Rolling Stone* magazine":** Kai 2022.

93 **"Jann managed to impart a sense of style":** Fong-Torres 1994, pp. 170–71.

93 **"Ben was my first glimpse":** Kai 2022.

94 **"So I started sending them reviews":** DeRogatis 2000, p. 51.

94 **Disappointed by the album, he submitted a scathing review:** DeRogatis 2000, p. 53.

95 **Once described as "a catalog of doom":** Flippo 1974, pp. 91–92.

95 **Readers seemed to think:** Carroll 2013.

95 **"Peter is very into the whole Sun, white Memphis thing":** SAP.

96 **"[Kingsbury] saw a lot of pictures":** Leibovitz 2003, pp. 208–9.

96 **"I was looking to be adopted":** Model Gene 2022.

96 **"Annie was one of the closest editorial collaborations":** Model Gene 2022.

97 **He didn't believe that rock and roll:** Marcus 1969, pp. 103–4.

97 **Even before Marcus began contributing album reviews:** Marcus 2006.

97 **"And two weeks later, I pick up the next issue":** Marcus 2022.

97 **"All anybody ever does is write about lyrics":** Levy 2017.

97 **"When I became record reviews editor":** Reynolds 2012.

98 **"I don't know whether Lester was fried":** DeRogatis 2000, p. 56.

98 **"Lester was the all-time oblivious, obnoxious houseguest":** DeRogatis 2000, pp. 56–57.

98 **"I got the feeling I was being totally condescended to":** DeRogatis 2000, p. 58.

98   **For these and other reasons, Marcus maintained:** Bangs 1987, p. xii; DeRogatis 2000, p. 51.

99   **It was *Creem*, Marcus wrote later:** Bangs 1987, p. xii.

99   **"One thing that really fucked me up":** Romano 2024, p. 257.

99   **"I was on Cloud 9":** Ward 2005.

99   **"I've always thought of John as my journalism school":** Ward 2005.

100 **"I called and got right through to Graham":** Ward 2014.

101 **That omission allowed her to recount:** Author interview with Sheila Weller.

101 **The Field Research Corporation found that:** SAP.

102 **"We have to drive the racist dog police out of communities or kill them":** Murray 1969.

103 **"Nothing I have read by the SDS":** Gleason 1969c.

103 **"Ralph's column, 'Perspectives: Is There a Death Wish in the U.S.?'":** Holzman 1969.

104 **"Thanks for sending on the proofs":** SAP.

104 **"It is truly unfortunate that *Rolling Stone*":** *Rolling Stone* 1969b.

Chapter 6. Wild West

105 **"As I flew in, I couldn't see the whole crowd":** Stone with Greenman 2023, p. 78.

106 **Olivier predicted that it would be:** Kramer 2013, pp. 99–100.

107 **"Rock and roll is now the energy core":** *Time* 1969.

107 **"As for Wenner, he remains, for the moment":** *Newsweek* 1969.

108 **"You can't ask for both our money and our love":** Graham and Greenfield 1992, p. 278.

108 **"*Don't touch me!*":** Graham and Greenfield 1992, p. 278.

108 **"I want the festival council to be expanded":** Kramer 2013, p. 120.

109 **A *Daily Cal* article concluded that the festival failed:** Kramer 2013, pp. 122–23.

109 **"The Wild West Show, the kind of venture":** Fong-Torres 1969.

109 **"The Wild West Festival, the glorious dream":** *Rolling Stone* 1969a.

110 **In "Perspectives: Festival Paranoia," he argued that the festival:** Gleason 1969b.

110 **"*What* change? Rock music hasn't stopped the slaughter":** *Rolling Stone* 1969b.

111 **"It's just about that. . . .":** Wenner 1969.

111 **Likewise, Mick Jagger told Jonathan Cott:** Cott 1968.

113 **"Leave a sign," Manson instructed his minions:** Sanders 1971, p. 201.

113 **Another said the crime looked like:** Sanders 1971, p. 226.

113 **"Prior to the murders," he recalled in his memoir:** Polanski 1984, p. 323.

116 **"Is this the new community?":** Gleason 1970.

116 **"There are no specific guilty parties":** Gleason 1971.

116 **"Sorry I didn't stay to see you":** SAP.

117 **As Booth wrote, "It was like blaming the pigs in a slaughterhouse":** Booth 1984.

117 **"If you knew how hard it was simply to survive the tour":** SAP.

117 **"We are going to cover this from top to bottom":** Marcus 2006.

118 **It opened with the eyewitness account:** *Rolling Stone* 1970.

118 **"Again, congratulations on the Altamont coverage":** SAP.

118 **"I know you may think that it's not big enough":** SAP.

118 **"Though I think *Rolling Stone* is the best rock magazine going":** SAP.

119 **Willis later admitted to her daughter:** Willis 2011, p. xvii.

119 **"Also, in the years I've been reading *Rolling Stone*":** SAP.

Chapter 7. Keep Growing

123 **"Did you read the coverage in *Rolling Stone*?":** Thompson 2000, pp. 261–62.

123 **"Your Altamont coverage comes close":** Wenner 2011, p. 9.

123 **"Having once read your Angels book":** Wenner 2011, p. 10.

124 **"Graphically, it was a fucking horror show":** Thompson 2000, p. 283.

124 **During one of those breaks:** Whitmer 1993, pp. 170–71.

125 **Thompson hoped Steadman's drawings:** Thompson 2000, p. 304.

125 **When Steadman's illustrations arrived:** Hinckle 2017, p. 91.

126 **Thompson compared the experience:** Vetter 1974.

127 **"The Gene Marine thing was kind of a disappointment":** SAP.

127 **Genet's first words were:** Winner 2018.

128 **"Jann was out of town":** Reynolds 2012.

128 **"It was literally a life-and-death matter":** Hagan 2017, p. 152.

128 **"Wenner thought he was training me":** Flippo 1974, p. 103.

128 **"It all came to a head at midsummer":** Flippo 1974, p. 99.

129 **"The advertisers (I learned from our ad side)":** Flippo 1974, p. 99.

130 **"Our core mission was the purpose of the music":** Hagan 2017, p. 161.

130 **"When Jann got back, I think he found that the paper":** Reynolds 2012.

131 **Winner agreed to rewrite the review:** Winner 1970.

131 **To alter a record review:** Author interview with Greil Marcus.

131 **"I really want to talk about":** Reynolds 2012.

132   **But the class went poorly:** Marcus 2022.

132   **The editorial turnover didn't damage:** *New York Times* 1971.

133   **It was further evidence of that movement's importance:** Felton and Dalton 1970.

134   **"Jerry's razzing and his pipe-dreams":** Bangs 1970.

134   **"And I mean that quite literally":** Perlstein 2014, p. 475.

134   **Hollingworth, who managed Quicksilver Messenger Service:** Perry 1984, p. 141.

134   **"Now and then I'll send you a column":** SAP.

135   **"I didn't know the difference":** Bernstein 2018.

135   **"Jann wants to make sure the staff is astrologically compatible":** Draper 1990, p. 89.

135   **The idea, Thompson explained to Steadman:** Thompson 2000, p. 320.

136   **"For me, that week in Chicago was far worse":** Thompson 1970.

136   **"This is my last press conference":** Thompson 2000, p. 332.

137   **"Talked to Janis Joplin, sort of":** SAP.

137   **A month earlier, an article claimed that Joplin screamed:** Glover 1968.

137   **"Keep growing," Leary wrote:** SAP.

138   **"I fancied myself his wingman":** Wenner 2022, p. 50.

138   **"He was some kind of visionary or saint":** Wenner 2022, p. 50.

138   **Lennon continued to develop the lyric:** Greenfield 2006, p. 358.

139   **"I hope you will write more stuff for us from jail":** SAP.

139   **"Thanks to the noble protection of the Black Panthers":** SAP.

140   **"All is perfect here":** SAP.

140   **"Great level of literary productivity":** SAP.

140   **"We're not in favor of violence":** Greenfield 1970.

140   **"Read the writings of Huey P. Newton":** Greenfield 1970.

141   **"I've been waiting to talk to you for years":** Greenfield 2006, p. 466.

141   **"A matter has come up about which I don't know what [the] policy is":** SAP.

Chapter 8. New Morning

143   **"We were just becoming stark-naked real":** Longfellow 2008.

143   **"Dear Jann, After many years of searching":** Wenner 2022, p. 115.

143   **"John was always full of enthusiasms":** Longfellow 2008.

144   **"When we walked out":** Wenner 2022, p. 116.

144   **The following weekend, the Wenners visited Lennon and Ono:** Wenner 2022, p. 116.

144 **Running in two parts one month later:** Wenner 1971a.

145 **"Never before had a rock star":** Anson 1981, p. 123.

145 **Lennon's candor exemplified the hippie authenticity:** Riley 2011, p. 509.

145 **"He was always brave":** Longfellow 2008.

146 **"It was shocking," Wenner said later:** Longfellow 2008.

146 **After the interview, Tim Riley noted:** Riley 2011, p. 509.

146 **"It was so far out that I enjoyed it":** Merryman 1971.

146 **"Oh, I hated it":** Gambaccini 1974.

146 **"There is a huge market out there":** *New York Times* 1970.

147 **On June 30, he told Wenner:** SAP.

147 **"By then, we felt that Jann was our ally":** Hagan 2017, p. 173.

147 **When the book was reissued:** Wenner 1971a, p. x.

148 **"Accustomed to a daily afternoon newspaper schedule":** Paul Scanlon Facebook post.

148 **With few other options for claiming media attention:** Burrough 2015, p. 5.

149 **As the Weather Underground moved away from guerrilla tactics:** Eckstein 2016, pp. 92–93.

149 **In that sense, Marcus claimed:** Marcus 1970.

150 **"The underground had run its course":** Burrough 2015, p. 362.

150 **One prosecutor said:** Burrough 2015, p. 203.

151 **Sifting through the evidence:** Thompson 1971c.

151 **Later, Hinckle found it difficult to credit *Rolling Stone*:** Hinckle 1974, p. 180.

151 **"He inherited Hunter":** Hagan 2017, p. 180.

151 **As for Gleason, Hinckle said:** Hinckle 1974, pp. 144–45.

152 **"It will not require violence to succeed":** Reich 1970, p. 4.

152 **During his visits to San Francisco:** Reich 1970, pp. 259–60.

153 **In that book's introduction, Reich claimed:** Garcia et al. 1972, p. xvii.

153 **Wenner reinforced Reich's endorsement:** Garcia ct al. 1972, p. ix.

153 **After growing up in Fort Worth:** Lewis 2005, p. 239.

153 **"You could be judged violently nonconformist":** Lewis 2005, p. 240.

154 **One longtime friend described Lewis:** Lewis 2005, p. ix.

154 **His version of Timothy Leary's famous dictum:** Anolik 2019, p. 102.

154 **"Splendor in the Short Grass" reported unguarded remarks:** Lewis 1971b.

154 **He also compared Duane Allman to:** Lewis 1971a.

154 **Finally, he quoted Allman's profane comment:** Lewis 1971a.

155 **"What [Lewis] wound up writing":** Trucks 2005.

155   **In an introductory letter to novelist Joseph Heller:** Anolik 2019, p. 100.

156   **"In every young man's life":** Anolik 2019, p. 44.

156   **"I was almost thirty":** Anolik 2019, p. 102.

156   **"Joan Didion told the people at *Rolling Stone*":** Anolik 2019, p. 103.

156   **"She came to my place":** Anolik 2019, p. 103.

157   **"Do you like what's been happening":** SAP.

157   **"The perspective on music is almost wholly white":** SAP.

157   **"I've explained to him that I would like to see your byline":** SAP.

157   **He was less enthusiastic about Seale's memoir:** Lester 1970c.

158   **Although he credited Kofsky's claims:** Lester 1971.

158   **In his reply to Bogart, Wenner explained that it was difficult:** SAP.

158   **Jon Landau also panned:** Landau 1971.

158   **"To Mr. Jon Landau":** SAP.

158   **Although Landau later conceded:** Author interview with Jon Landau.

159   **"All of us were freelancing":** Romano 2024, p. 131.

159   **The magazine felt established right away:** Author interview with Vince Aletti.

159   **That focus gave him a place:** Author interview with Vince Aletti.

159   **Landau considered Aletti "absolutely reliable":** Author interview with Jon Landau.

159   **"I started going to The Loft in '71 or '72":** Romano 2024, p. 131.

160   **Within six months, Christgau said:** Romano 2024, p. 130.

160   **"Tuesday nights, people standing on line":** Romano 2024, p. 133.

Chapter 9. Gonzo

162   **"Sooner or later, you'll see what your call":** Thompson 2000, p. 376.

162   **"I was assigned by Jann":** Draper 1990, p. 176.

163   **"Everybody was knocked out":** Wenner and Seymour 2007, p. 133.

163   **"We would be dealing, from the start":** Thompson 1972, p. 110.

163   **He was "a bit leery":** Thompson 2000, p. 406.

164   **"We knew we couldn't make it illegal":** Baum 2016.

164   **"The drug culture, the hippie elements":** *Observer* 2013.

165   **The FBI had performed that work in the past:** Weiner 2012, p. 296.

165   **Editors checked its facts:** Wenner and Seymour 2007, p. 134.

165   **Thompson later called the Las Vegas book:** McKeen 1990.

166   **"It has been called to our attention":** SAP.

166 **Duke passed his days on his veranda:** SAP.

166 **Abbie Hoffman also attached a postscript:** Hoffman 1971.

167 **"Recently we had a go-around with Abbie Hoffman":** Wenner 1971b.

169 **"We were somewhere around Barstow":** Thompson 1972, p. 3.

169 **"We had two bags of grass":** Thompson 1972, p. 4.

170 **"Probably we should leave it that way":** Thompson 2000, p. 406.

170 **"A very painful experience in every way":** Thompson 1972, pp. 22–23.

171 **"Whatever the FBI was doing":** Medsger 2014, p. 226.

171 **"It looks like we're terribly reckless people":** Mazzetti 2014.

172 **That was especially clear:** Thompson 1972, p. 68.

172 **"Now that the dust of the '60s has settled":** Algren 1979.

172 **Thompson suspected that *Rolling Stone*:** Thompson 1997, p. 209.

172 **"Who else would have given":** Carroll 1993, p. 273.

172 **When asked if any other outlet:** Shamberg and Rucker 1973.

173 **Every now and then, Duke says:** Thompson 1972, p. 67.

173 **"Like, did you even so much as ask me":** Thompson 2000, p. 447.

173 **"You don't know how fucking lucky":** Thompson 2000, p. 448.

173 **"Dear Oscar," he wrote in April 1972:** Thompson 2000, p. 476.

174 **"What do you think?" Rinzler asked:** SAP.

174 **"I've been silent on the subject":** Thompson 2000, p. 542.

174 **"I am already thinking of the third book":** Oscar Zeta Acosta Papers, University of California, Santa Barbara Library.

174 **"I am still looking to you":** Thompson 2000, p. 561.

175 **"Money-wise, I am desperate":** Thompson 2000, p. 562.

175 **"What in the fuck would cause you":** Thompson 2000, p. 562.

175 **"How would you like to publish":** SAP.

175 **"Why in the fuck won't you give me a break?":** SAP.

175 **"I am dismayed that you seem to":** SAP.

176 **"The reinvention of *Rolling Stone*":** Hagan 2017, p. 180.

176 **"It had life force":** Eszterhas 1992.

177 **"Anyway, read the fucker":** SAP.

178 **"I loved covering political stories then":** Leibovitz 2008, p. 190.

178 **"Unlike most other correspondents":** Thompson 1973, p. 4.

178 **"Hunter worked his ass off":** Wenner and Seymour 2007, p. 164.

179 **"It is entirely conceivable":** Thompson 1973, p. 135.

180 **"They shouldn't try to be objective":** Crouse 1973, p. 305.

180   **Leaving the cool analysis to others:** Thompson 1973, p. 118.

180   **"McGovern made some stupid mistakes":** Thompson 1973, p. 389.

181   **By April, however, *Newsweek* columnist:** Alsop 1972.

181   **Following Thompson's example:** Taibbi 2012.

181   **Even after becoming the magazine's star contributor:** Thompson 2000, p. 502.

182   **She wasn't invited to the Big Sur editorial conference:** Author interview with Robin Green.

182   **Later, Wenner noted that *The Partridge Family*:** Author interview with Jann Wenner.

183   **"If the PR man or Cassidy himself":** Green 2018, p. 126.

183   **"For many of the girls":** Green 1972.

184   **"It was Annie's naked photos":** Green 2018, p. 126.

184   **Instead, he said later:** *Rolling Stone* 2010.

184   **"I was pigeonholed as a teen idol":** Sullivan 2017.

184   **"I can't speak for Annie":** Green 2018, p. 127.

185   **"I wanted to produce a journalistic novel":** Krebs 1984.

185   **Such exchanges were a staple:** Marcus 2024.

185   **"Lots of times I don't think":** SAP.

185   **"I wasn't bothered or worried":** Wenner 2022, p. 171.

186   **"I try to describe the Weather position":** Findley 1972.

187   **According to Flacks, Hayden's remarks:** Author interview with Richard Flacks.

188   **"It is Nixon himself who represents that dark":** Thompson 1973, pp. 391–92.

189   **"This may be the year":** Thompson 1973, p. 389.

189   **"Ready or not," his first sentence read:** Brand 1972.

190   **Annie Leibovitz photographed the winner:** Baker 2016.

190   **Decades after that, Jobs praised:** Jobs 2005.

Chapter 10. Boys Club

193   **"Please do this favor for me, old friend":** SAP.

193   **"At this point, they are generally getting repetitive":** SAP.

194   **Instead, he intended to produce:** Thompson 1973, p. 8.

194   **"I will definitely need speed":** SAP.

194   **Rinzler laid in 40 pounds of supplies:** Thompson 1973, p. 2.

194   **Thompson's book described them:** Thompson 1973, p. 1.

195   **"Working with you has been":** SAP.

195   **Rinzler resisted the temptation:** Author interview with Alan Rinzler.

197 **"David was in jail, I was pregnant":** Tannenbaum 2019.

197 **"By the time I made contact":** Harris 1993, p. 92.

197 **"I didn't know what I wanted to do":** Author interview with Tim Cahill.

198 **"Graham: But let me tell you":** SAP.

199 **Relying heavily on police sources:** Author interview with Nicholas Schou.

200 **"Every time I went somewhere in Rome":** Eszterhas 1974.

201 **Such a salary, he wrote:** SAP.

201 **He also claimed that the magazine's:** SAP.

202 **"The fact is that Mike Salisbury":** Author interview with Roger Black.

202 **"He gave *Rolling Stone* a look":** Wenner 2022, p. 213.

202 **"So I'm ready for the interview":** SAP.

203 **"I am of course offended":** SAP.

203 **"Dear Ben," Geffen wrote:** SAP.

203 **"I was hooked":** Crowe 2025, pp. 59–60.

203 **"How could it be that my rock-writing hero":** Crowe 2025, p. 60.

204 **"Half the staffers hate you":** Crowe 2025, p. 125.

204 **"I was aware of that situation":** Paul 2023, p. 172.

205 **The charges against Ellsberg:** Ellsberg 2002, p. 454.

205 **The judge decided that:** Ellsberg 2002, p. 456.

205 **As Wenner noted, Ellsberg's remarks:** Wenner 1973.

207 **Wenner also admitted that he was starstruck:** Wenner 2022, p. 184; Hagan 2017, p. 285.

208 **"*Rolling Stone* readers would never read":** Draper 1990, p. 211.

208 **If Wenner was starstruck by Goodwin's connections:** Wenner 2022, p. 185.

208 **Klein turned down other offers:** Author interview with Joe Klein.

208 **"Dick had written three brilliant essays for us":** Wenner 2022, p. 184.

209 **It was another example, Klein said:** Author interview with Joe Klein.

209 **"He had done an impressive job":** Wenner 2022, p. 197.

209 **"When Jann said politics was":** Draper 1990, p. 227.

209 **Later, Klein said Wenner:** Author interview with Joe Klein.

210 **"There was a sign over Jann's secretary's desk":** Hopper 2018.

210 **Christine Doudna, who started as:** Hopper 2018.

210 **Sarah Lazin, who also started:** Author interview with Sarah Lazin.

211 **Later, she admitted she knew nothing:** Author interview with Marianne Partridge.

211 **"Marianne just talked to each one of us":** Hopper 2018.

211 **"She helped lead a remarkable":** Bernstein 2018.

211   **"It's sort of amazing":** Hopper 2018.

211   **"What is this shit?":** Author interview with Marianne Partridge.

212   **Wenner later said she wasn't as attuned:** Author interview with Jann Wenner.

212   **She wanted to change that:** Author interview with Marianne Partridge.

212   **"I was sitting next to Jann":** Hopper 2018.

212   **After it appeared, Willis encountered William Shawn:** Willis 2011, p. xi.

213   **"The times had changed":** Author interview with Marianne Partridge.

213   **"The single highest priority":** SAP.

214   **"Oscar was one of God's own prototypes":** Thompson 1977.

Chapter 11. After the Revolution

215   **"On the professional side":** SAP.

216   **"Re your pompous letter":** SAP.

216   **"I can speak for editorial":** Shamberg and Rucker 1973.

217   **"I had found someone with the same":** Wenner 2022, p. 124.

218   **"Janno—Just finished reading the manuscript":** SAP.

218   *Mystery Train* **was about rock and roll:** Gleason 1975b.

219   **Although he faulted Marcus:** Landau 1975.

219   **"I just finished reading the galleys":** SAP.

219   **"What wafted back to me":** Hagan 2017, p. 291.

219   **Acknowledging that the reader feedback:** Hagan 2017, p. 294.

219   **"If you want to be a *real* writer":** Crowe 2025, pp. 201–2.

220   **"Had it not been for the discovery":** Draper 1990, p. 270.

220   **"And then here's Cameron":** Draper 1990, pp. 270–71.

221   **The memo credited the magazine:** SAP.

222   **As Tim Crouse said later:** Beuttler 1984.

222   **"They have moved, shall we say":** Anson 1981, p. 236.

222   **"That's the period where *Rolling Stone*":** Hagan 2017, p. 292.

222   **"Last Thursday, at the Harvard Square Theatre":** Landau 1974.

223   **As Abe Peck observed, the magazine:** Author interview with Abe Peck.

224   **"On Straight Arrow Books, I cannot accept":** SAP.

224   **"Your note to Hunter":** SAP.

224   **"I am immensely fucking pissed off":** Thompson 2000, p. 610.

225   **"There has never been any 'verbal understanding'":** SAP.

226   **"If we're going to do this":** Hopper 2018.

227 **Marcus, who served as a consultant:** Author interview with James Miller.

227 **"Growing up in the 50s and 60s":** Hopper 2018.

227 **"At the outset," Miller wrote:** Miller 1976, p. 9.

228 **Advertisers had long known that selling aspiration:** Berger 1972, p. 134.

229 **"Hollywood is always the last to know":** Biskind 1998, p. 14.

229 **Director Billy Wilder, for example:** Lubin 2025, p. 233.

229 **Writer and critic Susan Sontag:** Biskind 1998, p. 17.

230 *Where the Buffalo Roam* **(1980) was a loose:** Nelson 1997.

231 **The company was "its own kind of god":** Kohn 1975a, p. 151.

231 **"Start writing," Wenner told Kohn:** Kohn 1975a, p. 151.

232 **Company officials, he wrote:** Kohn 1979b.

234 **According to one** *San Francisco Chronicle* **reporter:** Taylor 2014.

235 **Wenner later described the story as:** Wenner 2022, p. 204.

236 **So was his best friend of fifty years:** Thomas 1996.

236 **The following year, another FBI memo:** Bergman and Weir 1976.

237 **AIM leaders accused the FBI:** Weir and Bergman 1977.

238 **His Las Vegas piece:** McKeen 2008, p. 224.

238 **"When Hunter had problems":** Author interview with David Felton.

238 **"I don't think there's an editor":** Gabel and Hughes 2005.

238 **According to Thompson's wife:** Gibney 2008.

239 **"I would like to rescue our relationship":** SAP.

239 **"The attempt was enough":** McKeen 1991, p. 107.

Chapter 12. The Establishment

241 **"Just one thing," he said:** Jacobs 1995, p. 463.

241 **The year after that,** *Rolling Stone* **featured:** Zane 1971.

241 **The accompanying text maintained:** *Rolling Stone* 1972.

241 **Queerness, one historian claimed:** Boyd 2003, p. 2.

242 **By the 1950s, the gay bar had become:** Boyd 2003, p. 15.

242 **Decades later, a character:** Fritscher 1990, p. 155.

242 **The "gay stampede" that ensued:** Sides 2009, p. 84.

242 **In his memoir, which recounted his own:** Wenner 2022, p. 145.

242 **He also recalled a 1971 letter:** Wenner 2022, p. 144.

242 **"Fags still drink more than turned-on straights":** Burke 1973.

243 **Responses to Burke's article:** *Rolling Stone* 1973.

243 **"You went into the old gay baths":** Young 1973.

244 **In 1975, *Rolling Stone* profiled *The Advocate*:** Reid 1975.

244 **"I think the Continental Baths":** Kramer 1998.

244 **"We're close now to total sexual liberation":** Burke 1976.

245 **Mendelsohn described Bowie as:** Mendelsohn 1971.

245 **The same year, David Felton's cover story:** Felton 1971.

245 **"I haven't met anybody":** Jahr 1976.

246 **It was about time, one reader wrote:** *Rolling Stone* 1976.

247 **"He was surrounded by few of the trappings":** Klein with Sufian 1976.

247 **"Hunter couldn't stay away from Washington":** McKeen 2008, p. 221.

248 **"At the moment," he wrote:** Thompson 1976.

248 **After the story appeared, Wenner recalled:** Wenner 2022, p. 214.

248 **Partridge knew it was Wenner's privilege:** Author interview with Marianne Partridge.

248 **Much to Klein's dismay:** Author interview with Joe Klein.

249 **"I waved at [*Washington Post* publisher] Kay Graham":** Wenner 2022, p. 328.

249 **"This is the first time young people":** Wharton 2020.

250 **"I was spending more time in New York":** Wenner 2022, p. 194.

250 **"If you went to Earl's":** Anolik 2019, p. 48.

251 **"We all just hit it off great":** Hagan 2017, p. 327.

251 **When Wenner asked Tom Burke:** Burke 1976b.

251 **"Every weekend we went to the NBC studios":** Wenner 2022, p. 224.

251 **"It was totally inspired by Hunter":** Hagan 2017, p. 326.

252 **"He wanted to have an entire issue":** Wenner 2022, p. 208.

253 **"*Rolling Stone* would decide":** Wenner 2022, p. 208.

254 **Later, however, Wenner said he was:** Author interview with Jann Wenner.

254 **"It was a pleasure having Mr. Avedon":** Bush 1976.

255 **"Even for the people who were there":** Perry 1976.

255 **Back in the San Francisco office:** Draper 1990, p. 244.

255 **"I spoke to sad and long faces":** Wenner 2022, p. 216.

255 **"We're active in book publishing":** Meislin 1976.

256 **"I had given them my goddamn life's blood":** Draper 1990, p. 245.

256 ***Rolling Stone* had shown it could survive:** Wenner 2022, p. 216.

256 **"It was becoming clear that the cultural center":** Wenner 2022, p. 237.

258 **"The editors had these big corporate offices":** Draper 1990, p. 251.

258 **"*Rolling Stone* began to be run by":** McKeen 1990.

258 **According to CIA officials:** Bernstein 1977.

259 **Their reporting also revealed:** Kohn and Newman 1977.

259 **Appearing on *The Today Show*:** *Today Show* 1977.

Epilogue

262 **Along the way, Wenner declined:** Weir 1999.

262 **"We had a conventional":** Levy 2022.

262 ***Salon*'s first editor was David Talbot:** Author interview with David Talbot.

262 **But when the two outlets:** Walsh 2023.

262 **At that time, *US Weekly*'s average paid circulation:** Ember 2017.

262 **"At the center of it all":** Aswad 2017.

263 **The book critics at *The New York Times*:** Coscarelli and Ember 2017.

263 **Seymour claimed that the memoir:** Seymour 2022.

264 **"I feel that, of all the magazines":** Flippo 1974, p. 170.

264 **Indeed, Evelyn McDonnell, a journalism professor:** McDonnell 2019.

265 **As Abe Peck observed, Wenner knew how:** Author interview with Abe Peck.

265 **The proof that *Rolling Stone* was a good idea:** Mason 2017.

266 **As late as 2023, for example, prominent historian:** Foner 2023.

266 **In his reply, Springsteen mentioned:** Gilmore 1987.

267 **Countercultural values also found expression:** Roszak 1986b, p. 11.

267 **One environmental historian, Andrew Kirk:** Kirk 2007, p. ix.

267 **Kirk also emphasized Brand's role:** Kirk 2007, p. 206.

268 **"When I was young":** Jobs 2005.

268 **In one interview, he said that taking LSD:** Markoff 2005, p. xix.

268 **He also claimed that Microsoft founder:** Isaacson 2011, pp. 172–73.

269 **For him, the "mystic tendencies":** Roszak 1986b, p. 15.

269 **A more spectacular example:** Burning Man Project 2021.

270 **"Both Burning Man and the Internet":** Gates 2018.

270 **Mark Zuckerberg and Jeff Bezos:** Tremayne-Pengelly 2024.

271 **"It's not about building an alternative":** Slee 2015, p. 27.

271 **Writing for *The Nation*, Doug Henwood:** Henwood 2015; Barbrook and Cameron 1995.

271 **What seemed to be "an appeal to community":** Slee 2015, p. 163.

273 **Fifty years after Hunter S. Thompson:** Kupfer 2011.

273 **"Forms and rhythms in music":** Wenner 2023, p. ix.

Bibliography

In the notes, the abbreviation SAP refers to the Straight Arrow Papers, which include internal memos, correspondence, and corporate records from Straight Arrow Publishers Inc. I reviewed this material in the warehouse where they were stored.

Albright, Thomas. "The Environmentalists: The *Whole Earth Catalog* Gets Down to Business." *Rolling Stone*, Dec. 13, 1969.

Algren, Nelson. Book review of *The Great Shark Hunt*, by Hunter S. Thompson. *Chicago Tribune*, July 15, 1979.

Alsop, Stewart. "The Clothespin Vote." *Newsweek*, Apr. 17, 1972.

Anolik, Lili. *Hollywood's Eve: Eve Babitz and the Secret History of L.A.* Scribner, 2019.

Anson, Robert Sam. *Gone Crazy and Back Again: The Rise and Fall of the* Rolling Stone *Generation.* Doubleday, 1981.

Armstrong, Don. *The Life and Writings of Ralph Gleason: Dispatches from the Front.* Bloomsbury, 2024.

Aswad, Jem. "TV Review: Rolling Stone: *Stories from the Edge.*" *Variety*, Nov. 6, 2017.

Aykroyd, Dan, and John Belushi. "Jimmy Carter: New South Burn." *Rolling Stone*, Jan. 13, 1977.

Babitz, Eve. *Eve's Hollywood*. New York Review of Books, 2015.

Baker, Chris. "Stewart Brand Recalls First 'Spacewar' Video Game Tournament." *Rolling Stone*, May 25, 2016.

Bangs, Lester. Book review of *DO IT!*, by Jerry Rubin. *Rolling Stone*, June 25, 1970.

———. *Psychotic Reactions and Carburetor Dung*. Edited by Greil Marcus. Alfred A. Knopf, 1987; rpt. Anchor Books, 2003.

Barbrook, Richard, and Andy Cameron. "The Californian Ideology." *Mute*, Sept. 1, 1995.

Baum, Dan. "Legalize It All." *Harper's Magazine*, Apr. 2016.

Berger, John. *Ways of Seeing*. Penguin, 1972; rpt. 2008.

Bergman, Lowell, and David Weir. "Revolution on Ice." *Rolling Stone*, Sept. 9, 1976.

Bernstein, Adam. "Harriet Fier, 'Assertive and Savvy' Editor with *Rolling Stone*, Dies at 67." *Washington Post*, Feb. 24, 2018.

Bernstein, Carl. "The CIA and the Media." *Rolling Stone*, Oct. 20, 1977.

Bernstein, David W. *The San Francisco Tape Music Center: Emerging Art Forms and the American Counterculture, 1961–1966*. University of California Press, 2008.

Beuttler, Bill. "Meeting Citizen Wenner." Unpublished 1984 manuscript. Accessed Aug. 21, 2025. https://www.billbeuttler.com/meeting_citizen_wenner_11928.htm.

Biskind, Peter. *Easy Riders, Raging Bulls: How the Sex-Drugs-and-Rock 'n' Roll Generation Saved Hollywood*. Simon & Schuster, 1998.

Blauner, Bob. *Resisting McCarthyism: To Sign or Not to Sign California's Loyalty Oath*. University of California Press, 2009.

Booth, Stanley. "Altamont Remembered." *Rolling Stone*, Sept. 13, 1984.

Boyd, Nan Alamilla. *Wide Open Town: A History of Queer San Francisco to 1965*. University of California Press, 2003.

Brand, Stewart. "Spacewar: Fanatic Life and Symbolic Death Among the Computer Bums." *Rolling Stone*, Dec. 7, 1972.

Brower, Steven. "Mike Salisbury, the Biggest Design Multihyphenate You Don't Know." *Eye on Design*, Dec. 24, 2015.

Browne, David. "*Rolling Stone* at 50: Shaping Contrasting Narratives of Woodstock, Altamont." *Rolling Stone*, June 26, 2017.

Bumsted, Allison. *TeenSet, Teen Fan Magazines, and Rock Journalism: Don't Let the Name Fool You*. University of Mississippi Press, 2024.

Burke, Tom. "Violet Millennium or The Invert Comes of Age: Featuring Total License and the Consequences." *Rolling Stone*, Aug. 30, 1973.

———. "King Queen." *Rolling Stone*, May 6, 1976a.

———. "Saturday Night." *Rolling Stone*, July 15, 1976b.

Burning Man Project. "What Is Burning Man?" Accessed Aug. 21, 2025. https://burningman.org/about/.

Burrough, Bryan. *Days of Rage: America's Radical Underground, the FBI, and the Forgotten Age of Revolutionary Violence.* Penguin, 2015.

Bush, George H. W. Letter to the editor. *Rolling Stone*, Nov. 18, 1976.

Callahan, Mat. *The Explosion of Deferred Dreams: Musical Renaissance and Social Revolution in San Francisco, 1965–75.* PM Press, 2017.

Carroll, E. Jean. *Hunter: The Strange and Savage Life of Hunter S. Thompson.* Dutton, 1993.

Carroll, Jon. "A Conversation with Jerry Garcia." *Playboy Guide: Electronic Entertainment*, Summer–Spring 1982.

———. "Back in the Day with *Rolling Stone.*" *San Francisco Chronicle*, July 18, 2013.

Clark, Kenneth. "NBC's John Chancellor Leaving TV After 43 Years of Globetrotting." *Chicago Tribune*, June 20, 1993.

Cohen, Robert. *When the Old Left Was Young: Student Radicals and America's First Mass Student Movement, 1929–1941.* Oxford University Press, 1993.

Conners, Peter. *White Hand Society: The Psychedelic Partnership of Timothy Leary and Allen Ginsberg.* City Lights Books, 2010.

Coscarelli, Joe, and Sydney Ember. "Jann Wenner and His Biographer Have a Falling Out." *New York Times*, Oct. 18, 2017.

Cott, Jonathan. "Rolling Stone Interview: Mick Jagger." *Rolling Stone*, Oct. 12, 1968.

———. *Days That I'll Remember: Spending Time with John Lennon and Yoko Ono.* Doubleday, 2013.

Creem. Interview with the Grateful Dead. Nov. 1970.

Crouse, Timothy. *The Boys on the Bus.* Random House, 1973.

Crowe, Cameron. *The Uncool: A Memoir.* Avid Reader Press / Simon & Schuster, 2025.

Davis, Belva. *Never in My Wildest Dreams: A Black Woman's Life in Journalism.* PoliPoint Press, 2010.

Davis, Clive, with James Willwerth. *Clive: Inside the Record Business.* William Morrow, 1975.

DeRogatis, Jim. *Let It Blurt: The Life and Times of Lester Bangs, America's Greatest Rock Critic.* Bloomsbury, 2000.

Dickensheets, Scott. "Angry for All the Right Reasons: A Conversation with John Lombardi, Who Brought Hunter Thompson to *Rolling Stone*." *Las Vegas Weekly*, Feb. 15, 2007.

Didion, Joan. "Slouching Towards Bethlehem." *Saturday Evening Post*, Sept. 23, 1967.

Draper, Robert. Rolling Stone *Magazine: The Uncensored History*. Doubleday, 1990.

Eckstein, Arthur M. *Bad Moon Rising: How the Weather Underground Beat the FBI and Lost the Revolution*. Yale University Press, 2016.

Ellsberg, Daniel. *Secrets: A Memoir of Vietnam and the Pentagon Papers*. Viking, 2002.

Ember, Sydney. "*Us Weekly* Is Sold to *National Enquirer* Publisher." *New York Times*, Mar. 15, 2017.

Eszterhas, Joe. "Charlie Simpson's Apocalypse." *Rolling Stone*, July 6, 1972a.

———. "The Strange Case of the Hippie Mafia." *Rolling Stone*, Dec. 7, 1972b.

———. "The Strange Case of the Hippie Mafia, Part 2." *Rolling Stone*, Dec. 21, 1972c.

———. "The Getty Kidnapping." *Rolling Stone*, May 9, 1974.

———. "King of the Goons." *Rolling Stone*, June 11, 1992.

Farber, David. *Chicago '68*. University of Chicago Press, 1988.

———. *The Age of Great Dreams: America in the 1960s*. Hill and Wang, 1994.

Farhi, Paul, and Will Sommer. "The Rapid Downfall of Jann Wenner Was Years in the Making." *Washington Post*, Sept. 18, 2023.

Felton, David. "Elton John." *Rolling Stone*, June 10, 1971.

Felton, David, and David Dalton. "Year of the Fork, Night of the Hunter." *Rolling Stone*, June 25, 1970.

Findley, Tim. "Tom Hayden: The Rolling Stone Interview Part 2." *Rolling Stone*, Nov. 9, 1972.

Flippo, Chester White. "Rock Journalism and *Rolling Stone*." Master's thesis, University of Texas, 1974.

Foner, Eric. "Seeing Was Not Believing." *New York Review of Books*, Sept. 21, 2023.

Fong-Torres, Ben. "A Tidal Wave in the Wild West." *Rolling Stone*, Aug. 9, 1969.

———. "Love Is Just a Song We Sing but a Contract Is Something Else: A Discordant History of the San Francisco Sound." *Rolling Stone*, Feb. 26, 1976.

———. Introduction to *The Rolling Stone Interviews: Talking with the Legends of Rock & Roll, 1967–1980*, edited by Peter Herbst. St. Martin's Press / Rolling Stone Press, 1981.

———. *The Rice Room: Growing Up Chinese-American; From Number Two Son to Rock 'n' Roll.* Hyperion, 1994; rpt. University of California Press, 2011.

———. *The Hits Just Keep on Coming: The History of Top 40 Radio.* Miller Freeman Books, 1998.

———. *Becoming Almost Famous: My Back Pages in Music, Writing, and Life.* Backbeat Books, 2006.

Fox, Margalit. "Arthur Janov, 93, Dies; Psychologist Caught World's Attention with 'Primal Scream.'" *New York Times*, Oct. 2, 2017.

Frank, Thomas. *The Conquest of Cool: Business Culture, Counterculture, and the Rise of Hip Consumerism.* University of Chicago Press, 1997.

Fritscher, Jack. *Some Dance to Remember.* Palm Drive, 1990.

Gabel, J. C., and James Hughes. "Long Live the High Priest of Gonzo: An Oral History of Dr. Hunter S. Thompson." *Stop Smiling*, no. 22 (2005).

Gambaccini, Paul. "Paul McCartney: The Rolling Stone Interview." *Rolling Stone*, Jan. 31, 1974.

Garcia, Jerry, Charles Reich, and Jann Wenner. *Garcia: A Signpost to New Space.* Straight Arrow Press, 1972; rpt. Da Capo Press, 2003.

Gates, Anita. "Larry Harvey, the Man Behind Burning Man, Is Dead at 70." *New York Times*, Apr. 28, 2018.

Gibney, Alex, dir. *Gonzo: The Life and Work of Dr. Hunter S. Thompson.* Magnolia, 2008.

Gilmore, Mikal. "The Rolling Stone 20th Anniversary Interview: Bruce Springsteen." *Rolling Stone*, Nov. 5, 1987.

Gitlin, Todd. *The Whole World Is Watching: Mass Media in the Making and Unmaking of the New Left.* University of California Press, 1980.

———. *The Sixties: Years of Hope, Days of Rage.* Bantam Books, 1987.

Gleason, Ralph J. Letter to Alexander Hoffman, Sept. 2, 1963. In Ralph J. Gleason Letters to Alexander P. Hoffman, 1963, Bancroft Library.

———. "'The Family Dog': Liverpool in S.F." *San Francisco Chronicle*, Oct. 22, 1965a.

———. "The Times They Are A'Changin'." *Ramparts*, Apr. 1965b.

———. "The Children's Crusade." *Ramparts*, Mar. 1966.

———. "Like a Rolling Stone." *American Scholar*, Autumn 1967.

———. "Perspectives: Changing with Moneychangers." *Rolling Stone*, Feb. 24, 1968a.

———. "Perspectives: The Final Paroxysm of Fear." *Rolling Stone*, Apr. 6, 1968b.

———. *The Jefferson Airplane and the San Francisco Sound.* Ballantine Books, 1969a.

———. "Perspectives: Festival Paranoia." *Rolling Stone*, Sept. 6, 1969b.

———. "Perspectives: Is There a Death Wish in the U.S.?" *Rolling Stone*, Apr. 5, 1969c.

———. "Aquarius Wept." *Esquire*, Aug. 1970.

———. "Altamont Revisited on Film." *Rolling Stone*, Apr. 1, 1971.

———. *Celebrating the Duke: And Louis, Bessie, Billie, Bird, Carmen, Miles, Dizzy, and Other Heroes.* Little, Brown, 1975a.

———. "The Rainbow Trail Leads to Rock Studios." *San Francisco Chronicle*, June 15, 1975b.

———. "'Listen, Listen, Listen': Hippies, the Haight, and the Soundtrack of the Sixties." *Grateful Dead Studies* 1 (2013–14).

———. *Conversations in Jazz: The Ralph J. Gleason Interviews.* Yale University Press, 2016a.

———. *Music in the Air: The Selected Writings of Ralph J. Gleason.* Yale University Press, 2016b.

Glover, Tony. "Bands Dust to Dust." *Rolling Stone*, Nov. 23, 1968.

Goodwin, Michael. "Jerry Garcia at 700 MPH." *Flash*, Apr. 1971.

Graham, Bill, and Robert Greenfield. *Bill Graham Presents: My Life Inside Rock and Out.* Doubleday, 1992.

Green, Penelope. "Eve Babitz, a Hedonist with a Notebook, Is Dead at 78." *New York Times*, Dec. 19, 2021.

———. "Steve Ostrow, Manhattan Bathhouse Impresario, Dies at 91." *New York Times*, Feb. 11, 2024.

Green, Robin. "Naked Lunch Box: The David Cassidy Story." *Rolling Stone*, May 11, 1972.

———. *The Only Girl: My Life and Times on the Masthead of* Rolling Stone. Little, Brown, 2018.

Greene, Andy. "How Rolling Stone Got Those Patty Hearst and Charles Manson Scoops." *Rolling Stone*, Mar. 16, 2017.

Greenfield, Robert. "Tim Leary: or, Bomb for Buddha." *Rolling Stone*, Dec. 2, 1970.

———. *Dark Star: An Oral Biography of Jerry Garcia.* William Morrow, 1996.

———. *Timothy Leary: A Biography.* Harcourt, 2006.

Haber, Izak. "An Amerikan Dream: A True Yippie's Sentimental Education or How Abbie Hoffman Won My Heart & Stole *Steal This Book*." *Rolling Stone*, Sept. 30, 1971.

Hagan, Joe. *Sticky Fingers: The Life and Times of Jann Wenner and* Rolling Stone *Magazine.* Knopf, 2017.

Hanley, Jason. "Hall of Fame Interview with Inductee Jon Landau." Rock & Roll Hall of Fame, 2020.

Hard Road. Jerry Garcia interview. July 20, 1970.

Harris, David. "Ask a Marine." *Rolling Stone*, July 19, 1973; rpt. in Love 1993.

Harris, Mark. "The Flowering of the Hippies." *Atlantic Monthly*, Sept. 1967.

Hartlaub, Peter. "Grateful Dead 'Drug Bust' at 50: Nothing Left to Do but Smile . . ." *San Francisco Chronicle*, Jan. 9, 2018.

Helms, Chet. "Summer of Love 30th Anniversary Mission Statement." *Fun_People*, September 10, 1997.

Henwood, Doug. "What the Sharing Economy Takes." *Nation*, Jan. 27, 2015.

Hill, Steven. *Raw Deal: How the "Uber Economy" and Runaway Capitalism Are Screwing American Workers.* St. Martin's Press, 2015.

Hinckle, Warren. "A Social History of the Hippies." *Ramparts*, Mar. 1967.

———. *If You Have a Lemon, Make Lemonade: An Essential Memoir of a Lunatic Decade.* G. P. Putnam's Sons, 1974.

———. *Who Killed Hunter S. Thompson? The Picaresque Story of the Birth of Gonzo Journalism.* Last Gasp, 2017.

Hobsbawm, Eric. *Interesting Times: A Twentieth-Century Life.* Pantheon, 2005.

Hoffman, Abbie. Letter to the editor. *Rolling Stone*, Oct. 28, 1971.

Holzman, Jac. Letter to the editor. *Rolling Stone*, May 3, 1969.

Hopper, Jessica. "'It Was Us Against Those Guys': The Women Who Transformed *Rolling Stone* in the Mid-70s." *Vanity Fair*, Aug. 28, 2018.

Isaacson, Walter. *Steve Jobs.* Simon & Schuster, 2011.

Jackson, Blair. Interview with Robert Hunter. *Golden Road*, Feb. 1988.

Jacobs, Alexandra. Book review of *Like a Rolling Stone: A Memoir*, by Jann Wenner. *New York Times*, Sept. 11, 2022.

Jacobs, John. *A Rage for Justice: The Passion and Politics of Phillip Burton.* University of California Press, 1995.

Jahr, Cliff. "Elton John: It's Lonely at the Top." *Rolling Stone,* Oct. 7, 1976.

Jobs, Steve. "'You've Got to Find What You Love,' Jobs Says." *Stanford Report,* June 12, 2005.

Kai, Suzanne Jo, dir. *Like a Rolling Stone: The Life & Times of Ben Fong-Torres.* StudioLA.TV/XTR, 2022.

Kamin, Ira. "Playing for Nothing on a Hot Afternoon in Mill Valley." *Rolling Stone,* Sept. 17, 1970.

Kirk, Andrew G. *Counterculture Green: The* Whole Earth Catalog *and American Environmentalism.* University Press of Kansas, 2007.

Klein, Joe, with Vicki Sufian. "The Prince of the West." *Rolling Stone,* July 15, 1976.

Kohn, Howard. "Malignant Giant: The Nuclear Industry's Terrible Power and How It Silenced Karen Silkwood." *Rolling Stone,* Mar. 27, 1975a; rpt. in Love 1993.

———. "Shutdown at Oklahoma's Kerr-McGee: The End of a Plutonium Relationship." *Rolling Stone,* Dec. 4, 1975b.

———. "Karen Silkwood Was Right in Plutonium Scandal." *Rolling Stone,* Oct. 20, 1977a.

———. "Nuclear Politics: The Case of Karen Silkwood." *Rolling Stone,* Jan. 23, 1977b.

———. "Nuclear Power on Trial." *Rolling Stone,* May 4, 1978.

———. "Karen Silkwood Vindicated." *Rolling Stone,* June 28, 1979a.

———. "Karen Silkwood's Dark Victory." *Rolling Stone,* July 26, 1979b.

———. "The Silkwood Case Goes to Trial." *Rolling Stone,* Mar. 8, 1979c.

———. "Silkwood vs. Nuclear Power: The Courtroom Reaction." *Rolling Stone,* May 17, 1979d.

Kohn, Howard, and Lowell Bergman. "Reagan's Millions: Inside the Candidate's Closet Cabinet." *Rolling Stone,* Aug. 26, 1976.

Kohn, Howard, and Barbara Newman. "How Israel Got the Nuclear Bomb." *Rolling Stone,* Dec. 1, 1977.

Kohn, Howard, and David Weir. "The Lost Year of the SLA." *Rolling Stone,* Apr. 22, 1976.

Kramer, Larry. "Queer Conscience." *New York,* Apr. 6, 1998.

Kramer, Michael J. *The Republic of Rock: Music and Citizenship in the Sixties Counterculture.* Oxford University Press, 2013.

Krebs, Albin. "Truman Capote Is Dead at 59; Novelist of Style and Clarity." *New York Times,* Aug. 28, 1984.

Kupfer, David. "Against the Grain: Peter Coyote on Buddhism, Capitalism, and the Enduring Legacy of the Sixties." *Sun*, June 2011.

Landau, Jon. Album review of *Curtis/Live*, by Curtis Mayfield. *Rolling Stone*, June 24, 1971.

———. *It's Too Late to Stop Now: A Rock and Roll Journal*. Straight Arrow Books, 1972.

———. "Growing Young with Rock and Roll." *Real Paper*, May 22, 1974.

———. "'Mystery Train': Right on Time." *Rolling Stone*, Aug. 28, 1975.

Lebowitz, Fran. "Fran Lebowitz on the Glamorous Worlds of Camilla McGrath." *Literary Hub*, Oct. 28, 2020.

Leibovitz, Annie, ed. *Shooting Stars: The Rolling Stone Book of Portraits*. Straight Arrow Books, 1973.

———, ed. *American Music*. Random House, 2003; rpt. 2004.

———. *At Work*. Edited by Sharon DeLano. Random House, 2008.

Legaspi, Althea. "Breaking Through Rock Journalism's Boys' Club." *Rolling Stone*, Nov. 1, 2023.

Lester, Julius. Book review of *Conversations with Eldridge Cleaver: Algiers*, by Lee Lockwood. *Rolling Stone*, Dec. 2, 1970a.

———. Book review of *19 Necromancers from Now*, edited by Ishmael Reed. *Rolling Stone*, Nov. 12, 1970b.

———. Book review of *Seize the Time: The Story of the Black Panther Party and Huey P. Newton*, by Bobby Seale. *Rolling Stone*, Dec. 2, 1970c.

———. Book reviews of *Black Nationalism and the Revolution in Music*, by Frank Kofsky, and *Black Magic: Four Lives*, by A. R. Spellman. *Rolling Stone*, May 13, 1971.

Levy, Joe. "*Rolling Stone* at 50: How Magazine's Album Reviews Became a Cultural Fixture." *Rolling Stone*, Apr. 18, 2017.

Levy, Steven. "Why Jann Wenner Let *Wired* Start the *Rolling Stone* of Tech." *Wired*, Sept. 30, 2022.

Lewis, Grover. "Hitting the High Note with the Allman Brothers Band." *Rolling Stone*, Nov. 25, 1971a.

———. "Splendor in the Short Grass." *Rolling Stone*, Sept. 2, 1971b.

———. *Splendor in the Short Grass: The Grover Lewis Reader*. Edited by Jan Reid and W. K. Stratton. University of Texas Press, 2005.

Longfellow, Matthew, dir. *Classic Albums: John Lennon / Plastic Ono Band*. BBC, 2008.

Love, Robert, ed. *The Best of* Rolling Stone: *25 Years of Journalism on the Edge*. Doubleday, 1993.

———. "A Technical Guide for Editing Gonzo: Hunter S. Thompson from the Other End of the Mojo Wire." *Columbia Journalism Review,* May–June 2005.

Lubin, David M. *Ready for My Close Up: The Making of* Sunset Boulevard *and the Dark Side of the Hollywood Dream.* Grand Central, 2025.

Lydon, Michael. "An Evening with the Grateful Dead." *Rolling Stone,* Sept. 17, 1970.

———. *Flashbacks: Eyewitness Accounts of the Rock Revolution, 1964–74.* Routledge, 2003.

———. *Busy Being Born: A 60s Memoir.* Franklin Street Press, 2018.

Lydon, Susan Gordon. *Take the Long Way Home: Memoirs of a Survivor.* Harper San Francisco, 1993.

Marchese, David. "Jann Wenner Defends His Legacy, and His Generation's." *New York Times,* Sept. 15, 2023.

Marcus, Greil, ed. *Rock and Roll Will Stand.* Beacon Press, 1969.

———. "Chicago . . . and Santa Barbara and the Black Panthers and Beyond." *Rolling Stone,* Apr. 2, 1970.

———. *Mystery Train: Images of America in Rock 'n' Roll Music.* Dutton, 1975.

———. "The Early Years." *Rolling Stone,* May 18, 2006.

———. "The Whole World in a Song." *Letter in the Ether,* Sept. 2022.

———. "Ask Greil." *Letter in the Ether,* Apr. 19, 2024.

Markoff, John. *What the Dormouse Said: How the 60s Counterculture Shaped the Personal Computer Industry.* Viking Penguin, 2005.

———. *Whole Earth: The Many Lives of Stewart Brand.* Penguin, 2022.

Mason, Anthony. "Jann Wenner on *Rolling Stone* at 50." *CBS Sunday Morning,* Nov. 5, 2017.

Mazzetti, Mark. "Burglars Who Took on F.B.I. Abandon Shadows." *New York Times,* Jan. 7, 2014.

McDonnell, Evelyn. "It's Time for the Rock & Roll Hall of Fame to Address Its Gender and Racial Imbalances." *Billboard,* Nov. 15, 2019.

McKeen, William. Interview with Hunter S. Thompson. Mar. 1990; rpt. in Torrey and Simonson 2008 and Streitfeld 2018.

———. *Hunter S. Thompson: A Critical Biography.* Twayne, 1991.

———. *Outlaw Journalist: The Life and Times of Hunter S. Thompson.* W. W. Norton, 2008.

McMillian, John. *Smoking Typewriters: The Sixties Underground Press and the Rise of Alternative Media in America.* Oxford University Press, 2011.

Medsger, Betty. *The Burglary: The Discovery of J. Edgar Hoover's Secret FBI*. Knopf, 2014.

Meislin, Richard J. "*Rolling Stone* Planning Move to New York City in January." *New York Times*, Sept. 2, 1976.

Mendelsohn, John. "David Bowie? Pantomime Rock?" *Rolling Stone*, Apr. 1, 1971.

Merryman, Richard. Paul McCartney interview. *Life*, Apr. 16, 1971.

Miller, James, ed. *The Rolling Stone Illustrated History of Rock & Roll*. Random House, 1976.

———. *Democracy Is in the Streets: From Port Huron to the Siege of Chicago*. Simon & Schuster, 1987.

———. *Flowers in the Dustbin: The Rise of Rock & Roll, 1947–1977*. Simon & Schuster, 1999.

Model Gene. "Who Is Annie Leibovitz? Part 1 (Growing Up and *Rolling Stone* Magazine)." YouTube, Nov. 12, 2022.

Morgan, Edward P. *What Really Happened to the 1960s: How Mass Media Culture Failed American Democracy*. University Press of Kansas, 2010.

Murray, George Mason. "Panthers' Fight to the Death Against Racism." *Rolling Stone*, Apr. 5, 1969.

Music Journalism Insider. "Ed Ward Interview (*The History of Rock & Roll, Volume 2: 1964–1977: The Beatles, the Stones, and the Rise of Classic Rock*)." Nov. 19, 2019.

Nelson, Sara. "Interview with Hunter S. Thompson." *Book Report*, 1997.

Newsweek. "Rocking the News." Apr. 28, 1969.

New York Times. "American Notebook." Aug. 2, 1970.

———. "*Rolling Stone* Adds Edition Here." May 6, 1971.

———. "Ralph Gleason, Jazz Critic, Dead." June 4, 1975.

Observer. "Elvis Presley's Letter to Richard Nixon, 1970." Oct. 12, 2013.

Owens, Ernest. "It's Time to Kill the Silence." *Rolling Stone*, Nov. 1, 2023.

Paul, Alan. *Brothers and Sisters: The Allman Brothers Band and the Album That Defined the 70s*. St. Martin's Press, 2023.

Peck, Abe. *Uncovering the Sixties: The Life and Times of the Underground Press*. Pantheon, 1985.

Perlstein, Rick. *The Invisible Bridge: The Fall of Nixon and the Rise of Reagan*. Simon & Schuster, 2014.

Perry, Charles. "Is This Any Way to Run the Army?—Stoned?" *Rolling Stone*, Nov. 9, 1968.

———. "From Eternity to Here: What a Long Strange Trip It's Been." *Rolling Stone*, Feb. 26, 1976.

———. *The Haight-Ashbury: A History*. Random House, 1984; rpt. Wenner Books, 2005.

Polanski, Roman. *Roman by Polanski*. William Morrow, 1984.

Reich, Charles. *The Greening of America*. Random House, 1970.

Reid, John. "*The Advocate* Is the Best Gay News Medium in the Country." *Rolling Stone*, Oct. 9, 1975.

Reynolds, Simon. "Myths and Depths: Greil Marcus Talks to Simon Reynolds." *Los Angeles Review of Books*, Apr. 27, 2012.

Richardson, Peter. *American Prophet: The Life and Work of Carey McWilliams*. University of Michigan Press, 2005; rpt. University of California Press, 2019.

———. *A Bomb in Every Issue: How the Short, Unruly Life of* Ramparts *Magazine Changed America*. The New Press, 2009.

———. *No Simple Highway: A Cultural History of the Grateful Dead*. St. Martin's Press, 2015.

———. "Roots Music: The Beginnings of *Rolling Stone*." *California*, Winter 2017.

———. *Savage Journey: Hunter S. Thompson and the Weird Road to Gonzo*. University of California Press, 2022.

———. Book review of *Whole Earth: The Many Lives of Stewart Brand*, by John Markoff. *California History* 100, no. 1 (2023).

———. "The Music Never Stopped." *Alta*, Feb. 12, 2024.

Riley, Tim. *Lennon: The Man, the Myth, the Music: The Definitive Life*. Hyperion, 2011.

Robinson, Jackie. *I Never Had It Made*. Fawcett Press, 1972.

Rolling Stone. "Fears and Follies Kill 'Wild West.'" Sept. 6, 1969a.

———. Letter to the editor. Oct. 18, 1969b.

———. "The Rolling Stones Disaster at Altamont: Let It Bleed." Jan. 21, 1970.

———. "Random Shots." Dec. 7, 1972.

———. Letters to the editor. Sept. 27, 1973.

———. "The Inside Story: Tania's World." Oct. 23, 1975a.

———. "The Inside Story Part Two: Tania's World." Nov. 20, 1975b.

———. Letters to the editor. Nov. 4, 1976.

———. "*Rolling Stone*'s Biggest Scoops, Exposés and Controversies." June 24, 2010.

———. "The Last Word: Annie Leibovitz Looks Back on a Legendary Career." Oct. 23, 2017.

Romano, Tricia. *The Freaks Came Out to Write: The Definitive History of The Village Voice, the Radical Paper That Changed American Culture.* PublicAffairs, 2024.

Rorabaugh, W. J. *Berkeley at War: The 1960s.* Oxford University Press, 1989.

———. *American Hippies.* Cambridge University Press, 2015.

Rosenfeld, Seth. *Subversives: The FBI's War on Student Radicals, and Reagan's Rise to Power.* Farrar, Straus and Giroux, 2012.

Roszak, Theodore. *The Making of a Counter Culture: Reflections on the Technocratic Society and Its Youthful Opposition.* Doubleday, 1969; rpt. University of California Press, 1995.

———. *The Cult of Information: A Neo-Luddite Treatise on High-Tech, Artificial Intelligence, and the True Art of Thinking.* Pantheon, 1986a; rpt. University of California Press, 1994.

———. *From Satori to Silicon Valley: San Francisco and the American Counterculture.* Don't Call It Frisco Press, 1986b.

Rubin, Jerry. *DO IT! Scenarios of the Revolution.* Simon & Schuster, 1970.

Sanders, Ed. *The Family.* Dutton, 1971; rpt. DaCapo Press, 2002.

Schrecker, Ellen. "The 50-Year War on Higher Education." *Chronicle of Higher Education,* Oct. 14, 2022.

Selvin, Joel. *Monterey Pop.* Chronicle Books, 1992.

———. *Summer of Love: The Inside Story of LSD, Rock & Roll, Free Love, and High Times in the Wild West.* Dutton, 1994.

———. *Sly & the Family Stone: An Oral History.* Permuted Press, 1998; rpt. 2022.

Seymour, Corey. "Jann Wenner's Memoir Is the Story of a Man Who Built an Empire (and Changed the World)." *Vogue,* Dec. 29, 2022.

Shamberg, Michael, and Allen Rucker, dirs. *TVTV Meets Rolling Stone.* WNET, 1973.

Sides, Josh. *Erotic City: Sexual Revolutions and the Making of Modern San Francisco.* Oxford University Press, 2009.

Skipper, John C. *The 1964 Republican Convention: Barry Goldwater and the Beginning of the Conservative Movement.* McFarland, 2016.

Slee, Tom. *What's Yours Is Mine: Against the Sharing Economy.* OR Books, 2015.

Stone, Sly, with Ben Greenman. *Thank You (Falettinme Be Mice Elf Agin): A Memoir.* Auwa Books, 2023.

Streitfeld, David. *Hunter S. Thompson: The Last Interview and Other Conversations*. Melville House, 2018.

Stuckey, Fred. "Jerry Garcia Interview: It's All Music." *Guitar Player*, Apr. 1971.

Sullivan, Caroline. "David Cassidy Obituary." *Guardian*, Nov. 21, 2017.

Taibbi, Matt. Introduction to *Fear and Loathing: On the Campaign Trail '72*, by Hunter S. Thompson. Straight Arrow Books, 1973; rpt. Simon & Schuster, 2012.

Talbot, David. *Season of the Witch: Enchantment, Terror, and Deliverance in the City of Love*. Free Press, 2012.

Tannenbaum, Rob. "Joan Baez on 3 Days of Pregnancy and Priggishness at Woodstock." *New York Times*, Aug. 5, 2019.

Taylor, Michael. "Death to the Fascist Insect: Looking Back 40 Years, Does the SLA Make Any More Sense?" *California*, Sept. 16, 2014.

Thomas, Pat. *Did It! From Yuppie to Yippie: Jerry Rubin, An American Revolutionary*. Fantagraphics Books, 2017.

Thomas, Pat, with Christopher Gurk. "The Godfather of Rock Criticism: Paul Williams." *RockCritics.com*, Aug. 10, 2001. Archived on the Internet Archive's Wayback Machine.

Thomas, Robert Mcg., Jr. "Sidney Korshak, 88, Dies; Fabled Fixer for the Chicago Mob." *New York Times*, Jan. 22, 1996.

Thompson, Hunter S. "The Hashbury Is the Capital of the Hippies." *New York Times Magazine*, May 14, 1967a.

———. *Hell's Angels: A Strange and Terrible Saga*. Random House, 1967b.

———. "Presenting: The Richard Nixon Doll." *Pageant*, July 1968.

———. "The Battle of Aspen." *Rolling Stone*, Oct. 1, 1970.

———. "Fear and Loathing in Las Vegas." *Rolling Stone*, Nov. 11, 1971a.

———. "Fear and Loathing in Las Vegas: A Savage Journey to the Heart of the American Dream." *Rolling Stone*, Nov. 25, 1971b.

———. "Strange Rumblings in Aztlan." *Rolling Stone*, Apr. 29, 1971c.

———. *Fear and Loathing in Las Vegas: A Savage Journey to the Heart of the American Dream*. Random House, 1972.

———. *Fear and Loathing: On the Campaign Trail '72*. Straight Arrow Books, 1973; rpt. Grand Central Publishing, 2006.

———. "Third-Rate Romance, Low-Rent Rendezvous." *Rolling Stone*, June 3, 1976.

———. "The Banshee Screams for Buffalo Meat." *Rolling Stone*, Dec. 15, 1977.

———. *The Great Shark Hunt: Strange Tales from a Strange Time.* Simon & Schuster, 1979.

———. *The Proud Highway: Saga of a Desperate Southern Gentleman.* Edited by Douglas Brinkley. Simon & Schuster, 1997.

———. *Fear and Loathing in America: The Brutal Odyssey of an Outlaw Journalist.* Edited by Douglas Brinkley. Simon & Schuster, 2000.

Time. "A Bomb in Every Issue." Jan. 6, 1967a.

———. "The Hippies." July 7, 1967b.

———. "*Rolling Stone*'s Rock World." Apr. 25, 1969.

The Today Show. NBC, aired Oct. 24, 1977.

Toobin, Jeffrey. *American Heiress: The Wild Saga of the Kidnapping, Crimes and Trial of Patty Hearst.* Doubleday, 2016.

Torrey, Beef, and Kevin Simonson, eds. *Conversations with Hunter S. Thompson.* University of Mississippi Press, 2008.

Tremayne-Pengelly, Alexandra. "How Burning Man Has Inspired Silicon Valley Innovations over the Years." *Observer*, Aug. 27, 2024.

Trucks, Butch. "'Whipping Post'!" *New York Times*, May 8, 2005.

Turner, Fred. *From Counterculture to Cyberculture: Stewart Brand, the Whole Earth Network, and the Rise of Digital Utopianism.* University of Chicago Press, 2006.

Vetter, Craig. "Playboy Interview: Hunter Thompson." *Playboy*, Nov. 1974.

Walsh, Joan. "Just Another RFK Jr. Lie: I Know, Because It's About Me." *Nation*, June 22, 2023.

Ward, Ed. "Last Crumbs of February." *BerlinBites*, Feb. 28, 2005.

———. Comment posted on the WELL, Jan. 12, 2014.

Weiner, Tim. *Enemies: A History of the FBI.* Random House, 2012.

Weir, David. "Wenner's World." *Salon*, Apr. 20, 1999.

Weir, David, and Lowell Bergman. "The Killing of Anna Mae Aquash." *Rolling Stone*, Apr. 7, 1977.

Weller, Sheila. "LSD, Ecstasy, and a Blast of Utopianism: How 1967's 'Summer of Love' All Began." *Vanity Fair*, July 2012.

Wenner, Jann S. "Bob Dylan's T.B. and Acid-Rock." *Daily Californian*, Feb. 24, 1966a.

———. "Rock Around the Clock." *Daily Californian*, Mar. 10, 1966b.

———. "From the Editor." *Rolling Stone*, Dec. 7, 1968a.

———. "Musicians Reject New Political Exploiters: Groups Drop Out from Yip-In." *Rolling Stone*, May 11, 1968b.

———. "Rolling Stone Interview: Bob Dylan." *Rolling Stone*, Nov. 29, 1969.

———, ed. *Lennon Remembers*. Straight Arrow Books, 1971a; rpt. Verso Books, 2000.

———. "Letter from the Editor: On the Occasion of Our Fourth Anniversary." *Rolling Stone*, Nov. 11, 1971b.

———. "Daniel Ellsberg: The Rolling Stone Interview." *Rolling Stone*, Nov. 8, 1973.

———. "Ralph Gleason in Perspective." *Rolling Stone*, July 17, 1975.

———, ed. *Fear and Loathing at* Rolling Stone*: The Essential Writings of Hunter S. Thompson*. Simon & Schuster, 2011.

———. *Like a Rolling Stone: A Memoir*. Little, Brown, 2022.

———. *The Masters: Conversations with Dylan, Lennon, Jagger, Townshend, Garcia, Bono, and Springsteen*. Little, Brown, 2023.

Wenner, Jann S., and Corey Seymour. *Gonzo: The Life of Hunter S. Thompson*. Little, Brown, 2007.

Wharton, Mary, dir. *Jimmy Carter: Rock & Roll President*. Greenwich Entertainment, 2020.

Whiting, Sam. "John Burks, First Managing Editor of *Rolling Stone*, Dies at 83." *San Francisco Chronicle*, Feb. 26, 2021.

Whitmer, Peter O. *When the Going Gets Weird: The Twisted Life and Times of Hunter S. Thompson*. Hyperion, 1993.

Williams, Paul. "The Golden Road: A Report on San Francisco." *Crawdaddy*, June 1967.

———. *The Crawdaddy! Book: Words (and Images) from the Magazine of Rock*. Hal Leonard, 2002.

Willis, Ellen. "The Not-So-Groovy Side of Woodstock." *New Yorker*, Aug. 29, 1969.

———. *Out of the Vinyl Deeps: Ellen Willis on Rock Music*. Edited by Nona Willis Aronowitz. University of Minnesota Press, 2011.

Winner, Langdon. Album review of *McCartney*, by Paul McCartney. *Rolling Stone*, May 14, 1970.

———. "The Black Panthers: My Encounter with Jean Genet." *Langdon Winner on Politics, Technology and the Arts*, May 26, 2018. Archived on the Internet Archive's Wayback Machine.

Wolfe, Tom, with E. W. Johnson. *The New Journalism*. Harper & Row, 1973.

Young, Perry Dean. "So You're Planning a Night at the Tubs? Here's Some Advice Your Mother Never Gave You." *Rolling Stone*, Feb. 15, 1973.

Zane, Maitland. "Les Cockettes de San Francisco: Tinsel Tarts in a Hot Coma!" *Rolling Stone*, Oct. 14, 1971.

Index

Founded in 1893,
UNIVERSITY OF CALIFORNIA PRESS
publishes bold, progressive books and journals
on topics in the arts, humanities, social sciences,
and natural sciences—with a focus on social
justice issues—that inspire thought and action
among readers worldwide.

The UC PRESS FOUNDATION
raises funds to uphold the press's vital role
as an independent, nonprofit publisher, and
receives philanthropic support from a wide
range of individuals and institutions—and from
committed readers like you. To learn more, visit
ucpress.edu/supportus.